CISTERCIAN FATHERS SER

GEOFFREY OF AUXERRE: ON THE APOCALYPSE

CISTERCIAN FATHERS SERIES: NUMBER FORTY-TWO

GEOFFREY OF AUXERRE: ON THE APOCALYPSE

Translated by Joseph Gibbons, CSSP

Cistercian Publications
Kalamazoo, Michigan
2000

This translation has been made from
Geoffredo di Auxerre. *Super Apocalypsin*. Edited by Ferrucio Gastaldelli.
Rome: Edizioni di Storia e Letteratura, 1970.
Geoffrey of Auxerre (fl. 1050)

Cistercian Publications would like to thank John Leinenweber
for his help in the production of this manuscript.

Cistercian Publications
Editorial Office
Institute of Cistercian Studies
Western Michigan University
Kalamazoo, MI 49008

Available from

Cistercian Publications (Distribution)
Saint Joseph's Abbey
167 North Spencer Road
Spencer, MA 01562-1233

and

Cistercian Publications (UK)
Mount Saint Bernard Abbey
Coalville, Leicester LE67 5UL

The work of Cistercian Publications
is made possible in part by support from Western Michigan University
to The Institute of Cistercian Studies

Library of Congress Cataloguing available upon request.
ISBN 0-87907-4426 (hc)
0-87907-6429 (pb)

Printed in Canada

TABLE OF CONTENTS

Translator's Introduction

Geoffrey of Auxerre appears on history's scene in the midst of an enormous cultural, political, and religious revolution. Europe, finally free from centuries of invasion, was achieving the self-confidence to develop its own identity. This distinctly European genius had already found expression over the preceding century (1050–1140) in art, in a renewal and expansion of educational opportunities, in the beginnings of a distinctly European secular literature, in architectures, and in law. The Middle Ages had reached its noonday. This cultural explosion, dependent in large part on a revival of trade and commerce, is far too complicated for us to describe here.[1] We need only note that these amazing years gave birth to a number of different religious movements, all borrowing from the emerging consciousness of the times. Some went on to stamp the future but most appeared only to spice an already turbulent time.[2]

The Church, which had guarded Europe's patrimony during the previous centuries, had to find a new place for itself. This meant reform and updating. Influenced by, and in turn influencing, the spirit of the times, reform and reorganization reached a peak in the Gregorian reform and during the century following these efforts to establish the Church at the heart of European life.[3] The

[1] A good introduction to the background is: L. J. Lekai, 'Motives and Ideals of the Eleventh-Century Monastic Renewal', *The Cistercian Spirit*, CS 3 (Cistercian Publications, 1970) 27–47.

[2] See B. K. Lackner, *The Eleventh Century Background of Cîteaux*, CS 8 (Cistercian Publications, 1972), especially his very full bibliography.

[3] See A. Fliche, *La réforme gregorienne* (Paris: Champion, 1937) for a good introduction to the eleventh century movement in all its aspects.

Church under the direction of the reformers went about seeking an inner strength based on clear lines of control within and independence from influences without, a clericate welded together against powerful lay forces, a new fervor to which it could give direction and which it could use to expand its influence and its outsized claim to be judge of all the world. The success and the effects of this reform have been viewed in different lights by both its contemporaries and later historians;[4] it certainly contributed greatly to a reforming zeal already strong in the monastic establishment.[5] The Cluniac Benedictines had spread their influence throughout Europe and had given expression to the finest elements of an earlier feudal culture. Cluny was at its height when, in the closing years of the eleventh century, the Cistercian renewal began. The Cistercian reform makes sense, in fact, only against the massive backdrop of two centuries of Benedictine presence within medieval life and culture.[6] But new religious ideals were springing out of an altered world and were finding expression in a renewed primitivism—an interest in the earliest monasticism, and a desire to rid the Rule of Benedict from the accretions of customs and usages which had grown up around it.[7] The foundation of Molesme under Saint Robert in 1075 was one such attempt to live the Rule in all its literal purity. Twenty-three years later this abbot and monastery were to give birth to a still more radical primitivism: Cîteaux.[8]

[4] Lackner, *Eleventh Century*, 131–166, gives a fine introductory discussion on the monastic aspects of the reform.

[5] Ibid., 92–122.

[6] See E. Sackur, *Die Cluniacenser in ihrer kirchlichen und allgemeinachichtlichen Wirksamkeit bis zur Mitte des 11 Jahrhunderts* (Halle: Niemayer, 1892) for a full introduction. Lackner, *Eleventh Century*, presents the development of the monastic reform movement in its context. See also, A. Chagney, *Cluny et son empire* (Lyons: Vitte, 1949).

[7] *Cistercians and Cluniacs: The Case for Cîteaux*, a translation of two works by Idung of Prüfening by J. O'Sullivan, J. Leahey, and G. Perigo, CF 33 (Cistercian Publications, 1977) gives the Cistercian side of the argument. See also D. Knowles, 'Cistercians and Cluniacs: The Controversy between St. Bernard and Peter the Venerable', *The Historian and Character* (Cambridge: University Press, 1963) 50–57.

[8] J. Leclercq, 'The Intentions of the Founders of the Cistercian Order', *The Cistercian Spirit*, 88–133.

The early Cistercians conceived and described their undertaking as something new. This newness represented not only their break with the older monasticism represented by Cluny but became, especially in the writings of Saint Bernard, a central tenet of the Cistercian ideal.[9] By recalling monks to the gospel and primitive monasticism, Cîteaux was also making religious life relevant to an already-changed world; they became a new movement calling Christians to newness of life. In the year 1140 Bernard, the soul of Cistercianism and then at the height of his powers, delivered at Paris a discourse on conversion filled with these ideals.[10] Among his listeners was a bright and capable student of Peter Abelard named Geoffrey of Auxerre, who, without hesitation, left the schools for the cloister.

Little is known of the life of Geoffrey before his entrance into Clairvaux.[11] His sudden conversion apparently caused astonishment, especially when he left Abelard to enroll in a much more demanding discipleship to Bernard.[12] Five years after his entrance he became the abbot's principal secretary, a task that made good use of his considerable theological and literary talents and furthered his education under the tutelage of the genius of the twelfth century.[13] A close study of the first *Life of Saint Bernard*, which was based on Geoffrey's own notes and completed by him, gives some idea of the deep effect this close working relationship had on Geoffrey.[14]

[9] Ibid., 102–104.

[10] See Sermon 18 below for Geoffrey's mention of this discourse. See *S. Bernardi Vita Prima* 4; PL 185:327B.

[11] See *Histoire Littéraire de la France* (Paris: Imprimerie Nationale, 1733–1944) 430–451 for the life. Geoffrey is known both in manuscript testimony and by such early commentators as Geoffrey of Hautecombe and Geoffrey of Clairvaux; see the discussion in J. Leclercq, 'Les ecrites de Geoffroy d'Auxerre', *Recueil d'Études sur S. Bernard et Ses Écrits* I (Rome: Edizioni di Storia e Letteratura, 1962) 28–29.

[12] P. Pechenard, *Histoire de l'Abbaye d'Igny de l'ordre de Cîteaux au diocèse de Reims* (Reims: Imprimerie Coopérative de Reims, 1883) 90; see also, *Vita Prima*, 327B.

[13] J. Leclercq, 'Saint Bernard et ses secrétaires', *Revue Bénédictine* 51 (1951) 208–229, has shown the important creative work of men such as Geoffrey in the literary composition of Bernard's letters and sermons.

[14] A. H. Bredero, 'St. Bernard and the Historians', *Saint Bernard of Clairvaux*, CS 28 (Cistercian Publications, 1977) 31–32. See also R. Lechat, 'Les fragments de *vita et miraclulis S. Bernardi* par Geoffroy d'Auxerre', *Analecta Bollandiana* 50 (1932)

His position as secretary meant close companionship with Bernard on his numerous journeys.[15] This association in travel, the discussions that preceded and followed Bernard's discourses, the continual dialogue involved in composing Bernard's letters and editing his discourses, and the experience of being present at many important events of the day gave Geoffrey wide experience in the political and ecclesiastical events of the times. After the death of Bernard in 1153, the former secretary's life was, for the most part, divided between positions in the Order and political missions. As an intimate of Bernard he would have been considered in possession of something of the original spirit of the Cistercians; as a man trained under Bernard, he was seen to have the expertise to deal effectively with the sensitive politico-ecclesiastical events affecting the Cistercians and the Church.

In 1157 Geoffrey was chosen abbot of Notre Dame d'Igny.[16] Five years later he was elected abbot of Clairvaux, quite possibly to increase his prestige as he advanced the cause of Bernard's canonization. A request for canonization had to come from one in possession of the candidate's remains and Geoffrey, who had begun collecting material for the official *Life* while he was still Bernard's secretary, had practically completed the biography necessary for presentation to Rome.[17] For reasons which remain unclear, the request was denied and Geoffrey began revising his biography to present Bernard in a more discrete light.[18]

In 1165 Geoffrey resigned as abbot of Clairvaux in a conflict still subject to diverse interpretations. *The Chronicle of Clairvaux* claims that he resigned because of allegations enemies made 'justly

---

89–122; Bredero, *Études sur la 'Vita Prima' de saint Bernard* (Rome, 1960) 73–77. The *Exordium Magnum*, Edited by B. Griesser (Rome, 1961) 368, explicitly states: 'Dom Geoffrey was the holy abbot's secretary and was most highly esteemed by him'.

15 See, for example, *Vita Prima*, 395–416, on preaching the second crusade; N. M. Häring, 'The Writings against Gilbert of Poitiers by Geoffrey of Auxerre', *Analecta Cisterciensia* 22 (1966) 30–80, on the council of Reims.

16 Pechenard, 89–114; J. B. E. Carre, *Histoire du monastère de N. D. d'Igny* (Reims: Michaud, 1884) 83–103.

17 Bredero, 'The Canonization of Bernard of Clairvaux', *Saint Bernard of Clairvaux*, 63–100; esp., 84.

18 Ibid., 86–91.

or unjustly'.[19] The *Statutes* of the Order say that he was deposed.[20] A number of elements entered into the opposition to Geoffrey: the battle between Thomas Becket and Henry II of England—a conflict in which Geoffrey had implicated himself; failure of the 1163 canonization request and the consequently diminished appreciation for Geoffrey's portrait of Bernard; growing complaints about Geoffrey from people inside and outside the Order; and, perhaps the beginnings of the calcification which seems inevitable in a religious order after the death of a great leader.[21] Whatever the confluence of forces which led to his abdication, and the relative strength of known and unknown elements influencing this event, Geoffrey retired to Cîteaux as a simple monk.

But his simple life at the motherhouse of the Cistercians was to be short-lived. The conflict between Frederick Barbarossa and the curial cardinals had resulted in the election of the anti-pope, Victor IV. The ensuing schism had a deep effect on the now widespread Cistercians.[22] Geoffrey was invited to Italy in the capacity of delegate to help resolve the schism. The following two years saw him closely involved in the dispute between Henry II and the Archbishop of Canterbury. The moral authority he enjoyed owing to his friendship with Bernard, his own talents, and the immense diplomatic experience had gained in his eight years as Bernard's secretary singled him out for one important task after another. In 1171 he was chosen abbot of the monastery at Fossanova, and in 1176 abbot of Hautecombe. More than once he addressed the general chapter or spoke in its name at councils.[23] He seems to have retired to Clairvaux around 1188 and nothing else is known of his

[19] PL 185:1248A.

[20] J. M. Canivez, ed., *Statuta Capitulorum Generalium Ordinis Cisterciensis* I (Louvain: Bibliothèque de la RHE 9, 1933) 75–76.

[21] M. Preiss, 'Die politische Tätigkeit und Stellung der Cistercienser im Schisma von 1159–1177', *Historische Studien* 248 (1934) 84–92; S. Lenssen, 'L'abdication du Bienheureux Geoffroy comme abbé de Clairvaux', *Collectanea Cisterciensia* 17 (1955) 89–110; Bredero, 'Canonization', 90–94.

[22] Preiss, 88–90.

[23] J. Leclercq, 'Le témoignage de Geoffroy d'Auxerre sur la vie cistercienne', *Analecta Monastica*, II series (Studia Anselmiana 31, 1953) 177.

life or his death. He is honored among the Cistercians with the title 'blessed'.[24]

Geoffrey's literary works, published and unpublished, have been listed by Jean Leclercq.[25] This wide-ranging list includes work preparatory to the biography of Bernard as well as books three through five of the *First Life*. There is a collection of Bernard's letters, a series of sermons on the master and on various other important personages, and some occasional sermons commenting on contemporary events. He wrote a refutation of Gilbert of Poitiers, whom Bernard had opposed, a treatise on the mystical significance of numbers, and two major biblical commentaries—one on the Song of Songs, and the commentary presented here on the first three chapters of the Revelation of Saint John.

Geoffrey's Latin style, while it does not rival Bernard's best works in sheer power,[26] is elegant and nuanced. His wide vocabulary, sonorous language, and precise expression suggest that a fine literary and philosophical education had preceded any educational benefits stemming from Bernard's training.[27]

These twenty sermons were originally discourses delivered in diverse circumstances, probably liturgical, to cistercian audiences.[28] Gastaldelli's work on the manuscript tradition gives convincing proof of his hypothesis that toward the end of his life Geoffrey collected these sermons, reworked them to give the series a literary and thematic continuity, added an occasional doctrinal elaboration, and presented the whole as a biblical commentary.[29] The evidence points to a date sometime around the year 1188 for the collection,

[24] J. Leclercq, 'Textes et manuscripts cisteriens dans diverses bibliothèques', ASOC 12 (1956) 307; S. Lenssen, ed., *Menologium Cisterciense* (Westmalle, 1952) 252.

[25] Leclercq, 'Les ecrites de Geoffroy d'Auxerre', 27–46; see also, *DS* 6, 227–29.

[26] See C. Mohrmann, 'Observations sur la langue et le style de Saint Bernard', *S. Bernardi Opera* 2 (Rome: Editiones cistercienses, 19) 9–33.

[27] F. Gastaldelli, *Goffredo di Auxerre: Super Apocalypsin*, Temi e Testi 17 (Rome: Edizioni di Storia e Lettratura, 1970) 40–41.

[28] Ibid., 42.

[29] Ibid., 41–44.

while the final revision would have been completed in the years immediately following.[30]

The content of the sermons is wholly traditional and demonstrates a wide acquaintance with biblical and theological sources.[31] We have a fragmentary record of his feelings toward Joachim of Fiore, his younger contemporary and commentator on apocalyptic themes.[32] Perhaps the work of Joachim and the general interest in eschatological speculation to which the Calabrian abbot gave voice dictated Geoffrey's choice of a biblical book on which to preach and comment.[33]

Joseph Gibbons, CSSP

[30] Ibid., 47–51.

[31] See Leclercq, 'Le témoignage de Geoffroy d'Auxerre', 174–201, for an excellent summary of Geoffrey's theology of the monastic and Cistercian life, complete with long excerpts from his unpublished works.

[32] Ibid., 200–201.

[33] For Joachim, see H. Grundmann, *Neue Froschungen über Joachim von Fiore* (Marburg, 1950). For Bernard, B. McGinn, 'Saint Bernard and Eschatology', *Bernard of Clairvaux*, 161–185.

Table of Abbreviations

ASOC	Analecta Sacri Ordinis Cisterciensis; Analecta Cisterciensia
BMVP	Bibliotheca maxima veterum patrum
CCh	Corpus christianorum
CF	Cistercian Fathers series
CS	Cistercian Studies series
CSEL	Corpus scriptorum ecclesiasticorum latinorum
PL	Patrologiae cursus completus . . . series Latina
RB	Rule of Saint Benedict
SBOp	Sancti Bernardi Opera
SCh	Sources chrétiennes series

Sermon One

The Apocalypse of Jesus Christ, which God gave him, to make known to his servants the things which must soon come to pass. He communicated it, sending it by his angel to his servant John, who gave testimony to the Word of God and to the testimony of Jesus Christ, whatsoever he saw. Blessed is the one who reads and who hears the words of this prophecy and who keeps the things here written; for the time is near.† †Rv 1:1–3

THE BOOK OF THE APOCALYPSE, as this brotherhood well knows, is read by custom in the churches of Christ during these days. With the Lord's approval, we have drawn for you a sermon on its beginning sections. Its very depth, however, not to mention our own unworthiness and lack of expertise, make the task difficult.

Blessed Jerome asserted that this book not only has as many interpretations as it has words, but that the layers of its meaning exceed the number of its words as honey overflows the waxen cells of the richest comb.[1] For us to comment on the very book we

[1] Jerome, *Ep* 53.9; CSEL 54:463.

see that not only he but all the earliest and greatest doctors of the church avoided is quite difficult. Among the canonical scriptures it holds the last place, even though John's gospel certainly came later in time than the Apocalypse. But just as the Gospel of John is a fitting complement to those preceding it, so Scripture itself ends with the Apocalypse that the canon may find an incorruptible end at the hands of a virgin in whose book the Lord says: 'I am alpha
†Rv 1:8, 21:6 and omega, the beginning and the end'.†

Deservedly is it read in the church during these days, that at the time of the Lord's resurrection the glory of his own revelation may be more prominently preached. John's very person stands out as a marvelous example in so many ways: his apostolic office; his badge of virginity; the privilege of Christ's love; and the exile imposed for his devotion to the faith and his constancy in preaching. A cause demands an effect of the same degree, and to such an exile such a consolation was owed.

[John] never lost his special solicitude for the state of the churches. In this vision he mentions it before all else, to reprove those needing correction, to console the afflicted, to rejoice with those making progress, and to stir them to still more progress by his counsels. The Lord did not leave the disciple so dear to himself desolate but, as was fitting and profitable, gave him a manifestation
†1 Co 12:7 of the Holy Spirit for the common good.† How much less prudent and less healthy is envy of those who are occupying themselves with
†Ps 131:1 things too great and too marvelous for them,† of those who heed
†Lv 19:26 dreams contrary to the law,† of those who follow visions from which no edification is seen for themselves or their neighbors, but which instead provide an occasion for presumption and vanity. Thus we must judge their revelation an illusion more imaginary than spiritual, for none of them is proficient in humility, fear of the Lord, charity, or seriousness, and none is found to be fervent, solicitous, or earnest in penance, patience, and obedience. Not only the first vision of the Apocalypse, but the rest as well, were divinely shown blessed John to aid holy church, and to be especially useful in times to come, after the excesses of the present. By the Lord's revelation he realized that persecutions of the faithful were not to happen just in his own day, and at [the Lord's] command he wrote this down so that many

should know of them through him, and that the arrow should inflict less injury.[2]

As the first John, the Baptist, was said to be 'more than a prophet'† because he not only predicted the Saviour's coming but pointed him out when he came, so also this second John, the sharer of both his name and his grace, was no less 'more than a prophet' for he saw in the spirit equally things past, present, and future. Observing himself along with the other evangelists, and foreseeing the gospel he was going to write (where especially he showed he was 'more than a prophet') John prophesied of himself after Ezekiel, who had prophesied of him.† Showing the truth of his name, which means 'the grace of God',[3] he informs us that he is not only dear to God and acceptable, but also 'graced' in another sense, that is, 'grateful'—just as when Paul, admonishing his disciples to give thanks, says: 'Let the word of Christ dwell in you, and be grateful.'† Nor does he put his own name in the title, but, professing right at the start that he is a servant, he faithfully praises the author of his revelation, his teacher who loves him. Thus he begins: *The Apocalypse of Jesus Christ.*†

†Mt 11:9; Lk 7:26

†Ezk 1:10; Rv 4:7

†Col 3:16, 15

†Rv 1:1

Not only this book but all the rest of the New Testament, except the gospel of Matthew and the apostle Paul's letter to the Hebrews, was written in Greek. The word *apocalypse* is Greek and means 'revelation'. Revelation can mean the matter revealed, as in the revelation of secrets; it can mean the person to whom something is revealed, as in the song of Simeon: 'A light to the revelation of the nations';† it can refer to the one revealing, as when the Apostle says: 'Let me come to the revelations of the Lord'.†

†Lk 2:32

†2 Co 12:1

The Apocalypse, the revelation of Jesus Christ, should be taken to mean that something was revealed not to him but by him. For it goes on: *which God gave him to make known to his servants.*† If it had simply said, 'which God gave him', and had nothing following, it would seem to refer to things revealed to him rather than by him. But since Scripture makes absolutely no mention of anything revealed to him, it is evident that the Lord gave him this revelation

†Rv 1:1

[2] Gregory the Great, *Homiliae in Evangelia* 2.35.1; PL 76:1259C; CS 123:301.

[3] Jerome, *Liber interpretationis hebraicorum nominum* 69.16; CCh 72:146.

not for his benefit but that he might make it known to his servants. Whatever the Son has as a divine person, he has from the Father, seeing that he proceeds from him, not from himself. Nevertheless the Son is neither later nor inferior but in all things and in every respect coeternal and coequal. As a human person, however, he possesses what God has given him, what the Godhead has given, what the entire Trinity has given, seeing that (as blessed Augustine reminds us in commenting on the verse, 'and my prayer will be
†Ps 35:13 turned into my breast')† in Christ there is a humanity that intercedes with the divinity in himself.[4]

Furthermore, something called 'revelation' must deal with matters hidden and veiled. Yet since we know that a great deal lies hidden in this veiled revelation, none of us should presume on his own powers of exposition, especially when he reads that the revelation was given [to John] to be make known not to just anyone but to [God's] servants.

If the title *Apocalypse* demands at the onset a serious intention to investigate, then the listener is required to be still more attentive and well-disposed[5] at this reminder of Jesus Christ. Its usefulness for salvation and its gentleness in applying remedies are recommended—it is truly good because it is useful for salvation, and engaging because
†Si 38:78 it applies remedies.† While its very remedies may teach us all things, the words following the title make us teachable as well: *which God*
†Rv 1:1 *gave him to make known to his servants*.† There are different kinds of revelations, but because this one is so lofty and outstanding, it is granted greater certainty in proportion as it is proven more worthy and sublime.

Nor should we doubt that this revelation is profitably asked and hoped for only from him to whom God has given it to be made known to his servants. Let no one, no matter how learned, presume on his own efforts, but let anyone who desires this revelation mark well that it is made known only to servants. Indeed not all who bear the name Christian serve Christ as their Lord; some, sadly enough,
†Rm 16:18 serve their bellies instead.† Those who serve mammon cannot at the

[4] Augustine, *Enarrationes in psalmos* 34.5; CCh 38:316.

[5] *Glossa ordinaria* Ap 1; PL 114:710C. Augustine, *De doctrina christiana* 4.2: CCh 32:117.

same time serve Christ.† It is a service of idols,* with which there can †Mt 6:24; Lk 16:13
be no traffic. Remember what Saint Agatha said: 'We find the great- *Ga 5:20
est freedom when our service of Christ is put to the test.'[6] Serving
him is not only freedom; it is to reign.[7] Careful reflection shows us
that we here and now have no choice but to serve, for, if a person
finds himself in the grip of sin, he has become its servant. What
twisted freedom, for people freed for justice to be servants of sin!† †Rm 6:20
How much better to be freed from sin and made servants of God,
to bear fruit for sanctification, and to have eternal life as their goal.† †Rm 6:22

Now if Christ himself possessed only what he received from
God, who are you to glory when you have not as yet received?† †1 Co 4:7
If you want Rachel you must serve for her or you will not receive
her or have her.† Although the Lord said: 'I no longer call you †Gn 29:18
servants',† yet he advised [his disciples] that when they do all that †Jn 15:15
has been commanded they should admit that they are servants, and
useless ones at that.† †Lk 17:10

There is another possible way of understanding this: it is not said
that God would give the *Apocalypse* to Jesus Christ *to make known to
his servants* but to publish through it *the things which must soon come
to pass*.† Let us understand *apocalypse* as referring to these things, as †Rv 1:1
the vehicle for publishing *the things which must*—for good reason,
or inevitably—*soon come to pass*. What it commands or advises in
the fervor of the Holy Spirit must be put into effect without delay
or hesitation, and be accepted in exactly that way, for the One
who is known to be pleased only with a cheerful giver.† Just as the †2 Co 9:7
person who hesitates has shown his unwillingness[8] and one who
finds reasons for delay has no fear of the judgment awaiting the
sinner, so someone who gives *soon* gives twice over.[9] He deserves
greater grace who obeys God at the hearing of the ear† just as the †2 S 22:45; Ps 18:45
first apostles left everything and followed the Redeemer† at a single †Lk 5:11
word of command. Does not 'O God, come to my assistance, O
Lord, make haste to help me'† resound all day long in our mouths? †Ps 70:1

[6] See *Antiphonarium officii* III, n. 5053.

[7] *Gelasian sacramentary* n. 1476. Bernard of Clairvaux, *Sermones in psalmum 'Qui habitat'* 7.4, SBOp 4:415. *Ep* 377.1; PL 182:582B.

[8] Seneca, *De beneficiis* 2.5.4.

[9] Syrus Publius, *Sententiae* 274.

How bold would it be to ask and insist like this if we ourselves are negligent and dawdle![10]

†Dn 13:45; cf RB 63:6

I remember well seeing a new Daniel of our own time,† a talented and pious boy. He entered the monastery of Clairvaux as a youngster, and was received as a lay brother when his father and brother were received. His companions, older than he, congratulated him enthusiastically because he had taken on the Lord's yoke so early in life. 'I did not come soon', he replied. 'Blessed would one be who was born here'. He came close to feeling the singular joy which John [the Baptist] felt in his mother's womb.† After a few years he became worn out by protracted and severe illness, for he had contracted leprosy, and on Christmas Day he appeared to die—but really he came to life in Christ. When he was laid out in the brothers' choir those who had heard his words remembered them, and they rejoiced to see fulfilled the antiphon they were even then singing: 'Unto us a child is born!'[11]

†Lk 1:41

But why do people delay doing penance and working out their own salvation when God is calling them to conversion without delay? Why do they hesitate and make excuses—is it not because they love evil, and turning away from God pleases them more than turning to him? Are they not snatched away unwillingly from what they love so much.

No wonder—or rather, a real wonder, and a sad blunder—that we count it delightful to be under the briars,† that we put so little faith in the one who promises: 'Take up my yoke and you shall find rest'.† This refers not to the future but to the present, as we see straightway: 'For my yoke is sweet and my burden light'.† My beloved, I beg you, let us hasten, because if the things that certainly must *soon come to pass*† be delayed they can be irretrievably lost. Delay brings danger in its wake; it increases our chances of damnation, it lessens our reward, and the one who withdraws his hand from the proffered gift gravely insults the giver.[12]

†Jb 30:7

†Mt 11:29

†Mt 11:30

†Rv 1:1

[10] Ps 70:1 is the opening versicle and response of each monastic office throughout the day. RB 17:3, 18:1.

[11] Introit of the day Mass of Christmas, *Verona sacramentary* n. 1245.

[12] *Trahit ad se mora periculum, protrahit damnum, subtrahit lucrum et muneranti graviter detrahit, qui a tanto munere retrahit manum.*

If we hasten, so will he; he will quickly hasten to help us. He will soon hasten, he will soon help. He comes in giant steps while we come like tortoises. Let us unhesitatingly believe what Truth has foretold, what he promises will soon come to be, lest perhaps the delay seem longer than it really is and occasion arise for dissolute living, for unbelief and complaining. What is it the wicked servant says, that his lord is long in coming? He will come on a day not
counted on and at an hour unknown.† He will come and not delay;* †Lk 12:45–46
he alone knows when the time will be. It will soon come to pass *Hab 2:3; Heb 10:37
that our momentary and light tribulation will work for us an eternal
weight of glory.† He will soon come, and soon the end of all works †2 Co 4:17
and the distribution of rewards will come to pass.

He communicated it, sending it by his angel to his servant John.† †Rv 1:1
Although this is a revelation, a publishing forth, it comes by a
messenger, with a sign, with a mirror and a riddle,† as the neck- †1 Co 13:12
laces of the bride are inlaid with silver.† It takes its beginning †Sg 1:11
from God the Father; it comes through Christ, through the angel, through John; through their angels to the seven churches and now, through them, at last to us. No wonder that he who called himself a servant calls us servants, even though he was chosen among the first disciples, held a special place among these friends, and was singled out for the privilege of love. No wonder he was not puffed up by this great revelation, but calls himself a servant, for the angel says to him: 'I am a fellow servant with you and
your brethren'.† †Rv 19:10

Who gave testimony to the Word of God.† John endured a long †Rv 1:2
martyrdom, holding the present world in disdain and enduring many afflictions. Together with the other apostles he gave testimony
with great power to the Lord's resurrection.† He who hoped to †Ac 4:33
reign with him was not afraid to suffer with him. He who went out from the presence of the council rejoicing endured a long martyrdom, so often was he considered worthy to suffer reproach
for Christ.† He gave testimony by being boiled in oil, by tolerat- †Ac 5:41
ing exile, drinking the Lord's cup as he had said he would.† He †Mt 20:22
gave testimony by perseverant preaching, by his letters, by example and deeds, and by this very *Apocalypse*. Finally he gave testimony by writing his own gospel. There, as Peter, acting not from his
own power but from Christ's, did greater works [than Christ],† †Jn 14:12

such as curing the sick who lay in the streets not by the touch [†Mt 14:36; Ac 5:15] of his hem but merely by his shadow,† so we see John, no less inspired by Christ, saying something more sublime: 'In the beginning was the Word, and the Word was with God', and all that [†Jn 1:1] follows.†

If John had said 'to the words of God' (in the plural), this would seem to refer to the words the Lord spoke in the flesh, and he would be understood to be giving testimony to what he had heard [†1 Jn 1:1] and seen.† As it is, this refers to the divinity of the Word of God; [†Rv 1:2] *the testimony of Jesus Christ, whatsoever he saw*† refers to his humanity. *Whatsoever* does not mean singular events, but should be understood as referring to various generalized notions, like certain indications given by the humanity he assumed: examples of meekness and humility; cures and signs of diverse powers; the sufferings of the passion and the glory of the resurrection and ascension into heaven; and the visible form in which he sent the promised Holy Spirit to the disciples. He even ended the book of his own gospel later with [†Jn 21:25] the reminder that not everything was written therein,† nor indeed could be written.

[†Rv 1:3] *Blessed is the one who reads.*† He promises happiness to well-disposed readers who, marking the author, the subject matter, and the messengers, have become docile and attentive. For the first inducement to learning is the sublimity of the teacher;[13] the final inducement is the fruit of the labor, the reward of happiness.

Blessed is the one who reads, either to himself or to another, *and who hears* from another who is reading or teaching *the words of this prophecy*, of this vision, if he *keeps the things here written*. He keeps them by firmly believing, by faithfully complying with its admonitions and commands, by effectually desiring and awaiting the things promised, and by fearing and shunning its threats. Another translation has: 'those who hear and keep',[14] because many can hear what one person reads.[15]

13 Ambrose, *De virginibus* 2.2.7, I. Cazzaniga, ed. (Turin: 1948) 36.

14 This is the *Vetus Latina*; see Primasius, *Commentarium super Apocalypsim beati Iohannis libri quinque* 1.1; PL 68:797C.

15 *Glossa ordinaria*, Ap 1; PL 114:710D.

Blessed too are those who keep [these things], so that a good seed bears good fruit and is not trampled underfoot by people.† †Mt 5:13 Blessed are those who by holy zeal and the intention of virtue surrender their own passions, and even those of others, by its warnings and examples. Then the birds of heaven will not devour [the seeds], nor will evil spirits pluck them from their hearts† by †Mk 4:4, 15 contrary suggestions (as the serpent deceived Eve by its cunning†) †2 Co 11:3 so that their senses are seduced away from faith lest as believers they be saved and blessed. Let them keep these things lest plants weakly rooted dry out in the heat of tribulation, as James warns: 'Do not wander about in the heat.'[16] This means, do not wonder, do not consider it a novel wandering, if the heat of persecution comes your way. Let them keep these things, lest they be choked by the thorns and briars of the riches and cares that grow up alongside them. Let them keep these things perseveringly, not willfully omitting them through injustice, not deceived into losing them through imprudence, not seduced by others into rejecting them through intemperance, not allowing them to be violently taken from them through cowardice.

The faithful teacher, fearful for those undergoing tribulation, warns how short the time is even now, saying: *for the time is near.*† †Rv 1:3 To the afflicted there seems no more dangerous temptation than the broad range of vexations and the delay of consolation. Would that his warning could stay constantly before us, for the time of our promised blessedness is near. May it soon come to pass, may it soon come† and never again pass away. The faithful witness who †Is 51:14 is truthful and true,† God above all who is blessed for ever, has †Rv 3:14 promised. Amen.

[16] Geoffrey is quoting not James but 1 Peter 4:12.

Sermon Two

John to the seven churches which are in Asia, grace to you and peace from him who is and who was and who is to come, and from the seven spirits who are in his sight, and from Jesus Christ, who is the faithful witness, the firstborn of the dead and the prince of the kings of the earth. He loved us, and washed us from our sins in his own blood, and made us a kingdom and priests to God and his father. To him be glory and empire for ever and ever. Amen.† †Rv 1:4–7

JOHN TO THE SEVEN CHURCHES *which are in Asia.*† With the insight of the meekness and humility he learned from his master, the Lord's beloved disciple forbore inscribing his own name at the beginning of the book of the Apocalypse just as, later on, in the body of his gospel, he preferred to speak of himself by a paraphrase rather than by his own name. Here, recalling that the Apocalypse was sent by the Lord through his angel, he shows himself a faithful servant, not forbearing to write to them in his own person, for this revelation was sent for their edification, and he exercised ecclesiastical authority among them as Christ's agent. We are not to believe that the apostle received the name John, which means 'the

†Rv 1:4

grace of God', or 'in whom grace dwells',[1] without the consent of
him who numbers the multitude of spiritual stars and calls them
†Ps 147:4 each by name.†

Graced and accepted by God, he received the privilege of
this love. In and through everything he proved his gratitude and
fidelity. How fortunate is the person who has grace, in whom grace
steadfastly remains. As the Lord says: 'If anyone loves me he will
keep my word, and my Father will love him, and we will come
†Jn 14:23 to him and make our dwelling with him'.† John is therefore the
†Ac 9:15 disciple of love, just as Paul is the vessel of election†—they above all
others have commended the grace of love. Paul taught that nothing
†1 Co 13:3 is of profit without love;† John taught that God is love.* That Paul
*1 Jn 4:8, 16 labored more than all the others, that he labored with great effort,
that he brought forth fruit, even that he existed, he rightly attributed
†1 Co 15:10 entirely to grace† and not to his own foolishness.* And so richer
*2 Co 11:16–17 grace flowed out to him because he gave it back to the one from
whom it came.

No other debt or repayment of debt is comparable to the manifestation of grace and to thanksgiving. In a marvelous way our repayment renders both the Lord and ourselves for a time greater debtors. A person's merit grows in God's sight in proportion to his faithfulness in thanking. Since this is itself the gift of grace, which our gracious Remunerator bestows[2] that we may thank him, there is a sense in which God becomes more indebted to the person each time he accepts his thanks. But since any human merit is nothing but the gift of God, for every meritorious act of thanksgiving that he pays he owes yet more, just as by giving more back he has
more. Perhaps the words of the wedding song may commend this
†Sg 2:16 miraculous exchange of grace: 'My beloved is mine and I am his';†
†Sg 6:2 'I belong to my beloved and my beloved belongs to me'.† Each of
these refers to the gift and act of divine condescension, for, solely
by his goodness and kindness, he freely allows humans to be in debt
†Ps 16:2 to him and he to them. He has no need of our goods,† but knows
that we are utterly in need, and unworthy, of his.

[1] Jerome, *Liber interpretationis hebraicoru m nominum* 69.16; CCh 72:146.

[2] *Remunerator benignus. Verona sacramentary* n. 662.

John to the seven churches.† Those who write much about numbers †Rv 1:4
call seven 'virginal'[3] because it is unfactorable by prime numbers. It is quite amazing that authors not inspired by faith see virginity in terms of both the absence of union and the absence of the power to beget. Not without reason are the gifts of the Holy Spirit sevenfold, for by the Spirit occurred the virginal conception of Christ, different from all others. The same number consecrates the Apocalypse revealed to John, whom the privilege of virginity, by the power of the Word,
made the Virgin's son after Christ and in Christ's place.† Thus there †Jn 19:26–27
are seven visions in the Apocalypse and the number seven appears throughout.

Finally, [John] particularly directed seven churches, pre-eminent among which was the city of Ephesus. And although the Greeks' churches do not receive the vow of chastity from their ministers (using as a reason Saint Paul's text: 'I have no command from the
Lord concerning virgins, but I give my advice'†), by the connection †1 Co 7:25
we traced above between the number seven and virginity this church's minsters are warned that they must neither extend the human race nor increase it with their fleshly children. This may be because [Melchizedek], who is commended in the Old Testament as
the first priest of the Lord,† is said by the Apostle to have had neither †Gn 14:18
father nor mother nor offspring.† The renewal of his [priestly] order †Heb 7:3, 6
is promised in the psalms,† so that at his promotion to the priesthood †Ps 110:4
no partiality may be shown to his parents and after his promotion no succession may be expected by his sons. But like the number seven—which is, as we said above, unfactorable by prime numbers—he may beget sons purely spiritually, that is, by the gospel, and no one may boast of being his fleshly progeny. Now Melchizedek was, like other human beings, born of fleshly parents, but he is said to have been without them because Genesis makes no mention of them.

It is not new to you who, I assume, have your hearts set on new things, that 'synagogue' means 'assembled together' and 'church'

[3] Macrobius, *Commentarii in Somnium Scipionis* 1.6.18, J. Willis, ed. (Leipzig: 1963). Martianus Capella, *De nuptiis philologiae et mercurii* 7.738, A. Dick, ed. (Leipzig: 1925). Isidore of Seville, *Liber numerorum* 8; PL 88:186A. Thomas the Cistercian, *Commentarii in Cantica Canticorum* 6; PL 206:362C.

means 'called together.'[4] But it is fitting that you keep in mind
that the gospel tells of the learned scribe (which I certainly am
not) who is compared to a householder taking from his treasury
†Mt 13:52 things new and old.† Therefore God calls his churches, which he
†Rm 8:29 foreknew and predestined;† he calls them to come and cleave to
him; he calls them together to cleave to one another. He calls when
†Dt 6:5; Mt 22:37; Mk 12:30; Lk 10:27 he says, 'You shall love the Lord your God';† he calls them together
when he adds, 'You shall love your neighbor as yourself'.†a He
†aLv 19:18; Mt 19:19, 22:39; Rm 13:9; Ga 5:14; Jm 2:8 calls them to himself to be one spirit with him;†b he calls them
together to be one in him.†c Now we speak of an 'assembly' even
†bEp 4:4 of insensible or irrational things, and perhaps mystically endow
†cJn 17:11, 21 insensible beings with some emotion of piety, but irrational beings
have no understanding of truth.

Moreover we see from their difficult and dangerous location
how necessary the divine call is to these churches. [The text] says that
†Rv 1:4 they are *in Asia*.† The name of the province which comprises these
churches means 'rising' or 'risen'.[5] 'Wonderful are the risings of the
†Ps 93:4 sea', but far more 'wonderful is the Lord on high!'† Asia's rising is
marvelous, but unstable and apt to fall; the Lord dwells on a height
†1 Jn 5:19 stable, solid, and eternal. Asia is 'a world seated in wickedness'†
†Mt 18:7 to which was said: 'Woe to you on account of scandals',† perils, and continuous uncertainty. Happy are those whom 'he who
†Ps 113:5 lives on high'† calls together to himself! Happy those who do
not refuse when called, to whom his hand is stretched out when
†Ps 106:47 they cry 'Lord, save us!'† By grasping them, he saves those who
grasp him.

If we understand 'rising' in another way, as 'elevation', it can
mean God's lofty throne among the angels, which people refer
†Is 6:1 to as 'elevated'.† Among angels this elevation is solid, and their
sublime state belongs to their very condition; the elevation of humans follows after ruin. Thus the church especially 'elevated' is not inappropriately called 'Asia'. Its seven churches are not just the ones that John the apostle particularly led, but rather they comprise all the churches.

[4] Isidore of Seville, *Etymologiarum libri* 8.1.8, W. H. Lindsay, ed. (Oxford, 1911).

[5] Jerome, *Liber interpretationis hebraicorum nominum* 80.10; CCh 72:159.

Grace to you, he says, *and peace*.† He wishes grace to others in †Rv 1:4
whom grace dwells, and shows himself gracious, for he desires,
without envy, that his many neighbors participate in the gift of
grace. And rightly does he do this, for, as a fire suffers no loss when
light is borrowed from it, so the oil that the faithful widow poured
into borrowed vessels at Elijah's word did not cease until her son,
who was ordered to bring a vessel, answered that he had none.† †2 K 4:6
There are many kinds of grace,† but anyone who asks simply for †1 Co 12:4
grace wishes to receive it either in its simple form or in the various
manifestations necessary to salvation.

Because sometimes we do not know what to wish or pray for,
not only for others but even for ourselves, or what would be most
beneficial for us, we do well to commit the matter to the one who
loves souls.† For once he has given us the power of prayer, he whom †Ws 11:26
we are sure can neither deceive nor be deceived stands ready to bring
it to completion. And so, if we confess that all the present merits
of humanity, and all the present gifts and benefits of God here, are
to be genuinely attributed to his grace, we can wait for peace in
the happiness to come. Meanwhile, 'the life of a human is a warfare
upon earth',† where the Lord himself, as he says, came to bring a †Jb 7:1
sword, and not peace.† †Mt 10:34

But since he gives peace, 'since he gives to his beloved sleep'† †Ps 127:2
that they may sleep and rest in peace,† look to the Lord's in- †Ps 4:9
heritance,† where neither body nor world nor evil spirit nor any †Ps 127:3
adversary whatsoever can ever attack or overwhelm [us]. Not even
the least thing can come near to disquiet [us]. This is the peace
for which the prophet prays in the third of the gradual psalms:
'Let peace be in your strength, and abundance in your towers'.† †Ps 122:7
And speaking in another psalm to Jerusalem, he says: 'He has set
your borders at peace, and fed you with the finest wheat'.† This is †Ps 147:14
God's peace, which surpasses all understanding,† where his abode †Ph 4:7
has been established.† This is his rest, which he swore in his wrath †Ps 76:2
that those who err in heart would not enter.† This is the Lord's †Is 28:12; Ps 95:10–11
joy, which the servant who was faithful in a few things, and is
now to be set over many, will enter.† And woe to those wretches †Mt 25:21
who in the meantime cry 'peace and security', because sudden
destruction will come upon them, which they will not be able
to escape!† †1 Th 5:3

But since ecclesiastical commentators[6] understand *grace* here to mean the forgiveness of sins, we may well interpret *peace* to mean steadfastness in avoiding further sin. Thus reconciled we surely have
†Rm 5:1 peace with God† if we are not ungrateful for the forgiveness we have received, and do not refuse to pray as carefully as we can
†Is 59:2 never to repeat the fault. Our sins come between us and God,† and while repentance returns us to his grace, obedience will keep us henceforward in peace.

Let us look at this another way. Peace can mean the forgiveness of sins, and grace can mean gathering merits. It is not unusual in holy Scripture for superior or greater things to be put before the inferior or lesser. In the seven gifts of the Holy Spirit Isaiah begins with the supreme gift of the spirit of wisdom and works his way down to the
†Is 11:2–3 Vulgate spirit of fear,† which is the beginning of wisdom.* John therefore
*Ps 111:10 wishes *grace* for his disciples as a help to living soberly, piously, and
†Tt 2:12 righteously,† and adds to his prayer *peace* as well, that they may obtain
†Heb 4:16 mercy† for the times they have carelessly offended the Lord.

†Ws 4:15 Thus we read that 'God's grace and mercy are with his elect'.† And that they may realize who it is from whom they hope and ask these gifts, and to whom they should give thanks after they have received them, he goes on to add: *from him who is and who was and*
†Rv 1:4 *who is to come*.† Many have understood this to refer to the Son[7] because he is most often called 'he who is to come'. We are used to attributing coming in judgment to the Son because the Father has
†Jn 5:22 given all judgment to him.†

They say that in those days when the church was young the
†Mk 13:22 portents† of various heresies arose about the Son and the Holy Spirit, but not about the Father. Thus Blessed John, pondering where especially he had to issue a warning, and what he had

6 Pseudo-Alcuin, *Commentariorum in Apocalypsin libri quinque* 1.1; PL 100:1092D. *Glossa ordinaria*, Ap 1; PL 114:711B. Anselm of Laon, *Enarrationes in Apocalypsim* 1.1; PL 162:1502C. Richard of Saint Victor, *In Apocalypsim Ioannis libri septem* 1.2; PL 196:696A.

7 Primasius, *Commentariorum super Apocalypsim beati Iohannis libri quinque* 1.1; PL 68:798B. Ambrose Autpertus, *In Apocalypsim* 1; BMVP 13:414. Anselm of Laon, *Enarrationes in Apocalypsim* 1.1; PL 162:1502C. Rupert of Deutz, *In Apocalypsim Iohannis apostoli commentariorum libri XII* 1.1; PL 169:835A. Richard of Saint Victor, *In Apocalypsim Iohannis libri septem* 1.2; PL 196:696B.

most to commend to his readers, is silent about the person of the
Father, whose majesty and omnipotence are not in any question.
He mentions only the Son and the Holy Spirit, for he knew there
were some who understood and held forth about them in a way that
was not fitting. About the text on the Son this was their teaching:
who is means that he still is, for he was never killed and never died;
and who was, indeed, 'in the beginning with God',† for he did not †Jn 1:2
begin at a certain point, but 'the Word was God'† before all time; †Jn 1:1
and who is to come, but certainly not to judge the living and the dead† †1 P 4:5
and repay each person according to his deeds.† Yet surely he *who is* †Mt 16:27; Rm 2:6; Rv 2:23
and who was and who is to come is he of whom it is said: 'Christ Jesus,
yesterday, today and forever'.† Those who said, 'We were hoping that †Heb 13:8
he was the one to redeem Israel',† thought that he had not survived †Lk 24:21
and no longer existed. And those who said, 'You are not yet fifty
years old and have you seen Abraham?'† did not believe that he was †Jn 8:57
before Abraham.† And those whom the awesome anticipation of †Jn 8:58
the judgment† does not correct, who store up for themselves wrath †Heb 10:27
by their hardness and their impenitent hearts,† seem not to know †Rm 2:5
that he is going to come.

And from the seven spirits who are in sight of his throne.[8]† The person †Rv 1:4
of the Holy Spirit is one, but his gifts are many. So many things have been published by so many devout authors of our own time concerning these seven gifts that no one will berate us if we omit our own treatment of these matters and proceed to others.

God's throne is the church. The synagogue was also his chair, but
a humble one, not sublime, seeking the things of earth and relishing
the land of the promise, not the glory of the heavenly kingdom.
In sight of the church the Spirit is sevenfold that he may see every
way, that is, may see and be seen. So we read in the beginning
of Genesis† that he moved over the waters, over the prime matter †Gn 1:2
which was yet crude and confused,[9] warming and dominating it, but
not yet infusing and spreading about the love that is especially his
own throughout the hearts of the faithful.† There was no one in this †Rm 5:5
as yet unformed mass capable of love because no one sharing reason

[8] The Latin here reads: *Et a septem spiritibus, qui in conspectu throni eius sunt*; in the text at the opening of the sermon the word *throni* is omitted.

[9] Ovid, *Metamorphoses* 1.7.

was to be seen. *In sight of the throne* were *seven spirits* when 'there appeared to the disciples parted tongues as of fire, and' the Holy
†Ac 2:3 Spirit 'hovered over each of them'.† The distribution of tongues recalls the varieties of graces. And because an eye is present where there is love,[10] this *sight* signifies both the infusion and the spreading about of love, just as in this revelation the Lamb is described as having
†Rv 5:6 seven eyes 'which are the seven spirits sent into all the earth'.†

†Is 66:2 On this point, where we read 'upon whom my Spirit shall rest',† another version has 'I shall only look upon one who is humble and
†Ps 34:16; 1 P 3:12 peaceful'.[11] Would that as 'the eyes of the Lord are upon the just'†
†Ps 123:2 so also 'our eyes were always on the Lord'† who loves those who
†Pr 8:17 love him† and who grants more ample gifts of his grace to those he finds grateful and loyal to him.

Yet the Holy Spirit alone is not love, nor is Christ the son of the Holy Spirit, although he is the son of Love. Rather, in the Trinity love is sometimes an attribute of the substance common to the three persons, and sometimes especially an attribute of the person of the Holy Spirit. In the same way wisdom is at one time common to the three persons and at another proper to the Son. *In sight of the throne* is the Holy Spirit, seeing and helping others to see, loving and inspiring love.

†Rv 1:5 *And from Jesus Christ, who is the faithful witness.*† In accord with the nature of the godhead, [John], having praised the eternity of the Son, turns to him again to say yet more about his humanity. I remember reading in some commentary or other[12] that these three phrases must be referred to praise of the Trinity so that *from him*
†Rv 1:4 *who is and who was and who is to come*† is understood as said of the Father. We must believe that at the judgment the Father is present in the Son and with the Son, just as that same Son, speaking of the first coming, says: 'He who sent me is with me, and has not left me

[10] Richard of Saint Victor, *Tractus de gradibus charitatis* 3; PL 196:1202D–1203A.

[11] The Septuagint: see Jerome, *Commentarii in Esaiam* 18.3; CCh 73A:770. Gregory the Great, *Moralia in Iob* 5.45; PL 75:724C.

[12] Haymo of Auxerre, *Expositionis in Apocalypsin Beati Iohannis libri septem* 1.1; PL 117:944B. Berengaudus, *Expositio super septem visiones libri Apocalypsis* 1.1; PL 17:846B. Rupert of Deutz, *In Apocalypsim Iohannis apostoli commentarioum libri XII* 1.1; PL 169:835BC.

alone'.† To come to his own is not foreign to the Father, seeing that the Son promises to the one who keeps his words that his Father 'will love him, and we will come to him and make our abode with him'.† In our own language we usually think of 'who is to come' as if it means 'will be', but this is not true in Latin. It seems, then, that by these three words, *is* and *was* and *is to come*, an eternity made up of the three periods of time is commended to us. This is as if to say, 'is, and was, and will be, without beginning, without end', which Genesis meant by the simple verb 'is' when Moses was commanded to say to the children of Israel, 'He who is has sent me to you'.†

†Jn 8:29 †Jn 14:23 †Ex 3:14

And from Jesus Christ.† Ecclesiastical custom has always called the three persons 'Father, Son, and Holy Spirit', for the apostles were told to baptize all nations in their names.† Yet there is complete equality and coeternity among them; one of them is not prior to another in time, or greater in dignity. But because we cannot profess at the same time the three names of these persons we are to adore equally, we can best confess them in that order, because the Son is from the Father and the Holy Spirit is from both. When a reasonable occasion comes along, however, we are not forbidden to vary the order, as here Blessed John mentions the person of the Son in third place because he is going to continue speaking about him.[13]

†Rv 1:5 †Mt 28:19

My sermon must end here, but limitations of time do not mean we must end the subject. Rather, it seems best to devote an entire sermon to these matters, for your edification and for the glory of him[14] who with the Father and the Holy Spirit is one God over all, blessed for ever. Amen.

13 Venerable Bede, *Explanatio Apocalypsis* 1.1; PL 93:134C.

14 Bernard of Clairvaux, *Sermones super Cantica Canticorum* 3.6; SBOp 1:17; CF 4:20.

Sermon Three

JOHN, AS HE DESIRES GRACE AND PEACE for the churches from our Lord Jesus Christ, goes on to add, *who is the faithful witness*.† It is common knowledge that in Greek 'martyr' means witness, and 'martyrdom' means the testimony of a witness. The faithful witness therefore is Christ, the greatest martyr of all, who is both the model and the crown of martyrs.[1] Although in his passion he was silent as a lamb,† having no reproaches in his mouth,* yet several times he seized an opportunity to give witness to the truth since for this was he born and for this he came into the world.†

†Rv 1:5

†Is 53:7
*Ps 38:15

†Jn 18:37

Yes, he is indeed the faithful witness, to whose eyes all things lie naked and open† and whose jealous ear hears everything.* In the future he will bear faithful witness to what he has seen and heard in the meantime, for, as he says through the prophet, he is both witness and judge,† a *faithful witness* and a just judge. He covers over nothing that must be given in witness and neglects nothing that must be judged, witnessing in truth and judging in equity. He is the faithful witness to the testimony the three give in heaven.† How blessed is the one who so confesses him before humans that [Christ] may also confess that one in the presence of his Father!†

†Heb 4:13
*Ws 1:10

†Jr 29:23

†1 Jn 5:7

†Mt 10:32; Rv 3:5

[1] Bernard of Clairvaux, *Sermones super Cantica Canticorum* 47.5; SBOp 2:64; CF 31:7.

†Rv 1:5 *The firstborn of the dead.*† He arose from the dead, the first fruits
†1 Co 15:20 of those who sleep,† so that death may no longer have dominion
†Rm 6:9 over him† who is the first to pass through death to immortality. And
†Rm 8:29 he is the firstborn among many brethren,† who, dead to the world
†1 P 2:24 and dead to sin,† by adoption are born to God. He died not for
†Ps 69:5 his own sin but for ours; he paid for what he did not seize.† He is
firstborn, supreme, most excellent; he is above all, for he comes from
†Jn 3:31 heaven.† By his godhead he is the only-begotten; in his humanity
he deigned to become the firstborn, giving to those who receive
†Jn 1:12 him the power to become children of God† that they may be heirs
†Rm 8:17 of God and joint heirs with himself.†

Beloved, think of this birth, this adoption, this brotherhood, so
that all of who have been adopted may strive to be conformed to
this firstborn. Certainly if we die with him we shall also live with
†2 Tm 2:11 him,† as is said: 'For you are dead and your life is hidden with Christ
†Col 3:3 in God'.† He is not firstborn of the dead only that we may imitate
his patience, but that we may see in him, *the prince of the kings of the*
†Rv 1:5 *earth*,† a model of righteousness and the hope of glory.*
*Col 1:27

Through him and under him the faithful rule over their earthly
†Ps 49:2 bodies. Through him the earthbound and the children of men†
obtain the kingdom of heaven. By his choice all earthly powers stand
firm[2] as do the rights of all earthly kingdoms. Those who govern
the people faithfully, wisely, and for their good in his churches
throughout the world humbly serve him. If only our ecclesiastical
and secular rulers would always acknowledge the government laid
†Is 9:6 on his shoulder† and earned by his passion! If only they would pay
him careful honor, extol him with overt dignity, and give him glory
by honoring their commitments, giving due reverence to his greater
majesty instead of taking pride in the number of their subjects to
†Ps 21:3 Vulgate their own folly.†

If only they were always mindful of the government of this *prince*
†Rv 1:5 *of the kings of the earth*,† over and above their own, so that what was
said of the centurion, whose faith the Lord extolled to all Israel,
may be said of them: 'I am a man under authority, and have soldiers
†Mt 8:9 under me'.† If only they would strive to submit to him and serve
him, rather than presume to rule contrary to him and to defy him.

[2] *Verona Sacramentary* n. 872.

If only those who fight under them would attend to their superior prince, and render to God the things that are God's as faithfully and effectively as they render to Caesar the things that are Caesar's.† If only they were not afraid to proclaim in word and deed that they owe the kings of the earth nothing that is forbidden by *the prince of the kings of the earth.* †Mt 22:21; Mk 12:17; Lk 20:25

He loved us, and washed us from our sins in his own blood.† My brothers, we should listen closely to these words, and pay careful attention, because they concern the mystery of our redemption and of our welfare. We must diligently study four matters: the source, the work, the cause, and the means they commend. †Rv 1:5

The source: God and man; the work: our cleansing from our sins; the cause: love; the means: by his own blood. The source's divinity commends glory, his humanity, grace. His divinity raises us up, his humanity increases our affection. His divinity draws our attentive† souls upward; devout consideration of his humanity spreads to all people everywhere so that a person may communicate it to all his fellow humans for whom the God-man deigned to give himself up. †RB Prol 9

The work is the abolition of our sins, a work possible only to him. The greatest sinners used to say of it: 'Who can forgive sins but God alone?'† A difficult work, but of no little effect; a great work, and greatly needed for everyone touched by the stain of sin. Moreover, unless people receive complete forgiveness of their sins while still alive, so that after death they can be expiated by others, unforgiven faults and indelible stains will produce undying worms, so that the unquenchable fire† can neither cleanse the stains nor destroy the worms.[3] †Mk 2:7; Lk 5:21 †Mt 3:12; Mk 9:42, 9:44; Lk 3:17

The cause is a love freely given, very great, yes, even 'excessive', as the Apostle put it.† He means nothing negative by 'excessive'; rather he extols its excess as much and more than he could. Rightly do young women love excessively and are in turn loved excessively,† but in comparison with [God's] excess, all their excess is of hardly any moment; it is scarcely anything at all, if this 'anything' can be compared with so great an excess. †Ep 2:4 †Sg 1:2

[3]Bernard of Clairvaux, *Sermones de diversis* 29.2; PL 183:621A.

During the first years of my conversion, a lay brother named Yves, who was very devout, lay dying at the monastery of Clairvaux. To a brother who was visiting him, one who is still alive today and can bear witness today, he said: 'An angel of the Lord appeared to me, showing me his beautiful and joyful countenance as I lay here in my weakness. And he said, "You humans do well to desire the sight and presence of the Lord. If you knew how much he loves you, how much he wants you, with what longing he waits for you, you would hurry to him with far more fervent affection." ' These were his last words, to which his serene summons, which immediately followed, bore sufficiently trustworthy testimony.

But if you do not believe the words of an angel, or the words of a man soon to go to God, believe the works of the Lord,[4] believe the condescension by which the Word became flesh† for your sakes. God became a human for the sake of humans. Believe the bloodshed of the New Testament, believe him suffering, believe him dying, and descending into hell, 'for love is strong as death, and jealousy as hard as hell'.† No greater human love exists than to lay down one's life for one's friends.† Adamant can be rent by goat's blood,[5] and purple cloth, dyed with the blood of a shellfish,[6] is supposed never to suffer discoloration from the sun's heat or to be washed out by rain.

†Jn 1:14
†Sg 8:6
†Jn 15:13

Under the Old Testament the blood of animals poured out, and the sprinkling of a heifer's ashes, were held to cleanse the defiled and absolve the guilty.† Why could the blood of Christ not do the same? When it was shed, not inappropriately rocks were rent, tombs opened, the earth shook,† and the sun experienced dread. 'I will love you, Lord, my strength, my salvation, my hope, my God and my mercy'.† May my soul love you with its whole heart, its whole mind, and all its power.†[a] May it love you, desire you, wait for you, O victorious redeemer, strong helper, and kind support.†[b] May my soul desire one thing, ask for one thing, seek one thing†[c]—to please you, to cleave to you, to enjoy you. May it live for you who deigned

†Lv 16:15; Heb 9:13
†Mt 27:51–52
†Pss 18:2, 27:1, 71:5, 59:18
†[a]Mt 22:37; Mk 12:30; Lk 10:27
†[b]Pss 71:7, 42:10, 3:4
†[c]Ps 27:4

[4] Bernard of Clairvaux, *Ad clericos de conversione* 21.38; SBOp 4:114; CF 25:76.
[5] Pliny, *Naturalis historia* 37.15.
[6] Ibid., 9.60–61.

to die for it, so that you may wash away the stains of its sins in your own blood.

This utterly chokes out ingratitude. You would surely have given many other boundless gifts to the human race, but our excessively odious ingratitude made this complaint: 'Why should he not have been generous? It cost him nothing although it benefitted me! It may help me, and it is so easy for him!' What a crude, blasphemous and foolish way to think! Woe to you, wretch! Is the gift less important to you because it is not costly but freely given? Are you more pleased by its cost than by its usefulness to you? But so that you may realize how exceedingly he loves you, look, he gives a gift you can appreciate deeply, a gift he purchases with the great price of his blood, his death, his cross.

What a marvelous thing, beloved, if we can only keep thus firmly in mind the source, the work, the cause, and the means of our salvation, that this more than threefold cord may not be broken† in us without difficulty. If only these thoughts can draw, can entice, can firmly fasten and indissolubly bind and inseparably bind us to our Saviour! †Qo 4:12

And he made us a kingdom and priests.† Jesus means 'saviour' and Christ means 'anointed'.[7] The angel explained the name Jesus to the spouse of the blessed virgin Mary when he said, 'For he shall save his people from their sins'.† To the name Jesus therefore pertains the phrase *he washed us from our sins*,† and to the name Christ that *he made us a kingdom and priests*,† for he is called the anointed, a true king and priest, a powerful king† and the prince of kings,† a priest offering himself as a sacrifice to God the Father.* The anointing of kings and priests begun under the Old Testament continues today under the New. John himself mentions its grace and spiritual efficacy when he says in his epistle: 'And you have an anointing from the Holy One, and his anointing teaches you of all things'.† †Rv 1:6 †Mt 1:21 †Rv 1:5 †Rv 1:6 †Si 1:8 †Rv 1:5 *Heb 9:14 †1 Jn 2:20, 27

I pray that the priests of modern times may be mindful of the grace, and that they may direct their attention less to worldly honors than to spiritual greatness and constancy, for the priestly anointing

[7] Isidore of Seville, *Etymologiarum libri XX* 7.2.2 and 4.

is worthier than the royal. Kings are anointed only by priests; priests are not anointed by kings.

We read that under the Old Covenant some priests once exercised civil responsibilities. Not only were they not punished for this, they were even commended. But when one of the kings, Uzziah (one of the kings of Judah), who is otherwise highly praised, dared to exercise the priestly office, he was immediately punished by being struck on the forehead with leprosy.† [†2 Co 26:19] Ahijah the prophet, so we read, tore his cloak into twelve parts.† [†1 K 11:30] Ten of them he gave to Jeroboam, saving two for Rehoboam, the son of Solomon. So it came about that the remaining ten tribes in the kingdom of Israel were given over to Jeroboam. With the two tribes of Judah and Benjamin subject to Rehoboam, the thirteenth tribe, Levi, whose task was divine worship and not human rule, remained, and did not pass to the kingdom of Israel.

This twofold anointing, especially if understood spiritually, in that it ought to be common to all the faithful as members of the high priest and king, must be preceded by an ablution because, as it was set down above, *he washed us from our sins in his own blood*.† [†Rv 1:5] We read that Moses first washed Aaron and his sons and then consecrated them to the priesthood.† [†Lv 8:6, 12] In the same way Christ consecrates Christians who have been washed from their sins according to the text, 'Turn from evil and do good'.† [†Ps 37:27] To turn from evil means to renounce sin, something no one can do except in the power of the blood of the unblemished Lamb who alone has washed us and made us clean instead of unclean.† [†Jb 14:4] He alone, having been by the power of faith spread on the lintel, which means the intention of the heart, as well as on the two doorposts of word and work, snatched us from the sword of the destroying angel.† [†Ex 12:23] No one can do good unless he exercises a kind of royal power in bridling the unworthy tendencies and illicit appetites of his heart and body.

The task of the spiritual priest is to seek peace,† [†Ps 34:14; 1 P 3:11] to give God peace offerings† [†Ex 32:6; Lv 9:18] and a sacrifice of praise* [*Ps 50:14, 23] in contemplation, in prayer, and in devotion of mind. The ablution, then, refers to the remedy of penance, the kingdom to the exercise of justice, and priesthood to the study of wisdom. These three elements are commended by those persons beloved by the Lord who lived together in one house, Lazarus, Martha and Mary.† †Jn 11:1–2

Significantly, blessed John reminds us that we do not become kings, but *a kingdom*. We are the kingdom of the King of kings,† †1 Tm 6:15 who alone is blessed and powerful, and who reigns in us with joy and power. [John], in whom grace dwells, is always coming back to a commendation of grace. He removes an occasion for arrogance by frequently reminding us of the one without whom we can do nothing and are nothing. That one reigns in us if through him and under him we reign over ourselves and grow stronger than those who attack our cites, and not only subdue our bodies and bring them into subjection† but gain control of our souls as well. †1 Co 9:27

This same apostle of Christ, mindful of how a wise son should seek his father's glory in everything, adds, *to God and his father*.† This †Rv 1:6 is to be understood simply as 'to God the Father'. It is for his sake, I say, and not for ours, that the apostle recalls that we have been made a kingdom and priests. And he adds, *To him be glory and empire*. Well may this be understood of the Son, since glory and empire belong to him who washed us and made us a kingdom and priests to God his Father. I say, let the kingdom obey his empire, let priests glorify him with wholehearted service, and, as blessed Paul advises, let us glorify God in our hearts and carry him in our bodies—we have been bought at a great price.† †1 Co 6:20

To him be glory,† not to us, for all our good comes from him, †Rv 1:6 not from ourselves. *To him be glory* which, as Scripture says, he will not give to another.† *To him be glory* which it is neither right nor †Is 42:8 expedient for us to take for ourselves. *To him be glory* in the highest, and how wonderful if there should be grace for us and peace on earth for people of good will!† *To him be empire,* that we may obey †Lk 2:14 and serve him, Christ the Lord, and not our bellies,† not mammon;* †Rm 16:18 *Mt 6:24; Lk 16:13 the God of justice, not sin.

The words *forever and ever*,† which follow, encourage us so to †Rv 1:6 persevere that in every change of season or circumstance our meditation may glorify him and our lives serve his empire. Moreover, if we understand *ever and ever* as everlasting and consecutive with the present age, we have here not a petition or a desire—as it may seem—but gladness of heart and the emotion of rejoicing. This is not empty glory but glory that lasts forever. This empire is not like those of which Wisdom says, 'All sovereignty is short-lived',† and in another place, 'The crown is passed from one generation to the next'.† This glory is everlasting, and this empire remains for eternity, as the adoring multitude of angels sing in unison, *Amen*, so be it and so shall it be.

†Si 10:11 Vulgate

†Pr 27:24

'Amen' is a Hebrew word of affirmation[8] but, like 'Hosanna' and 'Alleluia,' it is retained in other languages without being translated. These three words bespeak an assertion, a prayer, and a cry of praise both joyous and proper.† If you judge it fitting, relate them to faith, hope and love, so that faith affirms, hope prays, and love with inexpressible cries of praise extolls the Lord their God to whom be *glory and empire forever and ever. Amen*.

†Ps 147:1

[8] Anselm of Laon, *Enarrationes in Apocalypsim* 1.1; PL 162:1503A.

Sermon Four

Behold, he comes with the clouds, and every eye shall see him, and those too who pierced him. And all the tribes of the earth shall weep over him. Even so. Amen.

I am Alpha and Omega, the beginning and the end, says the Lord God who is and who was and who is to come, the Almighty.† †Rv 1:7–8

B*EHOLD*, THE LORD *COMES WITH THE CLOUDS, and every eye shall see him, and those too who pierced him. And all the tribes of the earth shall weep over him. Even so. Amen.*† †Rv 1:7

His saints often spoke and wrote of the Lord's coming, and, among them, prophets like Isaiah were especially concerned to make known his coming. This occurred not only under the Old Testament but in the time of grace as well. John, whose name means grace[1] and who was especially loved because of his purity, was favored with an extraordinary vision during his exile, as a consolation for his patience. Pleasing and acceptable to God is not only the patience of penitents but, to a lesser extent, the purity of those who suffer tribulations. In John these virtues were all the more pleasing to the

[1]Jerome, *Liber interpretationis hebraicorum nominum* 69.16; CCh 72:146.

one who bestowed them, who himself overcame the sharp edge of a world which flatters deceptively and fights viciously. Such was John, prophesying in his Apocalypse of that coming at which every eye will see the Lord, and he recounts the words just put to you, words the angel announced to him.

†Rv 1:7 *Behold, he comes with the clouds*.† Behold, suddenly, unbeknownst to humans—just as in the days of Noah the flood swept over the unaware. *With the clouds*, with teeming legions of angels,[2] as the
†Heb 12:1 Apostle speaks of a great multitude as a 'cloud of witnesses'.† At his first coming only a few of those who saw him recognized him,
†Lk 10:23 and to them he said; 'Blessed are those who see what you see'.† Wretched to the same degree were those who saw and hated. All the more blessed, at his last coming, will be those who see him as he
†1 Jn 3:2 is, for they will be like him† and unhappy will they be who should have wept with bitter weeping over him. Those who believed while they did not see, who longed for him, who waited expectantly for him, they shall see him. Each of them shall see and rejoice, saying,
†Jb 42:5 'With the hearing of the ear I heard you, and now my eye sees you'.†

Non-believers, dissemblers, the careless—they shall see him as well. They shall see him and weep because they were careless, because they dissembled, because they refused to believe. They shall all see him, and nothing of all that they did, whether deserving of
†Jb 22:19 evil or good, shall they not see. The just shall see and shall rejoice,†
†Ws 5:2 the unjust shall be troubled with terrible fear.† The faithful shall
†Si 44:10; Is 57:1 see the one they obeyed, merciful men† the one they ministered to. The ungodly shall see him whom they dared to persecute—just as
†Ac 9:4 Saul heard his voice address him.† They shall see him whom they refused to serve when at the judgment he turns to speak to those at
†Mt 25:41 his left.† If we think about it, how lightly will we esteem the things we see now, mindful of this vision of him whom every eye, evil or sincere, is going to see in one way or another.

†Rv 1:7 What follows, *and those too who pierced it*,[3]† may be understood to refer to the eye, of which a wise man says, 'Piercing the eye
†Si 22:24 brings forth a tear, piercing the heart brings forth feeling'.† If this

[2] Jerome, *Commentariorum in Zachariam prophetam libri duo* 3.14; PL 25:1526C.

[3] The pronoun *eum* can refer to the eye, which is of the masculine gender in Latin, as well as Christ; the more common interpretation follows.

interpretation is accepted, we go beyond ordinary human vision, and we see that those who make a place in their lives for holy compunction receive a special promise: 'Those who sow in tears shall reap in joy'.† †Ps 126:5

Our eye should be pierced not with some material probe but with spiritual study, that it may bring forth tears deserving of divine consolation. The heart should be pierced with the thought of terrible threats, with a consideration of the perils hanging over it, with the recurring thought of its many sins, so that it may bring forth the beginning of wisdom—the sense of fear†—once the insensitivity of a foolish and false security has been dispelled. †Si 1:16; Ps 111:10; Pr 1:7, 9:10

So every eye—either to its joy or to its confusion—is going to see the humanity of Christ appearing in his flesh. But those who pierced their eye spiritually, who practiced compunction, are going to see the glory of the Majesty of which it is said, 'Take away the ungodly one lest he see the glory of God'.† †Is 26:10 Vetus Latina

But I prefer to understand *who pierced him*† of the Lord himself. I am persuaded to it by another prophecy preserved in the gospel: 'They shall look on him whom they have pierced'.† They shall see his head which they crowned with thorns, his hands and feet which they gouged with nails, his side which they opened with a lance†—not only the gentiles who did these deeds but also the Jews who encouraged them. They most of all, they pierced him more sharply, whose teeth are weapons and arrows, and their tongue a sharp sword.† Saul also pierced him, and he heard, 'Why are you persecuting me?'† Even now the Head is being pierced in his members, pierced in his church, in his beloved, who is among the daughters as a lily among thorns.† The thorny crown pierces his head in prelates who are afflicted by the offenses of their subjects so that the glory of their position becomes a piercing burden. He who said, 'Obey those set over you—who keep watch over your souls—that they may do this with joy and not with sorrow'† forbade his disciples to crown prelates with such thorns. †Rv 1:7 †Zc 12:10; Jn 19:37 †Jn 19:34 †Ps 57:5 †Ac 9:4 †Sg 2:2 †Heb 13:17

The Lord's body is the church;† his hands refer to men holding office, his right hand to spiritual ministries and his left to corporal deputies. In these he is no less pierced by the wicked, pierced by the ungrateful. They pierce his hands with nails when they abuse †Col 1:24

his ministers by their words and attack them by their actions. His feet designate his last and humble members. The two, right and left, are obedient action and penitent satisfaction; one of them directs, the other corrects, the steps of life.

How many times is the Lord pierced even in these, for what
†Mt 25:40 is done to one of his least ones is done to him.† We cannot doubt
that all who wish to live religiously in Christ have to put up with
persecution and piercing blows, and who more than they of whom
the Apostle says, 'For you are dead and your life is hidden with Christ
†Col 3:3 in God'?† Who more than they who seek and mind only things
†Col 3:2 above and not the things that are upon the earth?† When the wicked
do not spare even those dedicated to divine contemplation, it is as
†Jn 19:34 if they pierce the side of someone asleep. Water with blood† comes
out of their wound to enable them not only to bear it patiently
but to find refreshment, to rejoice, and to glory in their tribulation.
As water commends the desire that come from thirst, so too it
commends the consequence of desire when the Prophet calls those
†Is 55:1 who thirst to the water.† Not without reason does John underline
this very important commendation of his wound by saying, 'And
†Jn 19:35 he who saw has given testimony'.†

Now if *those who pierced him shall see him*, how shall *all the tribes*
†Rv 1:7 *of the earth weep over him*?† Will everyone weep, and no one acclaim
him? Will even the chosen weep, perhaps, because they were less
grateful to him, less loyal, less careful than they ought to have been,
less humble, less patient, less aflame with love? This hardly seems to
be the meaning, since the Lord tells his city Jerusalem through the
†Zp 3:11 prophet, 'On that day you will not be ashamed for all your doings'.†
†Rv 1:7 We can better understand *the tribes of the earth*† as those given
over to earthly desires, ensnared in earthly pleasure, intent upon earthly honors, and consumed with earthly business. People like these shall weep over him. They will weep when they consider one they never bothered to heed crucified for their salvation. They will weep for themselves, not for what belongs to them, although all that was theirs will have been destroyed; they will weep for themselves because they will have utterly perished. *The tribes of the earth* will weep because tribes given over to vices—who have acquired earthly goods by malice, greed, and intemperance, who have hoarded what

they acquired or wasted it in dissolute living†—will repent too late. †Lk 15:13
They will weep over him because they will never have learned from his teaching to despise the things of earth and to love the things of heaven.[4] They will weep over him, groaning for anguish of spirit,† †Ws 5:3
because they will have wandered from his way, and the Sun of justice cannot rise upon them.† They will weep over him for what they †Ml 4:2
have committed against him, recognizing now what earlier they had not bothered to see, that they have pierced one of his least ones.

The following phrase, *Even so. Amen,*† is a double affirmation. †Rv 1:7
John, more than the other evangelists, often used 'Amen. Amen'. Perhaps the angel who was speaking said, *Even so*, and John went on to add, *Amen*. This prophecy may echo the words of Zechariah, the eleventh of the twelve prophets, as the Apocalypse is found to have many phrases in common with earlier prophecies.

'They shall look upon me, whom they have pierced', says the Lord— almost saying, 'whom they have crucified'[5]—'and they shall weep as one weeps for an only child'.† Of this great weeping he †Zc 12:10
adds, 'families and families'† will weep, or, as we read in another †Zc 12:12
translation,[6] 'tribe after tribe, and their women apart'. This means that an unreconcilable separation is going to take place, and there will be no hope of solace in living together.

Where four families are expressly named—those of David, Nathan, Levi, and Shimei†—the royal, prophetic, priestly, and teach- †Zc 12:12–13
ing prerogatives are meant. From David the line of kings took its origin; Nathan, his prophet and seer, represents the counselors of kings and princes; Levi was the priestly tribe; and from Shimei, or rather Simeon, the examinations of the teachers arose.

Here it is well to recall that the patriarch Jacob called the two brothers Simeon and Levi 'vessels of iniquity, waging war.'† What †Gn 49:5
follows is usually referred to the Pharisees and priests who conspired in the Lord's murder: 'Cursed be their fury because it is obstinate, and their wrath because it is cruel'.† Otherwise it would hardly be †Gn 49:7
clear why blessed Jerome declared that the examinations of teachers

[4] *Verona sacramentary* n. 421.

[5] *Confixerunt . . . crucifixerunt.*

[6] The Septuagint; see Jerome, *Commentariorum in Zachariam prophetam libri duo* 3.13; PL 25:1515B.

arose out of that tribe.[7] Of course we should not take this man to
†2 S 16:5–13 be that Shimei who cursed David,† but the son of Libni of the tribe
†1 Ch 6:29 of Levi.†

And so we see weeping in these families, as it were of men who follow in their footsteps after vanity of mind, and who seek carnal pleasure among their women. Great will be the weeping of
†Jn 16:20 both types, never to be changed into joy† for them. Other 'families and families' will do the same; for their various crimes the weeds must be tied into bundles for burning. Hence it is that this future
†Zc 12:11 weeping is shown in Jerusalem,† which means among those who have received the sacraments of faith but have not performed the works of faith.

This section can be understood to refer to the Saviour's first coming, and the word may not be *comes* but *came*.[8] For [Christ] had already come in the mystery of the Incarnation by the time this apocalypse appeared to blessed John. It can also be understood in the present tense of [Christ's] coming to the gentiles, for the beginning of their conversion, like a fire consuming woodland and
†Ps 83:14 a flame setting mountains ablaze,† spread from one to another as the
†Ps 147:15 Lord's word ran swiftly.† And so he was coming with the clouds, with the apostles, and in them, and in other preachers who, like clouds, flying by, watered the earth to make it bear fruit by showers of wholesome teaching.

†Rv 1:7 *And every eye shall see him.*† Not yet face to face, of course, but
†1 Co 13:12 by faith, with a mirror by a riddle.† Not only shall people from all the gentile nations accept faith in him, but even from those Jews who pierced and crucified him.

†Rv 1:7 *And all the tribes of the earth shall weep over him.*† People from
†Rv 7:9 all the tribes of the gentiles,† not only from the twelve tribes of
†2 Tm 3:6 Israel, shall weep. They shall weep for their souls laden with sins,† not for their bodies covered with wounds or for their material losses; not over their frustrated hopes for transitory earthly things, or over hindrances to their own will. They shall weep, attributing to themselves alone everything in them they know they should

[7] Jerome, *Commentariorum in Zachariam prophetam libri duo* 3.12; PL 25:1516B.
[8] The word is the same in Latin: *venit*.

weep for. They shall weep, those built on the foundation which is Christ,† as they turn to penance; but those who weep just to complain, to kick against the goad,† to give up hope, are cut off from the foundation.

†1 Co 3:11
†Ac 9:5

Even so. Amen.† [John] uses two adverbs of affirmation to make his confirmation certain and his certitude sure. He uses two adverbs, but the Latin translator leaves the Hebrew word in the Latin text just as he found it in the Greek original.

†Rv 1:7

These two seem to harmonize with what follows: *I am Alpha and Omega, the beginning and the end.*† I am the cornerstone,†[a] making both one,†[b] the end of the law†[c] and the beginning of the gospel, the end of the wall coming from the circumcision, the beginning of the wall coming from the gentiles. I am *the beginning*,† as I told the Jews, by whom all things were made;† and I am *the end* through whom all things are to find their consummation when I shall hand over the kingdom to the God and Father.† I am *the beginning*, because in me at first is the predestination of the elect, and *the end*, because by me at last are all promises fulfilled. I am *the beginning* from which springs every good desire, and *the end* from which comes perfection and perseverance in good works; rightly do my faithful followers offer me first fruits and tithes.

†Rv 1:8
†[a]Is 28:16; Ep 2:20
†[b]Ep 2:14
†[c]Rm 10:4
†Jn 8:25 Vulgate
†Jn 1:3
†1 Co 15:24

Alpha is the first letter of the Greek alphabet and Omega is the last. Thus what he says first, *I am Alpha and Omega*, is immediately explained, *the beginning and the end.*† He *who is* says this, that is, the unchanging one, who changes everything else while remaining the same; *and who was* with the Father before the world was;† *and who is to come* for judgment at the end of time.†

†Rv 1:8
†Jn 17:5
†Is 3:14

What follows, *the Almighty*,† can be taken simply in answer to the question, 'Now who is the Lord of whom you speak?' *The Almighty*! Israel sang to the Lord, among other texts, 'Almighty is his name!'† as also in the psalm, 'the Lord is his name!* We can refer this back to what preceded, *who is and who was and who is to come, the Almighty*. He is *almighty*, so we may hope for help from the mighty and all help from the almighty. He is *almighty*—on him we may lean confidently, not on the hollow staff of our own merits, our own wealth, our own prudence, or on any human gift. He is *almighty*, but he manifests his omnipotence most by pitying and

†Rv 1:8
†Ex 15:3
*Ps 68:5

showing mercy.[9] He was *almighty* who said, 'I am,' and laid out a host of enemies solely by the power of his word.† He shall come *almighty*, not weak, as he earlier showed himself; in all things and through all things he will powerfully show forth his omnipotence in his strength, appearing with the Father and the Holy Spirit, one God, who is blessed throughout the ages. Amen.

†Jn 18:6

[9] *Gelasian sacramentary* n. 1198.

Sermon Five

I, John, your brother and sharer in tribulation and in the kingdom, and in patience in Jesus, was on the island which is called Patmos, because of the word of God and the testimony of Jesus. I was in the spirit on the Lord's day, and I heard after me a loud voice like a trumpet saying . . .† †Rv 1:9–11

I, JOHN, YOUR BROTHER AND SHARER *in tribulation and in the kingdom, and in patience in Jesus, was on the island which is called Patmos.*† In writing to the churches, John began with the †Rv 1:9
customary greeting.† Beyond the usual style of writing, he paused to †Rv 1:4–5
mention the Saviour, thereby satisfying his own devotion and trying to edify those to whom he was writing. He begins to describe the revelation at this passage, and will discuss who, where, how, when and what[1] he saw.

Who: the person reporting is John, already known and respected by them, their brother by their common holy baptismal

[1] Primasius, *Commentariorum super Apocalypsim Beati Iohannis libri quinque* 1.1; PL 68:799. Beatus Liebanensis, *In Apocalypsin libri duodecim* 1.3.55, H. Sanders, ed. (Rome: 1930). Venerable Bede, *Explanatio Apocalypsis* 1.1; PL 93: 135B. *Glossa ordinaria*, Ap 1; PL 1214:712A.

regeneration and by the grace of divine adoption—even though whether the apostles actually were baptized is an open question. He is their brother, son of the same father, God, and the same mother, the church.

†Rv 1:9 *Your* brother†—a relationship we ought not pass over lightly
because he was, with the other apostles, also Christ's brother in
†Jn 20:17 accord with what he said to Mary Magdalene, 'Go to my brothers'.†
Even more than they is John Christ's brother, for the Lord says to
†Jn 19:26 the greatest Mary of all, his own mother, 'Behold your son',† and to
†Jn 19:27 him, 'Behold your mother'.† John may well have called himself the
father of those whom he had begotten by the gospel, but he chose to
say *brother* as a caution to himself and a kindness to them, reserving
†Mt 23:9 paternal authority to the common Father of all the chosen.†

†Rv 1:9 *And sharer in tribulation.*† He does not place on their shoulders
†Mt 23:4; Lk 11:46 a heavy burden he would not lift a finger to move,† but he reminds
them that they must bear the tribulation he shares. *And in the kingdom*, which can be entered only through many tribulations. It behooves us to remember, therefore, that by sharing this present tribulation we shall all of us share in the kingdom of God, that
†Ps 122:3 Jerusalem on high which is built as a city.† *And in patience*, which
†Rm 5:3 tribulation produces during this time,† for without tribulation patience cannot be put in practice. *And in patience*, which arises when we consider how slight and fleeting is our tribulation and how full
†2 Co 4:17 and how lasting is its reward.† Through patience will we possess
†Lk 21:19 our souls,† even if our goods are taken from us and our bodies are afflicted. Patience brings peace, and lightens and relieves burdens, even heavy ones, just as impatience exacerbates them, however slight they may be. Thus does a single tribulation bring a two-fold reward: the heavenly kingdom to come, and patience here and now.

In all this John refers to his Jesus, because in him and through
†Rm 11:36; Col 1:16 him,† not by his own merits and strength, he is present with the Lord's chosen faithful in their tribulation, and aspires to share in the heavenly kingdom. For by the gift of patience we attain that kingdom, not only by hoping for it but by having it now as a pledge and earnest.

†Rv 1:9 *In Jesus*,† which follows, can be taken to mean a sharer in him.
†Ps 122:3 For 'Jerusalem is built as a city, and all share in it'.† Those who

are sharers in Jesus have no merely partial union among themselves; there must be one heart and one soul† among those whose whole †Ac 4:32 substance is Jesus alone. The patience that the faithful receive from him and through him they can receive in Jesus and not from themselves. In the gospel Truth himself not undeservedly calls earthly riches deceitful because they are divided among many heirs; common use diminishes them and parceling out disperses them. Meanwhile companionship lessens the present tribulations of those who bear them bravely and faithfully, and the glory of the heavenly kingdom is enhanced by the number of those reigning with us. Patience, like the other virtues, shines more brightly when it is exercised in common. Thus John is their companion and a sharer in everything, and so the faithful find him acceptable and above suspicion in and through everything.

As a final indication of the way he shares their tribulation he adds, *I was on the island which is called Patmos.*† But why, when he was †Rv 1:9 writing this, did he say that he *was* on the island rather than that he *is* there? Had he perhaps already left it when he wrote what he had seen there? The unanimous opinion of all the commentators is that he sent out his Apocalypse from the place where he wrote it. The Lord commanded this: 'Write what you see in a book and send it to the seven churches'.† When he returned from exile, however, he †Rv 1:11 did not send it to Ephesus, but he went there himself, to the place where he made his home and where he later died a blessed death.

Did he perhaps, in the prophetic manner, change the tense? Yet I cannot recall any prophecy using the past for the present. Or, already anticipating a share in the future kingdom, was he considering the hardships of the exile he was then suffering as already a thing of the past? This would be in accord with the words of the psalm, 'Our feet were standing in your courts, O Jerusalem',† when the †Ps 122:2 rejoicing is solely in anticipation, as is indicated by the preceding verse, 'I rejoiced at what was said to me, "We shall go into the house of the Lord" '.† †Ps 122:1

Or was it because he was writing the Apocalypse chiefly for those coming after him to read, and chose to use a verb in the past tense because he knew his readers would recall it only as past? Or could it be because he had already seen the vision long before he began to write it there, and did not want to refer to it in the present because he might have to change it at once? My learned listeners may smile at my pausing over the tense of a verb; I am not offended if they recognize in this my own dull understanding.

†Rv 1:9 *I was on the island which is called Patmos*,† he says. The Lord has promised that at the judgment he is going to name six tribulations, †Mt 25:35–40 and the kindness shown or denied to those who experienced them.† In those who belong to him he himself suffered hunger, thirst, nakedness, sickness, wandering, and prison. In these tribulations some people ministered to him, and some did not. In his exile John was both a wanderer and confined to the vast harsh prison of the sea. By citing his own example of the Lord's promise that he would repay his faithful splendidly he offers the helpful solace of his own visitation to an imprisoned wanderer.

As once Noah, whom the Lord found just, prepared an ark for the deluge, so even now the Lord's loving-kindness provides an island for his faithful in the midst of this great sea. Although the cravenness of the foolish considered it and referred to it as *Patmos*, which means 'whirlpool' or 'raging sea',[2] it is not a whirlpool or a raging sea but an island. Although it is in the high sea it is not sea, not undulant, but firm. Those who discuss such matters say that 'raging' refers to a rough[3] and rolling sea. But Patmos is an island, in the deep[4] yet not of the deep, as apostles are in the world yet not †Jn 15:19 of the world.†

Why are you complaining, my brother? Why are you making excuses? Why are you growing fearful[5] and weak? You are mistaken when you call this a raging sea, or think of it as such. It is not sea but land; it is not a whirlpool, it is an island. Woe to those wretches, woe to the servants of the wicked king, who fire the furnace by their own distorted vision, when the Lord has caused in the midst †The song of Azarias 27 (Dn 3:50 Vulgate) of the furnace the blowing of a wind bringing dew!† And so they

[2] Pseudo-Alcuin, *Commentariorum in Apocalypsim libri quinque* 1.1; PL 100:1095C. Haymo of Auxerre, *Expositionis in Apocalypsin Beati Iohannis libri septem* 1.1; PL 117:949C. *Glossa ordinaria*, Ap 1; PL 114:712B.

[3] Isidore of Seville, *Etymologiarum libri XX* 13.17.2.

[4] Ibid., 14.6.1.

[5] Bernard of Claivaux, *Epistolae* 2.12; PL 182:87A.

wander away and do not enter. They stand before the furnace which tests men, whether they are acceptable† in the trial of tribulation. †Si 2:5 And the Angel of great counsel,† of great comfort, comes down †Is 9:6 LXX to them†—for the psalm says that [God] hears a person crying and †The song of Azarias 26 (Dn 3:49 Vulgate) answers, 'I am with him in tribulation',† beyond any doubt to make †Ps 91:15 the way easy for him.

A hotter flame burns those servants of the king of Babylon, those servants of Satan, who battle against themselves and heat up the furnace by their own exaltation. They will have to walk in the fiery flame that they have stirred up. When the Lord goes down into the furnace to walk with those who have not turned away, who have not fled and sought hiding places, he causes a wind bringing dew and refreshment, not heat. And so, do not fear the trial of the furnace, beloved, because the angel of the Lord went down into it, making a fourth with Azarias and his companions; and the angel stood not alongside it but in its very midst.† The stumbling block †Dn 3:25 (3:92 Vulgate) lies not in the road but alongside it—though the flame mount up above the furnace forty-nine cubits,† that is, seven times seven. †The song of Azarias 24 (Dn 3:47 Vulgate)

Seven frequently indicates 'many', as in 'seven women shall take hold of one man'.† The flames mount up above the furnace seven †Is 4:1 times seven cubits—as much do craven people reckon the annoyance of discipline, so that it grows immense and is exaggerated twice over. They brood over the painful aspects of affliction, or its duration. Nothing here on earth should be considered weighty by those of us dedicated to penance if we consider how much our Saviour bore for us and how much more our wickedness deserves. Nothing here on earth will be judged annoying if we ponder properly the joys of our reward and its immensity.

What then is more foolish than to count the moments, to worry about what unknown catastrophe the next day may bring? Let it be thirty, sixty, or a hundred years that this great annoyance of yours is drawn out, what is it compared to eternity, to the prospect of a blessedness that will have no end?† Year will not crowd upon year, †Lk 1:33 nor month upon month, nor day upon day, nor hour upon hour, nor can one moment overtake the previous moment. You imagine an immense reservoir menacing you, and you cannot endure its water sweeping over you. Consider how gently it drops, what tiny droplets flow down upon you, one after another, so that none is joined to another! Paul considered this sevenfold threat as nothing when he said, 'Our tribulation, which is light and of but a moment's duration, is bringing about in us an eternal weight of glory, sublime †2 Co 4:17 beyond all measure'.†

†Ph 2:2 Have this same mind in you,† beloved, and remember that the foolish call your disciplined way of life 'Patmos', and consider it a 'raging sea', restless, turbulent, and intolerable. But the faithful find it instead an island. Know by experience that the angel of the Lord, going down with Azarias and his companions, makes the middle of the furnace like a wind bringing refreshment. Azarias means 'the Lord's help'; Ananiah means 'sheep'.[6] 'Blessed is the man whose †Ps 84:6 help is from you, O Lord!'† Fortunate too the need that forces us to †Jn 15:5 better things.[7] Since we can do nothing without the Lord,† we must hurry back to his help, we must ever lean on him, not on our own merits, not on our skill in planning, not on the hollow staff of earthly goods or any human favor. Fortunate is he who hears his Shepherd's voice here on earth—he will find himself standing with the sheep †Mt 25:33 on the Lord's right hand,† and will be led into his kingdom.

The name 'Azarias' can also aptly refer to the Lord's helpers, those who wish to be found co-operating with him as well as they can in the work of their own salvation and that of their neighbors. Likewise too, the name 'Ananiah' fits those who obey them meekly. The name 'Misael' is said to mean 'interrogation',[8] and, in our context, not simply questioning but questioning by torture. Thus we read that the impious said beforehand of the Saviour: 'Let us †Ws 2:19 *Ps 100:3 interrogate him by outrages and torture'.† 'The sheep of his pasture'* are therefore linked with the Lord's helpers, and those who, for love of him, question and torture themselves that he may spare them for what they do not spare themselves, and may pardon every offense of those whom he sees avenging the wrong done to him. Such †Is 9:6 LXX persons need not be afraid, because the Angel of great counsel† and

[6] Ananias, Azarias, and Misael are the Septuagint names for Shadrack, Meshach and Abednego. Jerome, *Liber interpretationis hebraicorum nominum* 40.19; CCh 72:109. Isidore of Seville, *Etymologiarum libri XX* 7.8.25.

[7] Augustine, *Epistulae* 127.8; CSEL 44:28.

[8] Jerome, *Liber interpretationis hebraicorum nominum* 14.5; CCh 72:76.

of refreshment goes down with them into the furnace to make it a wind bringing dew.

Thus did our father Bernard remind us, especially during our novitiate, that the Lord would devise work in keeping his precepts,[9] where one taking up his yoke would find rest for his soul.† And he used to say, 'Is not this work he devised a light burden, a sweet yoke and, as in the rite for dedicating churches, an anointed cross? Was not the one who devised work in keeping his precepts the one who tempted Abraham by ordering him to sacrifice his beloved son Isaac?'[10] †Mt 11:29

According to the literal meaning, on the other hand, the island is called Patmos because the seething and roaring sea around it beats on the shore with vehement force. It is not a pleasant place; it would seem a wretched and discouraging place of exile for no greater cause than punishment. And so John goes on to add, *because of the word of God and the testimony of Jesus*† to explain the unflagging constancy of his testimony to the Lord Jesus Christ and his preaching of the gospel in word and deed.[11] †Rv 1:9

Here we must surely recall reading that the apostles bore testimony with great power to the resurrection of our Lord Jesus Christ.† One of their number is aptly called Philip, a name meaning 'the mouth of a lamp' or 'the mouth of a hand'.[12] Teaching by example shines more brightly than teaching by word. An exhortation coming from 'the mouth of a hand' is quite effective, especially from those whose discourse is corroborated by the signs which follow. †Ac 4:33

And so, because of God's word which he constantly preached, and the testimony of Jesus which he steadfastly demonstrated in his deeds and his many virtues, blessed John, having been dispatched into exile by the godless, was on the island of Patmos. These, his preaching and testimony, were what they hated and persecuted in him. John's godliness bore faithfully, patiently, graciously, and

[9] Bernard of Clairvaux, *Liber de praecepto et dispensatione* 1.2; SBOp 3:225; CF 1:106–107.

[10] Geoffrey of Auxerre, *Declamationes de colloquio Simonis cum Iesu ex S. Bernardi sermonibus collectae* 47; PL 184:467CD.

[11] Bruno of Segni, *Expositio in Apocalypsim* 1.1; PL 165:611B.

[12] Jerome, *Liber interpretationis hebraicorum nominum* 64.23; CCh 72:140.

generously the exile that Domitian's godlessness cruelly imposed
†Rv 1:9 because of this, *because of the word of God and the testimony of Jesus*.†

So he was there on the island of Patmos because of the word of
God, according to the text, 'Because of the words of your lips I have
†Ps 17:4 kept to a difficult path'.† [He was there] because of the testimony of
Jesus, because of the good confession he gave under Pontius Pilate:
'My kingdom is not from here. If my kingdom were from this world,
my servants would certainly be fighting against my being handed
†Jn 18:36 over to the Jews'.† [He was there] because of the testimony of Jesus,
so that John, like Paul, might make up in his own body what was
†Col 1:24 lacking to the sufferings of Christ.† [He was there] because of Peter's
reply to the Lord, who had asked whether the apostles wished to
go away as others had: 'Lord, to whom shall we go? You have the
†Jn 6:69 words of everlasting life'.† [He was there] because of his testimony
concerning the one of whom John himself said, 'He is the faithful
†Rv 1:5 witness'.†

†Rv 1:10 *I was in the spirit on the Lord's day*,† John says. There are different
types of revelations. We read that angels sent by divine command
have appeared in visible form to some, and have spoken in human fashion. They did this with such familiarity as to answer the
questions asked them. Angels from heaven coming to Abraham,
Zechariah, the blessed virgin Mary, the shepherds, and the women
at the Lord's tomb revealed their visions and utterances as if without
†1 Co 13:12 mirror and riddle.† Others, awake or in dreams, have imaginary
visions, and things are shown or said to them which can only be
interpreted by another—as Joseph did the dreams of the Egyptian
†Gn 40:1 butcher, baker, and Pharaoh,† and as Daniel did for the kings of
†Dn 2, 4 Babylon.† Others are taught directly by a revelation, like Daniel
†Dn 7, 8, 10–11; Am 7–8; Ezk 1, 40ff and certain prophets,† and as the Magi were warned in a dream
to avoid Herod on their return.†[a] In spirit and in an ecstasy of
†[a]Mt 2:12 mind the apostle Peter saw a platter filled with reptiles and heard its
†[b]Ac 10:11 secret.†[b] Paul was swept up to paradise and into the third heaven,
†2 Co 12:2 not knowing whether he was in or out of the body.†

†Rv 1:10 John saw this present revelation *in the spirit*,† not his own, of
course, but God's. It is the Spirit, who breathes where and how he
†Jn 3:8 chooses,† who speaks and shows mysteries. After he was called by
the Lord, John was never without the Spirit, especially after he and

the other disciples received its fullness† by having the risen Lord breathe upon them† and fiery tongues descend that Pentecost.* †Jn 1:16 †Jn 20:22 *Ac 2:3–4

That he mentions that he was *in the spirit*† is significant, since he was not only rising above the flesh but even above his own mind; in a marvelous way he was higher than himself through the Spirit who had seized him totally for himself. He had become oblivious not only to the experiences of his bodily senses, but he was also free from his thoughts and the affections of his heart. We are not saying anything new, seeing that long before the likeness of 'an eagle over all the four', of which it was one, appeared to the prophet Ezekiel.† †Rv 1:10 †Ezk 1:10

Up to this point, in addition to the material treated in the beginning of this book—which shows us whose Apocalypse it was, who bestowed it on him, by whom and to whom it was sent—the usefulness of reading, hearing, and heeding it is commended here not only by the person of John, the divinely appointed recipient and trusted writer, but also by the place of writing, and the reason why he was there when the revelation was granted to him. A remote place is suited to a spiritual vision,[13] a place remote from physical pleasure, and especially an exile imposed solely by hatred of godliness and borne for the love [of Christ] not only calmly but generously. It is also commended by the means used, which was not a sensible or imaginary vision, but a spiritual one.

A commendation by time follows: all these things were seen or heard *on the Lord's day*.† Indeed, O Lord, yours is the day and yours the night,† not one of them but all. The foolish children of humans have dedicated your days, which you made, to the heavenly lights you created.† They have fallen into serious blasphemy by this mistake, misunderstanding the right order of things, and attributing to creatures what belongs to your might alone. This pagan custom of naming the days is not only common among the unlearned but, what is worse, this habit has endured among the educated. †Rv 1:10 †Ps 74:16 †Gn 1:16

The Roman Pontiff once summoned a certain venerable abbot from France. I was there and heard an eminent bishop ask him, shortly before he set out, when he intended to undertake the journey. 'On the second Lord's day', he replied, 'I have decided

[13] Anselm of Laon, *Enarrationes in Apocalypsim* 1.1; PL 162:1504C.

to commend the assembled brethren to the Lord and to set out with their blessing'. The bishop, not a little agitated, replied, 'I sincerely hope, I very sincerely hope that you will not set out on the Lord's day!' I must confess that I could not restrain myself from immediately bringing out these words, 'I sincerely, most sincerely hope that he will not travel on the Lord's day!'

People do not realize what God did when he began the division
†Gn 1:4 of his works on that day.† They do not realize what he did when
†Mt 28:1 he rose on the Lord's day.† We see that pagans honored this day to the extent of assigning it to the sun, the greater of the heavenly lights. He, however, who divided created light from darkness, who rose from the dead on that day, who willed it to be called both the first day and the eighth—just as Noah was eighth in the line of the patriarchs, and was found worthy to become the founder and first of the second generation—gave it greater honor.

Quite rightly then is this day especially called the Lord's, and is especially consecrated to the Lord. On this day, it is believed, the Saviour was born of the Virgin, and on this same day he poured out the Holy Spirit in tongues of fire on the children of adoption. The hallowed observance of this day clearly began with the apostles, as we can see from Paul's command to the Corinthians to meet on the first day of the week—which had taken the place of the now abolished sabbath as the day of public reverence—and to take up a
†1 Co 16:2 free-will collection to be sent to help the saints at Jerusalem.† On this day especially dedicated to divine worship John was *in the spirit*, as he himself testifies. But whether he saw all these things then or over a period of time the learned have left open, and perhaps nothing stands in the way of either opinion.

†Rv 1:10 *And I heard after*[14] *me a loud voice like a trumpet.*† Admonished by the law and the prophets, [he heard] from posterity, arising out of what had gone before. The Holy Spirit had swept him up from all earthly things, and even from himself, to things to come, as if a voice resounding from posterity was wonderfully calling him to care and provide for the churches of Christ. Even if he heard a voice

[14] *Post me* is most often taken to mean 'behind me', but Geoffrey's next words, *A posteribus,* indicate that he understands *post* in a temporal sense.

behind him, it predicted such things concerning what would come *after* him.

The *voice* was not *loud* in its sound but in its effect, *like a trumpet* summoning to battle. Thus the Lord deigned to speak to his disciple as was fitting, so that he in turn might speak to his churches, and not to them only, but that the form might be handed down to generations to come. *Like a trumpet*, which sometimes makes a loud sound but at other times is muted. So our preaching, if it is not pompous but springs from us as humble exiles, will prove the more efficacious for others. The poet laughs at the braggart who promises, but delivers nothing worth his high-flown style;[15] he extols the modest beginning which goes on and accomplishes its task.

The Lord's voice is *heard*, as it were, *after* us, as often as it deigns to go before the souls of our hearers by our admonitions. As the psalm says, 'Who will lead me to the fortified city?'† It speaks †Ps 60:9
before us when our hearers, who may know more than we, allow themselves to be taught by our preaching. People are at different places on the Lord's path, so when the trumpet of salvation calls them to his army, one fights one way and another another way. Fortunate is the man who receives a divine indication of what his duty is, and the endeavor and the training by which he must serve.

Fortunate the one who fights for him, in those circumstances too in which he has placed him. Blessed John was fighting even in exile, fighting effectively for his king, when he saw what the king revealed, and wrote it down in a book at his command. He was fighting a good fight,† not only for himself but for the many †1 Tm 1:18
churches he enabled to fight by giving them weapons mighty to God,† faith, and a good conscience.* His pen was a keen sword †2 Co 10:4 *1 Tm 1:19
turned against the spiritual forces of evil.† Even today, through his †Ep 6:12
writings, those who already happily reign with God are valiantly fighting for him.

The Lord's voice is *heard*, as it were, *after us*, to rouse and to encourage us, *like a trumpet saying: 'Write in a book what you see'*.† †Rv 1:10–11
An articulate voice does not come from such instruments, nor is intelligible speech ordinarily formed by them. The loudness of this

[15] Horace, *Ars poetica* 138. Peter the Venerable, *Epistolae* 229.4; PL 182:400D.

voice is compared to a trumpet because its sound reaches many and is broadcast far and wide. Clearly there was no real trumpet; the simile is used at the pleasure of the Spirit of truth, to make the idea clear to the soul attentive to it, for the edification of the churches of our Lord Jesus Christ, who with the Father and the same Holy Spirit is one God above all, blessed forever. Amen.

Sermon Six

Write what you see in a book and send it to the seven churches which are in Asia: to Ephesus, Smyrna, Pergamum, Thyatira, Sardis, Philadelphia, and Laodicea.† †Rv 1:11

WRITE WHAT YOU SEE IN A BOOK *and send it to the seven churches which are in Asia.* I know that my betters know of my ignorance, my insufficiency, my uselessness. They know whether I am right to lament this, since I expect no more consideration than I deserve or than they can honestly give. Committing the duty of teaching to one untaught is no better than having a blind man lead†—dangerous for the blind, and ridiculous to those who can see. †Mt 15:14; Lk 6:39

That the prophets of old were called seers is common knowledge.[1] Doubtless this esteemed group is expecting good advice from a wise man and a sermon from a seer. Prophets came before evangelists because seeing must precede reporting. 'The law and the prophets held sway until John', says the Lord; 'since then the kingdom of God is proclaimed'.† In other words, no longer is †Lk 16:16

[1] Isidore of Seville, *Etymologiarum libri XX* 7.8.1.

it prophesied, but it is being reported. And so John, though an evangelist, was more than a prophet† [†Mt 11:9; Lk 7:26] because he prophesied even of himself. He had not yet written his gospel when he saw himself among the four living creatures.† [†Rv 4:6–7] Indeed he was far more than an evangelist, and even superior to himself, seeing that he was the likeness of an 'eagle over all the four'.† [†Ezk 1:10] John is the best example of his own saying, 'He gave testimony to Jesus Christ, whatsoever he saw'.† [†Rv 1:2]

Write what you see in a book.† [†Rv 1:11] I have no doubt that your entire mind stands docile and attentive to receive his teaching, as a book lies ready to be written in. How marvelous if each person who sees great things, who contemplates spiritual things, may be ordered to write in this book, which you may send to your churches!

Liber[2] is the inner bark of a tree, the part that carries its life and growth. For you to forego this work of the inner bark to give yourselves to outer reality is not fitting. A person whose concerns are fastened on outer, transitory things, and who neglects the health of souls, goes from the inner to the outer bark. What is seen is of time, what is unseen is eternal. The outer bark is necessary for those whose duty it is to handle things seen, to dispose of earthly matters, and, in a sense, to expose themselves to danger in order to protect and preserve the inner bark and the internal strength of the whole tree.

You know that you are responsible for the labors of Martha who, like rough outer bark, was full of care and bothered by many things† [†Lk 10:41] from which the inner bark is free. The splendor and glory of the fine linen, scarlet, purple, and blue within is owing in part to sackcloth. And the ten of these must protect the eleven, which they cannot do without.[3] On the other hand, the inner bark, with its living fluid, maintains the tree's strength and gives life to the outer bark. How marvelous if today this thought were written not on tablets and paper but in your minds and hearts for you to give to your seven churches for their edification!

[2] *Liber*, the word translated 'book' in Rv 1:11, has as its first meaning the inner bark of a tree, on which the ancients used to write.

[3] The strange ideas in these two lines seem to be based on Exodus 26 and 36.

'Church' means a large group of persons, and seven churches a large number of church congregations, or perhaps churches endowed with the renowned sevenfold gifts of the Spirit.† And what was first commanded to be written in a book and sent to the seven churches is written to the angels of each of the churches. Thus it will reach the churches through the ministry of their leaders, in accord with what is written, 'May the mountains receive peace for the people'.† The Apostle says, 'I have handed on to you what I also received'.†

†Is 11:2–3 Vulgate
†Ps 72:3
†1 Co 11:23

Because the act of calling together gives churches their name, you will see who he calls their angels and from where and to which he will call them. Of him, indeed, the prophet sings in the psalm: 'The Lord's voice is powerful, the Lord's voice is exalted!'† He calls the predestined, he justifies those called, and he exalts those justified.† He does not now call the absent, but he calls back the lapsed, and he calls together those who approach. [Hear the] voice of the one who calls: 'Come to me, you who labor and are heavily burdened'.† [Hear the] voice of the one who calls back: 'Return, return, O Shulammite'.† [Hear the] voice of the one who calls together: 'Behold how good and how joyous it is for brothers to dwell together in unity'.†

†Ps 29:4
†Rm 8:30
†Mt 11:28
†Sg 6:13 (or 6:12 or 7:1)
†Ps 133:1

All of you serve one another with the grace you have received 'as good stewards of the manifold grace of God'.† You must be mindful that your churches, or more correctly, the Lord's churches, whose ministers and angels you must be, are *in Asia*.† 'Asia' means 'exalted'.[4] Sacred scripture scarcely recommends exaltation, so we can understand *Asia* to mean the turbulence of this world, of which it is said, 'Marvelous are the exaltations of the sea'.† Do not let this scandalize you or weaken your resolve, because more marvelous still is the Lord on high† who commands the wind and the sea when he chooses.† The Song of Songs sings that the locks of the bride are like the exalted branches of palm trees.† Perhaps we may praise these exalted things, as when Isaiah sees 'the Lord seated on a high and lofty throne'.† I believe we find him 'high' in the angels who did not fall, and even in the faithful synagogue of those who persevered in

†1 P 4:10
†Rv 1:11
†Ps 93:4
†Ps 93:4
†Mt 8:26
†Sg 5:11
†Is 6:1

[4]Jerome, *Liber interpretationis hebraicorum nominum* 80.10; CCh 72:159.

faith and the observance of the law from the time of the patriarchs. We find him 'lofty' in the human race—fallen in the first man's transgression and raised up by the assistance of the second—or in the gentile church which, lying in the dust of infidelity and wickedness
†Is 51:17 and given over to demons, yet hears the call, 'Be exalted!'† He is also 'high' in those who have maintained their innocence, 'lofty' in those who have repented; he is 'high' in those who serve actively, and 'lofty' in those given to contemplation.

†Rv 1:11 The first church is called *Ephesus*,† a name meaning 'will' or 'counsel'.[5] The first fruits of salvation and the foundation of all good lies in a will that has had counsel, that lacks neither divine zeal nor knowledge. The second is *Smyrna*, meaning 'their song',[6] or common joy, since the good is more beautiful when practised in common. Self-centered people always seem to sing their own song one by one and to rejoice in their own joys. The third is *Pergamum*, which means 'a riven valley' or 'divided horns'.[7] That church, those called by the Lord, must thoroughly consider that they are bound to one another. They must consider that this valley will be riven in two, that the Lord will break 'the horns of sinners, and the horns
†Ps 75:10 of the righteous will be exalted'.† Thus the three names commend deliberation on the salvation set before us, the sharing of spiritual joy, and fear and hope of a twofold retribution.

†Mt 13:44–50 The threefold parable in a single reading from the gospel† corresponds to these three. The treasure in the field is in the heart's choice, and consists in the merit of an action and the intention that gives its name to the deed. The peerless pearl is the grace of sacred communion. One who tarries by the shores of the sea, mindful of death and awaiting the fearful judgment—so that what must there be done with respect to persons he himself now does here in discernment of what he has done, thus throwing out the bad fish and putting the good ones into baskets—rives the valley and turns the high valley wall into a fortress; such a one divides the horns.

[5] Ibid., 80.17; CCh 72:160.
[6] Ibid., 81.4; CCh 72:160.
[7] Ibid., 81.1; CCh 72:160.

The next name, *Thyatira*,† means 'enlightened',[8] enlightened through penance by him who calls from darkness into his own marvelous light;† not enlightened by the true light, but by the one who illumines everyone, because no one else came into the world without darkness. *Sardis* is 'the commencement of beauty',[9] the beauty of chastity, that beauty whereby the Saviour recreates our humble body, conforming it to the body of his glory.† *Philadelphia* means 'brotherly love'.[10] *Philos* is 'love', and *delphis* is interpreted 'brother'. It is the love of that brother who is the son of David and Lord, who showed himself a neighbor to the man who fell among thieves.† If we interpret it as 'preserving an inheritance' it still means the same, for love of this brother makes us his joint heirs.† Looked at in a different way, charity preserves our inheritance, for nothing is of profit without it. *Laodicea* means 'the lovable tribe of the Lord'[11] and brings humility to mind, for the Lord has specially regarded it in blessed Mary† and found her acceptable. For he says, 'Whom shall I regard, and upon whom shall my Spirit rest, save upon one who is humble and quiet?'[12] Therefore, he says, 'When you have done all that is required of you say, We are worthless servants'.†

†Rv 1:11 †1 P 2:9 †Ph 3:21 †Lk 10:30 †Rm 8:17 †Lk 1:48 †Lk 17:10

To these four [cities] we can connect as many virtues, for prudence enlightens us to do penance; temperance lays a foundation for beauty; magnanimity, through brotherly love, preserves our inheritance; and justice finds fulfillment in humility. And all of this, in accord with the Lord's word to John, that he may make for him a 'loveable tribe'.

A tribe is made up of three classes, as the Romans were once divided into senate, army, and commoners.[13] In our day we have in the church a similar threefold order[14] represented by Noah, Daniel, and Job. Moreover to the first churches, too, the four

[8] Ibid., 72.8; CCh 72:149.

[9] Ibid., 81.4; CCh 72:160.

[10] Venerable Bede, *Explanatio Apocalypsis* 1.3; PL 93:140B.

[11] Jerome, *Liber interpretationis hebraicorum nominum* 80.23; CCh 72:160.

[12] Is 66:2 LXX. Jerome, *Commentarii in Esaiam* 18.3; CCh 73A:770. Gregory the Great, *Moralia in Iob* 5.45; PL 75:724C.

[13] Isidore of Seville, *Etymologiarum libri XX* 9.4.7.

[14] Gregory the Great, *Homiliae in Ezechielem* 2.4; PL 76:976BC.

natural affections can be joined so that desire corresponds to the
will, joy to the song, fear to the division of horns, and sadness to
the enlightenment of penance in accord with the words, 'One who
†Qo 1:18 increases knowledge increases sorrow as well'.† Moreover, if you
fully understand from our discussion of the churches' names what
we are to emulate in their conduct, as we are certain you have, it is
fitting for you to give full consideration to your own name.

For [John] goes on: 'To the angel of the church in Ephesus
†Rv 2:1 write',† and to the others in the same vein. All of sacred Scripture
was written to you, beloved. It belongs to you, and you are under
the gravest obligation to meditate continually on the apostolic
†Rm 15:4 injunction: 'Whatever was written was written for our instruction'.†
[It was written] for your instruction in two senses: that first we may
be taught by it, and then that we may teach in accord with it. You
are not to neglect what was written to you. They err who do not
know the Scripture, and erring leaders mislead rather than lead in
the way of life. Those who do not know the Scriptures cannot know
the power of God either, as Truth himself said to the Jews: 'You err,
†Mt 22:29 knowing neither the Scriptures nor the power of God'.† About you
was the command given that the poles bearing the ark never be
†Ex 25:15 drawn out of their rings.† Besides, what will you announce but the
word of him whose messengers you ought to be always attentive
to him?

He says, 'Write' to the angel of one or the other church.
Angels of the Lord, angels of little ones, I beg you to turn your
attention to the meaning of your name. People seek the law from
†Ml 2:7 your mouths† because you are the angels of the Lord, they seek
your prayer because you are the angels of little ones. Angels of
the Lord—as is commanded of shepherds under another figure—
must be like pastors who know well the face of their flock so that
they may know what to say to each one. The angels of little ones
†Mt 18:10 continually look on the Father's face† so that they may surround
them with paternal affection and paternal care. The angels of the
Lord break bread for the little ones when they ask for it. They
†2 Tm 4:2 are constant in season and out of season.† Angels of the Lord
continually proclaim the Lord's will, which is good, acceptable, and
†Rm 12:2 perfect.† The angels of little ones tell their beloved of those who

are faint for love,† whether wretchedly in love, or happily because of love. †Sg 2:5

I beg you, defend the angelic name which is truly your own; manifest angelic purity in yourselves, readiness to serve toward your charges, and faithfulness toward God. No suspicion of corruption is found among the angels, not even a hint of it; no ambition is found among the angels, no presumption, no jealousy or wrangling. What a great thing if, when our angels come together, there be someone present who will put a tile in front of us, someone ignorant of wrangling, someone who will say, 'If it is yours, take it'.[15]

The raven loves gold; angels do not lay up money in hiding places, in chests, or in strong boxes. In regard to your neighbors, 'admonish the unquiet, console the faint-hearted, and be patient with all of them'.† You are angels, they are little ones; nevertheless, you are their angels. If the Spirit's manifestation is given to each for profit,† your words must always be spoken with discretion, adapted to each person. You have taken on an arduous and difficult task, to serve a variety of temperaments.† †1 Th 5:14 †1 Co 12:7 †RB 2:31

Paul preferred to say five words with his mind rather than ten thousand words in a tongue,† and you also must prefer this. Five words, I say; words of knowledge, of consolation, of exhortation, of entreaty, and, although less freely and therefore less frequently, of reproof.† The shortcomings of disciples are your responsibility.* This is a heavy burden, but heavier still the blame the shepherd will bear wherever the father of the household finds that the flock has yielded no profit.† †1 Co 14:19 †2 Tm 4:2; RB 2:23 *RB 36:10 †RB 2:7

And how difficult is the freedom which your lawgiver, [blessed Benedict], has proposed for your relief: 'He shall be free only if all diligence has been brought to bear and every care has been taken'.[16]† †RB 2:8

[15] *Verba Seniorum* 17.22; PL 73:977C; *Western Asceticism*, Owen Chadwick, ed. (Philadelphia, 1958) 186.

[16] The word *liber*, translated 'free', does not appear in the authentic text. See *RB 1980* (Collegeville: Liturgical Press, 1981) 172. Justin McCann observes, 'This is a difficult piece of Latin and was revised by the correctors in various ways', one of them being this version quoted by Geoffrey. See *The Rule of Saint Benedict* (London: Burns Oates, 1952) 171, note 20.

And who is up to all this?[17] How rare is such a man—if one such can be found at all—whom this consolation does not bind more than it loosens, does not burden more than it frees! Who can boast that he has left nothing undone?

Let us return to the passage from the Apostle which we put before you. He says that he prefers to say five, that is, few words, with his mind, that they may return to the place from which they issued, and that as they come forth from the heart they may move the heart—rather than saying ten thousand, that is, many words, in a tongue, that come forth from the surface of the lips and do nothing but strike the ears.

I also prefer to offer a few words for edification rather than many words for ostentation. Quickly, then, we recall that the five words are of knowledge, exhortation, consolation, entreaty, and, now and then, reproof. The first word is directed to the ignorant, the second to the slothful, the third to those suffering affliction, the fourth to the devout, and the fifth to the bad and undisciplined.

Knowledge is concerned with three things: what ought to be believed, what ought to be done, and what must be avoided. We can break it down another way: what must be done, what can be done, what is the best possible thing to do. The Apostle spoke
†1 Co 7:6 sometimes by way of precept, sometimes of concession;† where he
†1 Co 7:25 has no precept he gives an opinion.†

In exhortation, we should propose the delightful character of the virtues on their own account, their advantages on account of the recompense, and their easiness through examples. Examples show especially clearly that the Lord's commands are a light burden, not a
†Mt 11:30 heavy one.† Do you have any doubts that you can do what so many others have done?

Likewise, in consolation we should show the requisite compassion, our belief in forgiveness, and the promise of divine assistance. Taking on the duty of consoling means weeping with those who
†Rm 12:15 weep,† convincing the repentant of the certainty of forgiveness, and promising the support of grace to those who turn back from sin.

[17] Bernard of Clairvaux, *Sermones super Cantica Canticorum* 57.11; SBOp 2:126; CF 31:105.

When we entreat others we must remind the devout of God's
superabundant love for humans, his untiring patience with those
who stray, his care and concern for his chosen ones. The prophet
says: 'The Lord takes thought for me';† and the Apostle: 'He takes †Ps 40:17
care of us'.† †1 P 5:7

To reproof belong detestation of sin, so unworthy in itself; the menace of death, as the most certain event in human life, though we are uncertain of its time; the clear picture of future damnation, that the torments prepared for the wicked may somehow be brought before the eyes, depicted by our mournful representation.

I have kept you a long time, but there is yet something I must
say about fidelity to the divine majesty. Remember that you are the
Lord's angels. 'The kings of the gentiles lord it over them, but you
must not do so'.† And in another place, 'When a servant becomes †Lk 22:25–26
king, the earth is shaken'.† Do you not know that you are servants? †Pr 30:21–22
The heavenly angel said to John, 'I am a fellow servant with you
and your brothers'.† There are faithless, reprobate, pseudo-angels, †Rv 22:9
lying messengers, who propose their own teaching in place of God's.
'They say, "Says the Lord", when the Lord has not sent them'.† They †Ezk 13:6
spoke, but not on my behalf, declares the Lord; they do not speak
my truth, but a lie flowing from their own hearts. They avenge their
injuries and call holy whatever pleases them; whatever is not to their
liking they say is forbidden.† Judging by their own likes and dislikes, †RB 1:9
they kill souls that should not die and keep alive souls that should
not live.† May we, his angels gathered together today, be freed now †Ezk 13:19
and always from these perils by the Angel of great counsel† who, †Is 9:6 LXX
with the Father and the Holy Spirit, is one God above all, blessed
for ever. Amen.

Sermon Seven

And I turned to see the voice that was speaking with me. And when I had turned I saw seven golden lampstands, and, in the midst of the seven golden lampstands, one like the Son of Man, clothed in a long robe, and with a golden sash across his chest. His head and his hair were bright as white wool, bright as snow, and his eyes were like a flame of fire; his feet were like fine brass as in a burning furnace, and his voice was like the voice of many waters. And he held in his right hand seven stars, and from his mouth came a sharp, two-edged sword, and his face was like the sun shining with full strength.† †Rv 1:12–16

HOW HAPPY AND HOW JOYOUS today's celebration of the Lord's appearance ought to be is evident when we consider, beloved, at what an evil point people in this world would have been so long as they were without God. But now, thanks to him, the great mystery of our religion has been made known to the gentiles†—while a mother fondles a baby at her breast, and a †1 Tm 3:16 heavenly star points him out in marvelous manner. If the Creator of the stars caused a new star to shine in the sky, he made another shine on earth as in a sea great and wide.† No faintly glowing star †Ps 104:25

appeared to the Magi, abandoning its heavenly course and stopping
†Mt 2:9 over the place where the child was.† Not in word or speech, but in
†1 Jn 3:18 deed and in truth,† it proclaimed by its rays, 'This is the one you
seek; here you will find the king with his family, the boy with his
mother'. Far brighter, however, is the star of the sea—as the Virgin's
name, Mary, is interpreted[1]—than the star of heaven which made
known the baby she had borne. The sight the star presented to the
eyes of the Magi was not as marvelous as the joyful miracle Mary
showed to the citizens of heaven.

In a second appearance divine things are joined to human.
When the one who was to be baptized bowed beneath the hands
of a servant, the Holy Spirit came down on him in bodily form as a
dove, and the Father's voice was heard: 'This is my beloved Son in
†Mt 17:5 whom I am well pleased'.† In Cana of Galilee an equally marvelous
†Jn 2:1–11 manifestation of kindness and power appeared.† The Lord of majesty
revealed his presence to the guests at a human wedding. That he who
came into the world without marital intercourse should come when
invited to be among the guests at a wedding is not less marvelous
than his power to turn water into wine.

The appearances I have just mentioned you have heard about
so much and so often that I cannot hope to add anything new today.
But I do not believe that it would be out of place if I spoke of another
marvelous appearance of the Lord. Many times and in many ways
†Heb 1:1 has he not only spoken† but he has even often appeared to those
whom he loves. Of all of these, the apostle John received the grace of
a loftier revelation as he had also received a special privilege of love.

†Rv 1:12 *And I turned*, John says, *to see the voice that was speaking with me*.†
He remembers that he turned because, as he said earlier, he heard
†Rv 1:10 someone's voice speaking after him.† This type of turning is not
ordinarily necessary because that voice, which is also the true light,
has no particular place. The Son of God, incomprehensible word
†1 Tm 6:16 and inaccessible light† before he took on human nature, afterwards
deigned to speak humanly to humans through the human nature
he had assumed, and not only to be heard but to be seen as well.

[1] Isidore of Seville, *Etymologiarum libri XX* 7.10.1. Bernard of Clairvaux, *In laudibus Virginis Matris* 2.17; SBOp 4:34; CF 18:30.

[John's] turning was spiritual, his discourse was spiritual; his hearing and seeing were mystical.

Blessed John in describing these adds many elements. Although the number seven is apparently central, he also gives the number twelve a place. Both are made up of the same factors, three and four, the first by addition and the other by multiplication. The first contains three plus four, the other three times four. As twelve thousand were sealed from each of the twelve tribes,† and twelve gates† and as many foundations* are described as being in the holy city, so at the beginning of this marvelous vision he mentions twelve elements: place and form, robe and sash, color of head and of hair, eyes and feet, voice and right hand, mouth and face.

†Rv 7:5–8
†Rv 21:12
*Rv 21:14

And when I had turned I saw seven golden lampstands.† He turned within, he turned to the one who cleanses the hearts of his people and dwells therein by faith. He was not cast out like Cain, the killer of his brother, who became a fugitive and a wanderer;† he was not poured out† like Reuben, receiving a curse in place of a blessing;†[a] nor in life does he cast away his bowels.†[b] These lampstands are said to be of gold owing to faith, wisdom, and love: faith tested by the fire of tribulation does not fail; wisdom achieves the beauty of a lightning flash; and, as the value of gold exceeds all other metals, so love surpasses all other virtues.

†Rv 1:12
†Gn 4:12
†Gn 49:4 Vulgate
†[a]Gn 27:12
†[b]Si 10:9 (10:10 Vulgate)

John mentions seven lampstands. In the literal sense they refer to the seven churches mentioned earlier in the same vision; mystically, however, they refer to the spiritual gifts enjoyed by these churches, and by all churches. As the Spirit of the Lord is called one and manifold,† so the church assembled by that same Spirit is sevenfold and one. And as there are many members in one body, so one church exists in many churches.

†Ws 7:22

John saw seven lampstands; Moses constructed one lampstand with seven lamps. Three arms extended to each side from the central shaft,† and those six arms with the central shaft had the same significance in the tabernacle as the seven lampstands in the Apocalypse. As the middle shaft of Moses' lampstand signified the primitive Jewish church from which six arms extended among the Greeks and the Latins, so in the Apocalypse Christ, the servant of the circumcision,† appeared in the midst of the seven lampstands.

†Ex 37:18, 23
†Rm 15:8

†Rm 11:24 But with the natural branches cut off and the wild olive grafted in,† the place of the middle shaft is taken by the Roman church, whose faith has never failed, even if one of its popes cuts himself off from the fundamental catholic faith. This is said of a certain pope Leo who was quickly punished.[2] The three arms, or three lampstands, on one side refer to the churches of Constantinople, Alexandria, and Antioch, whose language has always been Greek. The three arms, or three lampstands, on the other side represent the churches using Latin, spread throughout the other parts of the world, to the south, west, and north.

There is another way of understanding this: the central shaft, †Jn 12:32 being lifted up, draws all things to itself;† it summons everyone from every side, offers itself to all, and rejects no one. O foolish man, why do you flee, why do you turn away, why do you look for hiding places? Truth has no liking for corners, nor does love look for resting places. He who made himself a palanquin inlaid its interior †Sg 3:10 with love.† We can delay no longer, I am afraid, on the meaning of this central shaft, but must hurry on to other things.

†Rv 1:13 *I saw*, John says, *one like the Son of Man*.† I do not doubt that the Son of Man preferred to have his beloved disciple fully recognize him, affectionately receive him, and joyfully gaze on his ordinary form. At one time [John] used to contemplate that lovable image, and in the same way he would now embrace more warmly his ampler glory. Beloved, we firmly hope and believe that in his kingdom we †Jn 6:45 will all be taught by God,† and with him as our teacher we all will know everyone most fully. When we regard our revered fathers, our beloved brethren, the dear companions of our early education, the memory of their presence and their love, do we not believe that nothing can be added to our joy? With what charm did our holy father Bernard promise us,[3] while he was alive, that as we were approaching we would recognize with all quickness and ease the great mansion within the enclosure of paradise belonging to

[2] Anacletus II, or Peter the Lion, was elected pope in 1130, and claimed the Roman See until 1139. He was opposed by a rival, Innocent II (1130–43), who in the end proved victorious. Bernard of Clairvaux supported Innocent vigorously. See his *Sermones super Cantica Canticorum* 24.1; SBOp 1:151; CF 7:42.

[3] Bernard of Clairvaux, *Sermones de diversis* 22.2; PL 183:596B.

himself and his own, and that we, his sons, would find with him there the great multitude of those who had gone before us.

In the meantime, each of us should meditate on these things with prayer and desire, as the Spirit leads each of us. And this must be our prayer: that we may enjoy the eternal sight of those for whom we give thanks as we recall them now.[4] Let us give thanks for John, now happily contemplating his beloved and loving Lord and Master in glory, as he delightedly reflects upon his likeness, which he once saw in humble state. It is our belief that when he saw him shining in glory among the golden lampstands he affectionately remembered how he had once seen him living meekly among his humble disciples, and how he had at the last gazed at him hanging ignominiously among thieves.

When he saw him *clothed in a long robe, and with a golden sash across his chest,*† did he not picture how he had seen him at the Last †Rv 1:13
Supper put aside his garments, take a basin and pour water, and, wrapped in a towel, wash and dry the feet of his disciples?† Did †Jn 13:5
he recall his nakedness as he was crucified by the godless, as his garments were divided, and as lots were thrown for his tunic?† His †Jn 19:23–24
ankle-length robe pointed to the church which will continue until the end of time and to the ends of the earth.

The *golden sash* which appeared *across his chest*† symbolizes the †Rv 1:13
perfection of the heavenly wisdom by which those who when in their right mind† offer his little ones appropriate and nourishing †2 Co 5:13
milk are transported in mind to God. And since God the Father foreknew them, he predestined them to be like the image of his Son, that he may be the firstborn among many brothers.† He presents †Rm 8:29
him clothed in the way that he wills a multitude of his saints to imitate him.

The Greek word *pos* is translated 'foot'. It gives its name to the *poderis*, a full-length garment.[5] In ancient times priests wore a *poderis*, and the true Priest is thus clothed, for he offered himself as a spotless sacrifice to God the Father.† Nothing is more necessary †Heb 9:14

[4] *Verona sacramentary* n. 278.

[5] Geoffrey continues: 'as the *talaris* [an ankle-length garment] takes it name from the *talus* [ankle]'.

for the salvation of his faithful than perseverance in good works and custody of their hearts. The *golden sash* is the faith that binds their hearts, and the love that controls their fleeting and mutable thoughts. But, as will appear more clearly in what follows, the truly spiritual men who adhere closely to the Lord must mold themselves in the image of his meekness and chastity according to their individual gifts.

†Rv 1:14 *His head and his hair were bright as white wool, bright as snow.*†
Christ, the head of his body, is compared in the Song of Songs to
†Sg 5:11 the finest gold.† The hair firmly rooted in that head shows us this
single experience of life, that it draws nourishment and grows from
what is insensible. It can be twisted, teased, cut, and burned, but it
cannot be pulled from the scalp without pain.

Wool indicates meek patience, and *snow* holy chastity. Wool rises
out of flesh on account of its tenderness. We recall that 'if anyone
is discovered in some fault, you who are spiritual are to instruct
such a person in a spirit of meekness; consider yourself, lest you too
†Ga 6:1 be tempted'.† Snow falls from heaven and signifies celibate chastity.
[God] bestows snow or wool according to his desire to see us, as it
†Gn 25:25 were, hot or cold. Esau, a rough† and hairy man, wore not lamb's
wool but camel's hair; Jacob, the great shepherd, wore wool, and
†Gn 27:11 therefore was smooth.†

Among the varieties of wool and camel's hair, we can distinguish
and find some black fibers and some white in both. White wool
signifies the patience of the innocent, of which Peter says in his
epistle, 'It is a gift if, being aware of God, someone bears sorrow
†1 P 2:19 while suffering unjustly',† and, 'It is better to suffer doing good, if
†1 P 3:17 this is the will of God, than doing evil'.† Christ dressed in white
†Ps 69:4 wool because he paid the price for what he did not steal.† The thief
hanging on the cross was dressed in black wool when he said, 'We
[have been condemned] justly, for we are getting what we deserve
for our deeds', and he indicated Christ's white wool when he said,
†Lk 23:41 'But this man, what has he done?'† Declaring his fellow thief's black
camel's hair he says, 'Do you not fear God, seeing that you are under
†Lk 23:40 the same sentence?'† Those aware of holiness, who bear tribulation
patiently, are clothed in white camel's hair. The admiring friends of
blessed Job were trying to put him in black wool, covering over a

solid vessel.† No doubt they considered even black wool better than †Si 50:10
white camel's hair.

The marvelous vision continues: *his eyes were like a flame of fire*,† †Rv 1:14
an all-knowing flame, an avenging fire, a flame from which nothing
is hidden, a fire leaving no evil unpunished. Would that the first
parents of the human race had been wise enough to know those eyes
and to heed them well! Then they would neither have hidden themselves among the trees, nor so hastily sewn perishable loincloths.† †Gn 3:8, 7
The king sitting upon his throne scatters all evil with a glance
of his eyes,† offering terrible punishment or forgiving clemency. †Pr 20:8
This flame enlightened Peter to acknowledge guilt; this fire turned
his self-assuredness into bitter tears when he was warming himself
before the charcoal fire,† as cold in heart as he was in body, in the †Jn 18:18
Lord's sight.† †Lk 22:61

In another sense, *his eyes* signify the teachers and pastors appointed to see and foresee within his body, that is, the church.† †Col 1:24
If what is said of his precursor, 'He was a burning and shining
lamp',† be found to apply to them, they are deservedly compared †Jn 5:35
to a flame and to fire, seeing that the flame instructs their own and
their people's minds, and the fire inflames their hearts.

His feet were like fine brass as in a burning furnace.† If we consider †Rv 1:15
these extremities and the terrible tribulation they will undergo, we
will count whatever now comes upon us as delights rather than
afflictions. In these latter days gold grown pale seems like brass; it
looks like brass but costs like gold. Meanwhile we must be afraid
lest the brass glitter deceitfully like gold but not be gold.

But if instead we understand [*his feet* to be] the Lord's purpose,
of which he says, 'The things concerning me have achieved their
purpose',† and the apostle James, 'You have heard of the patience of †Lk 22:37
Job, and you have seen the purpose of the Lord',† we immediately †Jm 5:11
recognize why in the *burning furnace his feet were like fine brass*. The
Jews said to Pilate, 'If this man were not a criminal, we would
not have handed him over to you'.† What greater insult could the †Jn 18:30
godless have leveled at faithful Christians than that they believed in
a man whom the Jews had crucified?[6] † †Ac 5:28

[6] Cf. Tacitus, *Annales* 15.44.

He who conferred on many of the martyrs such wonderful consolation that they could laugh at their torturers and executioners took no measure of that kind of consolation for himself. Instead he drank wormwood without honey in order to give others a draught mixed with the greatest sweetness. For Azarias and his companions
†The song of Azarias 27 (Dn 3:50 Vulgate) he made the midst of the furnace like a wind bringing dew,† but his own furnace of tribulation reached such burning proportions that
†Lm 1:12 there was no sorrow like his sorrow.† Was there anyone else whose
†Lk 22:44 sweat became like drops of blood falling down on the ground?†
†Jn 19:31 Pilate wondered if he had already died,† not realizing all he had borne. *His feet*, each of them humble and in the lowest place, while they burn so painfully, are embellished like fine brass.

†Rv 1:15 *His voice was like the voice of many waters*.† We seldom attribute a voice to inanimate things. Inanimate objects have a sound, not a voice. But this same Apocalypse claims that many waters are many
†Rv 17:15 peoples.† Do we not have a saying that the people's voice is the Lord's voice? It is not given to everyone to say, 'I will hear what the
†Ps 85:8 Lord God will say in me'.† Perhaps not even John could find words for all he heard, but he says summarily that his voice is the church's voice; his voice is the voice of those to whom the Lord said, 'He
†Lk 10:16 who hears you hears me'.†

†Rv 1:15 *His voice was like the voice of many waters*† has another meaning as well. In his holy preachers he considers the capacity of their hearers so that he may speak through and in each of them according to their strength—through those of whom it is said, 'There are no speeches
†Ps 19:3 or words whose voices are not heard'.† Can we understand the *voice* of the *waters* to mean only what the preachers heard but not what they preached? Today you sang a psalm verse that may help us here: 'The voice of the Lord is upon the waters; the God of majesty has
†Ps 29:3 thundered; the Lord is upon many waters'.[7] †

†Rv 1:16 The *seven stars* he held *in his right hand*† either represent the magnificent burden of his powers, or his light-filled miracles, as the
†Sg 5:14 Vulgate bride in the Song remembers: 'His hands are filled with hyacinths'.† Perhaps the souls of the just that he holds in his powerful right
†Ws 3:1 hand,† and which none can snatch away, are called *stars*. We should

[7] Psalm 29 (Vulgate 28) is the first psalm sung at the night office on the feast of the Epiphany.

not, however, go beyond what our author has said. He has clearly shown the meaning of the mystery of the *seven stars*: they are the angels of the seven churches. Do not be surprised that they will appear *in* Christ's *right hand* before the day of judgment, not to be judged, but to sit with him and give judgment when he enters into judgment with the elders of his people.† †Is 3:14

And from his mouth came a sharp, two-edged sword.† How I wish, †Rv 1:16
beloved, that a living and effective word† would come from his †Heb 4:12
mouth to our hearts today, how I wish it would cut deep, how I wish it would wound us to our salvation! How I wish it would not return empty, but would accomplish what it was sent forth to do, to bring us to fear and love! Otherwise, what profit is there either for you or for us in all our wordiness if—God forbid!—no profit come to our souls from it? Do not, I beg you, do not harden your hearts today† against the sword of his word, but let one of its edges inflict †Ps 95:8
fear and sorrow, and the other bring joy and love.

There is something in a single word of what follows which, if we take it seriously, will move the intention of our heart either to right or to left. For what is more terrible to sinners or more desirable to the devout than to appear before the face of the Sun of justice *shining with full strength*.† The prophet says of him, 'Who will †Rv 1:16
consider the day of his coming, or who will stand to see him?'† †Ml 3:2

His face, says John, *was like the sun shining with full strength*.† The †Rv 1:16
psalmist who said, 'Turn your face from my sins',† was anxiously †Ps 51:9
shrinking away from this face. Yet, filled with an equally great desire for that face he said, 'My heart has said to you: My face has sought you; your face, O Lord, will I seek';† and in another psalm he says, †Ps 27:8
'When shall I come and appear before the face of the Lord?'† †Ps 42:2

His face is compared to the sun simply because nothing more splendid exists. For *the sun shines with full strength*† when no cloud †Rv 1:16
of any sort blocks it, and it gleams in all the purity and fullness of its light. The moon shines too, but not in its own strength, because it does not shine of itself, they say,[8] but by the sun's light. So also will the righteous shine like the sun in the kingdom of their Father.† †Mt 13:43

[8] Isidore of Seville, *Etymologiarum libri XX* 3.53.2. Honorius of Autun, *De imagine mundi* 1.68; PL 172:138C.

They will shine in the Lord's strength, not their own, for as they
†1 Jn 3:2 see him as he is they become like him.† How truly and fully blessed
†Mt 5:8 will the pure of heart be, because they will see God!†

Meanwhile, I beg you, beloved, let us come into the presence of
†Ps 95:2 that face with thanksgiving,† with the thanksgiving that cleanses the
stains on our hearts that can block so blessed and beatific a vision.
Let us come into the presence of that face with thanksgiving and
praise, as the psalm writer says: 'We will give thanks to you, O God,
†Ps 75:1 we will give thanks'† to you. And all the while we are consoled
†Tt 3:4 by the appearance of the goodness and loving-kindness,† by the
†Tt 2:11 appearance of the Saviour's grace,† until he fills us with joy with his
†Ps 21:6 countenance† in that last appearance of which the prophet says, 'I
†Ps 17:15 shall be satisfied when your glory shall appear!'† Would that all of us
may be like him, and become sharers in his brightness at that clear,
complete and continuing manifestation! For he is God over all and
blessed forever. Amen.

Sermon Eight

[And when I saw him I fell at his feet as though dead. And he placed his right hand on me, saying, Do not be afraid; I am the first and the last, and the living one. I was dead, and see, I am alive forever and ever; and I have the keys of death and of hell. Now write what you have seen, what is, and what is to take place after this. The mystery of the seven stars that you saw in my right hand, and the seven golden lampstands: the seven stars are the angels of the seven churches, and the seven lampstands are the seven churches.]† †Rv 1:17–20

WHEN HE ADDS, "*And when I saw him I fell at his feet*,"† †Rv 1:17 Blessed John makes known that among the many things which he recalls having seen above him and before him, when he saw one like the Son of Man in the midst of the seven golden lampstands,† he fell down forcefully before him. You recall †Rv 1:13 that we said that his feet indicate the Lord's purpose, and we brought forth the apostolic testimony of blessed James: 'You have heard of the patience of Job, and you have seen the purpose of the Lord'.† †Jm 5:11

'His feet were like fine brass as in a burning furnace'.† Is there †Rv 1:15 anyone among the faithful who would not hesitate, would not

lose courage, would not leave his pride behind when he considers
†1 Co 2:2 Christ, and him crucified,† when he gazes upon gold grown pale
in a burning furnace, not even to be esteemed 'like fine brass' but
rather crushed under foot? The one who said, 'He had no form
†Is 53:2–3 or beauty for us to esteem him',† had seen him in such a state. At
this sight Habakkuk was afraid and trembled, for he saw him in the
†Hab 3:2 LXX middle of two living things†—the Lord of glory crucified between
and Vetus Latina two thieves. Those who had come to this spectacle returned home
†Lk 23:48 beating their breasts.†

He foretold to his apostles, among whom was John, that they
†Mt 26:31 would all be scandalized.† He said it, and it came to pass.[1] The sun
†Lk 23:41 grew dark,† unable to look upon this sight or to make it possible
†Mt 27:51 for others to look. The earth quaked, rocks were split.† Is there a
human mind that does not take fright, does not swoon, is not struck
dumb? Is there anyone who is not humbled because the Son of God
†Ph 2:8 was humbled to the point of death, even death on a cross?†

†Rv 1:17 *I fell as though dead.*† For, 'if one has died for all, then all have
†2 Co 5:14 died'.† I fell, dying with him that I may come to life with him,* as
*2 Tm 2:11 †2 Co 6:9 it is written: 'As dying, and see, we are alive!'†

If we take the Lord's feet as his least members,[2] his faithful, beset
as the world nears its end by the most painful tribulation such as
†Mt 24:21 never will be,† as if about to be cast into a burning furnace, with
good reason did John fall down before them as if dead. He feared
†Mt 24:24 that even the elect, if possible, might be led astray.† If we take his
feet to be his lowest and humblest members, those choosing an
outcast state in the Lord's house, there is still another meaning that
we are free to take as long as the text does not say otherwise. To fall
before them as though dead is for one of them not to be cast down
even in his own thought, but to be as though immune from carnal
sensibility. When tribulation comes, such as these do not consider
the heat of the furnace.

†Rv 1:17 *And he placed his right hand on me.*† Anyone who sees the Lord
during this period of time sees his own stains and blemishes as well in
that glorious light. As the Lord becomes sweet to him, he becomes

[1] Terence, *Andria* 381.

[2] Haymo of Auxerre, *Expositionis in Apocalypsin Beati Iohannis libri septem* 1.1; PL 117:956B.

bitter to himself. The more worthily a person receives the Lord, the more does he despise himself. And so, on seeing the Lord John immediately falls at his feet as if to beg pardon for the many sins that crowd his soul. Thus when Peter saw the Lord looking at him he wept bitterly.† Thus Mary fell at his feet, and asked forgiveness with humble tears, kisses, and obsequies.† When a person falls at his feet, the Lord lays his right hand on him, not only to forgive the offense but to grant a grace that far exceeds† the sins committed.

†Lk 22:61
†Mt 26:6ff; Lk 7:36ff; Jn 12:3ff
†Rm 5:20

How many times Saint Bernard discoursed in our presence, in his sermons on the Song of Songs, on the kiss of the mouth,† and on kisses on hands and feet as well![3] You have at hand those sermons, and you are able to reflect with pleasure that the Lord lays his hand on the one who falls at his feet. But take care, I beg you, that when you fall at the Lord's feet you fall prostrate like one dead. Otherwise, you who are still living to sin will beg forgiveness in vain. No fault is remitted if it is not dismissed; none is remitted while it is committed.[4] While it lingers by action, or consent and intention of the heart, a disgrace, a crime, and a sacrilege is effected. No prayers, no tears, no reparation by one repenting in this way are sufficient to expiate a fault without it actually being renounced in deed.

†Sg 1:2

And he placed his right hand on me.† When the bride said, 'His left hand is under my head, and his right hand will embrace me',† she was looking for his hand, longing for his hand, desiring that it be stretched out to her. Although sometimes the Lord's *right hand*, especially when used absolutely, refers to his present assistance and the gift of the virtues, more often it indicates eternal happiness, in accord with the scriptural passage: 'Length of days is in his right hand, in his left are riches and glory'.† Fortunate is the one whose mind, whose principal purpose—for whose preservation those who would be prudent as serpents† put forth their other parts—presses down and rises above what pertains to the left hand, while he seeks and sets his mind on the things that are above at the right hand,† where there are pleasures forevermore.†

†Rv 1:17
†Sg 2:6
†Pr 3:16
†Mt 10:16
†Col 3:1–2
†Ps 16:11

[3] Bernard of Clairvaux, *Sermones super Cantica Canticorum* 3.4; SBOp 1.14–21; CF 4:19.

[4] The Latin reads: *Non remittitur culpa si non dimittitur; non remittitur, dum committitur.*

†Pr 31:30 Below lies deceitful glory, and vain is the beauty† of earthly
riches. Silver glistens and gold shines; the carbuncle burns, topaz has
the gleam of gold, the emerald is greener than grass, sapphires seem
blue as the sky. A young planting of sons, and the attire of daughters
†Ps 144:12 exhibiting the likeness of the splendor of a temple,† are pleasing.
†Ps 144:13–14 Sheep heavy with young, fat cattle,† treasure houses, granaries, full
†Ps 144:13 storehouses,† lofty bulwarks—these delight us. We find pleasure in
broad estates. But these things contain no true happiness. Under
†Qo 1:2–3 the sun there is only vanity of vanities, and all is vanity.†

Nor is the possessor of these truly happy, though he is falsely
said to be so. Rather, happy is the one upon whom the Lord now
places his right hand. He hopes for the one thing, he asks and longs
for the one thing beside which all else pales by comparison. He
does not agree to take any delight in these things, but refuses every
consolation. I beg you, beloved, set your minds on the things that
†Col 3:1 are above, where Christ is at God's right hand.† He is your treasure,
your love and desire, your sweetness, your welfare, and your life.

Yet because as we sing in the psalm, 'The Lord will bestow
†Ps 84:11 favor and glory',† we may well take the right hand laid upon us as
referring to his present help as well. He places his right hand on us
†Rm 8:15 to free us, lest we receive a spirit of slavery again in fear,† which
belongs to the left hand.

On that account, in laying his right hand on us he says, *Do not*
†Rv 1:17 *be afraid*.† He places his hand on us for warming, for blessing, for
protecting, just as once the prudent shepherd placed rods of poplar,
†Gn 30:37–38 almond, and plane before breeding sheep.† The poplar signifies a
medicinal balm to warm and heal, the almond a blessed food to
eat, and the plane tree a protective shade for secure covering from
the heat of temptation. This is why the text continues, *Do not
be afraid*.

We may ask why here and in some other visions we are told
not to fear when sacred Scripture and our own experience teach us
that fear is necessary for justification. There are two kinds of fear,
just as there are two kinds of love. We read in the letter of this same
†1 Jn 4:18 John, 'There is no fear in love, but perfect love casts out fear'.† Yet
the psalm seems to teach the contrary, that the holy fear of the Lord
†Ps 19:9 endures forever.† But because fear is described and is experienced

as having to do with punishment,† there seems to be a discrepancy †1 Jn 4:18
between the first text saying that fear must be cast out and the other claiming that it endures.[5]

This apparent contradiction disappears when we realize that the feeling of fear disappears but its fruitful effect remains, just as we sing in the psalm that the patience of the poor does not perish forever,† †Ps 9:18
yet the Apocalypse itself will later say that their deeds follow those who die in the Lord.† If we believe that the feeling of fear will †Rv 14:13
endure, even in the depths of our hearts, we are not to associate it with punishment, but with joy and delight based in the full and delightful reverence of love.

Zechariah, the father of John the Baptist, included this verse in the hymn he sang at the naming of his son: 'that being freed from the hand of our enemies we may serve the Lord without fear'†—and †Lk 1:74
this despite the prophet's admonishing us in the psalm to serve him in fear.† No doubt we are wise to fear the one who frees us from fear †Ps 2:11
of our enemies. But for the priest Zechariah, for the blessed virgin Mary, for the shepherds at the Lord's birth, for the women seeking him when he had arisen, for John himself—told in this place not to be afraid—it is not a matter of divine fear, but of that common human fear, neither good nor evil, that besets human minds when they see such visions. There is no doubt that he who heard, *Do not be afraid*,† fell down terrified. But you should not tremble before †Rv 1:17
feet in a furnace, feet like fine brass,† 'for the things concerning me †Rv 1:15
have a purpose'.† †Lk 22:37

I am the first and the last.[6] *I was dead and I am alive.*† And you, †Rv 1:17–18
then, if you have fallen as though dead, add as well that you are alive, as I proclaimed to you and to your fellow disciples, 'Because I live, you too will live'.† I am the first, and the firstborn before every †Jn 14:19
creature,† yet the 'least of men',* 'a worm and not human, the scorn †Si 24:5 Vulgate *Is 53:3
of humans and the outcast of the people'.† The 'least of men', as the †Ps 22:6

[5] Augustine, *In epistolam Ioannis ad Parthos* 9.5–8; SC 75:386–394; *Love One Another, My Friends: St. Augustine's Homilies on the First Letter of John* (San Francisco, 1989) 92–95.

[6] Geoffrey omits here the first phrase of verse eighteen in the Vulgate, 'and the living one', and modifies the third, 'and see, I am alive for ever and ever'. Later he will quote the second and third phrases as they appear in the Vulgate.

prophet says, accounted a leper, a man of sorrows acquainted with
†Is 53:3 weakness†—assuredly he learned it from what he suffered. Now he
is alive by his magnanimity and his immunity from all sin. Sin is
the soul's death. I have committed no sin, and no deceit was found
†1 P 2:22 in my mouth,† so they were utterly mistaken who said, 'Not for a
†Jn 10:33 good work do we stone you, but for blasphemy'.† I am one person
in three substances, first by the majesty of the Word, least by the
weakness of the flesh, and alive by all inner holiness and power.

†Rv 1:18 *I was dead.*† Truly, without any deception—even though no one
†Jn 10:17–18 took my life; rather I willingly laid it down.† I tasted death, and did
not reject it at once and refuse to drink, even though my vineyard,
†Jr 2:21 turned into a bitter and alien stock,† produced sour wine for me.
†Ps 3:5 I lay down and slept,† not to rise at once, but to wait from the
ninth hour of the day of Preparation until the first hour of the first
day of the week. This was the prediction I made while still alive,
†Mk 14:58 and of which the Jews reminded Pilate,† that this evidence given by
enemies may be more persuasive.

Earlier, while he was living in the world, he fasted forty days, and he did not feel hungry until they were completed, thus making known both his true power and his voluntary weakness. He lay dead for forty hours, four, that is, on the day of Preparation, and thirty-six during two nights and a day, thus proving beyond doubt that he was indeed dead. After his resurrection he appeared openly
to his disciples during that same number of days, speaking of the
†Ac 1:3 kingdom of God,† reminding them of what he had said previously,
coming and going among them, showing them his hands and his
†Jn 20:20 side,† eating and drinking in their company, and demonstrating the
†Ac 1:3 reality of his resurrection by many proofs.†

Thus he could say, in the vision we have under consideration,
†Rv 1:18 *I was dead, and see, I am alive.*† They had to be sure of the reality
of his death, but, much more, of his resurrection, in accord with
†Rm 8:34 the Apostle's words, 'Christ Jesus who died, yes, who arose'.† *See*,
he says, *I am alive forever and ever.* See what is new here: no long delayed resurrection, as the resurrection of others is delayed until the end of time. I am alive, not to die a second time as did Lazarus and some others who returned to life to die again. Indeed Christ,

rising from the dead, now dies no more, nor will death any longer have dominion over him.† †Rm 6:9

For, as he adds, he holds *the keys of death and of hell*.† At his command the dying have to enter, and at his command those arising will some day have to leave. If we take hell to be the depth,[7] for his soul has not been left in hell,† he even led out many with him. He who holds these keys will say to the godless: 'Go into eternal fire'.† They will be forced to obey him, and none of them will ever come back out. †Rv 1:18 †Ps 16:10 †Mt 25:41

Now write what you have seen, what is, and what is to take place after this.† This vision obviously refers to past, present, and future. To communicate it by word of mouth is not enough; write it down as well. Tell others by the living character of your actions what was divinely revealed to you, *what is* stored in your mind, *and what is to take place after this*, what I have disposed for myself or imposed on others. †Rv 1:19

The mystery of the seven stars that you saw in my right hand, and the seven golden lampstands.† Let us here understand: 'These are the things you must write'. He gives us a partial revelation, opening an approach, and giving the wise a chance to become wiser still. †Rv 1:20

The seven stars are the angels of the seven churches.† He calls their servants *stars*, and he calls them *angels*. Is it any wonder that he seeks, that he exacts from his stewards that they be found trustworthy,† that his stars give light, that his angels declare his will and not their own? If only our stars may not fall from heaven, but remain in the Lord's right hand! If only the Lord may not discover wickedness even among the angels!† †Rv 1:20 †1 Co 4:2 †Jb 4:18

And the seven lampstands are the seven churches.† If only the gold of wisdom and the gold of faith may shine in the churches, and not the gilt of hypocrisy and pretense! If only their light may shine before God for their own salvation and before people for their edification†—all under the rule of the true light* who is one with the Father and the Holy Spirit, God above all and blessed forever. Amen. †Rv 1:20 †Mt 5:16 *Jn 1:9

[7] Bernard of Clairvaux, *Sermones de diversis* 20.2; SBOp 6/1:166. Gregory the Great, *Dialogi* 4.44:301–302.

Sermon Nine

And to the angel of the church at Ephesus write: He who holds the seven stars in his right hand, who walks among the seven golden lampstands, says this: I know your works, your toil, and your patience. I know that you cannot bear evildoers, and have tested those who claim to be apostles and are not, and have found them to be liars. And you have patience, and have borne up for my name's sake, and have not given up. But this I hold against you: you have abandoned your first love. Remember then from what you have fallen and repent. Do your former works. Otherwise I come to you and will move your lampstand from its place. You have this in your favor: you hate the deeds of the Nicolaitans and I, too, hate them. Let anyone who has an ear hear what the Spirit says to the churches. To the one who conquers I will give permission to eat from the tree of life that is in the paradise of my God.† †Rv 2:1–7

AND TO THE ANGEL OF THE CHURCH *at Ephesus write.*† Ephesus was the first of the churches to which John was commanded to write. 'Ephesus' has three consonant meanings: it can be interpreted 'my will', 'their purpose',[1] or 'my soul †Rv 2:1

[1]Jerome, *Liber interpretationis hebraicorum nominum* 68.27; CCh 72:145.

in it'.[2] This purpose does not consume but rather consummates; it
belongs rightfully to the church's children, and thus it is the will
of God and his good pleasure, which is what 'his soul in it' means.
The letter is written to its angel, that is, to its bishop, about matters
known to pertain to that church, so that he may accept what is
enjoined on him by it. How different from the clever serpent of
†Gn 3:1 old, who bypassed the man and got around the silly woman!† The
faithful messenger tells the bishop what is best for the people; for,
if they hold the pastor in contempt, deception will be charged to
the audacity of the flock. Not inappropriately then is the letter
concerning matters which refer to that particular church addressed
to the angel, for he is responsible for whether his disciples conduct
†RB 36:10 themselves well or fall short.†

†Rv 2:1 *He who holds the seven stars in his right hand says this*.† The person
of John, and also of the angel through whom the letter comes to
him, must receive all reverence from the leader and his church. Yet
the writer adds besides that these are the Lord's words, not theirs.
He has already stated that the stars are the churches' angels, and the
lampstands their churches; stars of such a kind must never decline
to his left hand, where are riches and glory, but must remain in his
†Pr 3:16 right hand, where there is long life.† Otherwise the order of things
would be reversed, as if we were to say, 'As with the people, so
†Is 24:2 with the priest',† and, 'As with the flock, so with the shepherd'.
Stars should remain fixed in the sky; lampstands shed their light
†Mt 5:16 on earth in good works.† These stars do not suppose that they can
remain steadfastly in the Lord's right hand by their own strength
or merit or zeal; for, unless he holds them, the stars—which God
forbid!—would fall from heaven.

Moreover, he who holds the stars in his right hand *walks among*
†Rv 2:1 *the lampstands*† not only by his own presence but also through the
radiation from those same stars. So also Paul, when he was among
the disciples, decided that he knew nothing except Jesus, and him
†1 Co 2:2 crucified.† Thus when John the Baptist saw Jesus walk by he said,
'Behold the Lamb of God. Behold him who takes away the sins
†Jn 1:36, 29 of the world'.† The Lord holds the stars in his right hand, that

[2] Jerome, *Commentariorum in Epistolam ad Ephesios libri tres* 3; PL 26:547A.

they may raise their minds to God in that heavenly stability; at the same time he walks by their light among the lampstands, through the dispensation of his human nature, so they may know that they should walk as he has walked. He walks among them to show them the paths his journey took, for 'all his paths are mercy and truth'.† Yet not to everyone does he show this, but 'to those who seek his covenant and his testimonies'.† This means, 'the kingdom of God and his righteousness'.† The same psalm continues: 'that he may make known to them his covenant';† 'his testimonies' are the gifts of grace by which his Spirit bears testimony to us that we are children of God.†

†Ps 25:10
†Ps 25:10
†Mt 6:33; Lk 12:31 Vulgate
†Ps 25:14
†Rm 8:16

I know your works.† In holy Scripture God's 'knowledge' frequently signifies not only cognition but also approval. Both meanings are suited to making us careful and circumspect, because everything is naked to the eyes of the one to whom we speak,† to whom an account must be rendered for everything.† Not even the smallest act done rightly will he leave unnoticed by disdaining it, nor disdain by not noticing it.

†Rv 2:2
†Heb 4:13
†Rm 14:12

In this passage he gives his approval to works of devotion, physical labor, the bearing of tribulation, zeal for justice, and a striving for discretion. Alms are more acceptable when they come from the fruits of labor and not from ill-gotten gains or excess wealth. Hard work willingly done piles up merits if a person also patiently bears the opposition of others. Patience with personal injustice, or any other affliction, never so saps the fervor of a just and zealous person that he is less able to give timely corrections to those who stray, and if one suspects that he is being carried away by hasty judgment, he can carefully imitate the caution of blessed Job: 'The cause I did not know I most diligently searched out'.† The fifth clause of this letter pertains to this: he tests *those who claim to be apostles* and finds *them to be liars*.†

†Jb 29:16
†Rv 2:2

But returning to the *patience* in which God takes so much pleasure, it is commended equally with perseverance in patience because a sheep or an ox that lacks an ear or a tail cannot fulfil a vow.† Do not think that patience and perseverance are opposites: they are not, for a person who may at first be unable to bear something may later be praised for bearing it and not giving up. [The church

†Lv 22:23 Vulgate

at Ephesus] does not *bear evildoers*—zealous in its faith, it separates itself from communion and concord with these people. Bearing up under persecution, it does not give up. Although physical training
†1 Tm 4:8 may be of some value† in that it involves toil, [the church at Ephesus] is admonished not to hate laborious work or the farm work created
†Si 7:15 by the Most High.† Futher, because godliness is valuable in every
†1 Tm 4:8 way,† he charges it with its lack, and complains, *But this I hold against*
†Rv 2:4 *you,*† and so on. Notice carefully that he remains aware that he holds the seven stars in his right hand, and that this and the other charges made in different places seem to refer more to churches than to individuals. Thus the Lord threatens this church with moving a lampstand, and not a person, from its place.

†Rv 2:4 *But this I hold against you: you have abandoned your first love.*†
†1 Co 13:8 Hearing that 'love never fails',† some question whether love once possessed can ever be lost.[3] We leave such questions to those with greater leisure; what others have written on this point must suffice. One thing is clear, that love's unchanging nature is not found immediately at its beginning or in some stage of its growth, as is sometimes claimed when the subject of lost love is discussed. Paul
†1 Co 9:27 claimed that he chastised his body lest he be disqualified,† and no one would presume to believe he was wanting in love. If there is a stage after which no one can fall, I believe that it can never be recognized either in oneself or in another apart from some clear revelation.

It is apparent from this reproof that in commending this church's *works* at the beginning of the passage he meant its works of love. He admonishes them to repent and do their earlier good works, suggesting that by an omission of them they abandoned love. If the omission of love demands penitential amends, then doubtless the commission of evil requires more serious expiation. If good works omitted require repentance, how much more effective must be the penance for bad deeds admitted!

Do you wish to do penance and bring forth fruits worthy of
†Lk 3:8 repentance?† *Remember then from what you have fallen,** he says. Clearly
*Rv 2:5 it is from the perfection of love, where you once stood. Repenting,

[3] Peter Lombard, *Libri IV sententiarum* 3.31.1.

however, is not enough, henceforth do the earlier works lest, by neglecting them again, you must repent again.

Otherwise I come to you.† Fortunate is the necessity that compels †Rv 2:5
us to do right.[4] After a reminder he adds a warning, saying *Otherwise.* Then he adds a promise: *To the one who conquers,*† and so on. †Rv 2:7
According to God's foreknowledge all, both elect and condemned, must come to their own places and occupy their places. By the merit of their earthly lives both sorts move during this present time as they change. As an example of the latter, Judas went to his place.† As an †Ac 1:25
example of the former, Matthias obtained his place by lot.† †Ac 1:26

Yet perhaps he is not yet threatening Ephesus with eternal damnation, but with a lessening of some temporal dignity or spiritual grace or future glory, in some not unprofitable persecution. Telling them 'I will come to you' seems to imply 'for your own good', to visit the fault of abandoned love with the rod of correction. Or we can take 'I will come to you' to mean simply that, 'I will not overlook this, I will not forbear'. Remember that the Lord sometimes avenges himself on superiors by bringing earthly punishment on their subjects, as he laid the punishment for King Hezekiah's pride on those who came after him.† Hezekiah realized †2 K 20:12–19=Is 39
how his successors would suffer punishment unless he paid no mean penalty for his fault.

But *you have this in your favor: you hate the deeds of the Nicolaitans.*† †Rv 2:6
The four animals, when they appear in several forms as symbols of the holy ones, are seen to be full of eyes within and without, in front and behind.† And rightly so, for who would dare be negligent once †Rv 4:6
he is aware that everything he does is being assiduously scrutinized by this great judge?

See how the loving Lord who loves souls† wrote to this priest, †Ws 11:26
for he himself wrote what he commanded be written. In this writing the Lord was the one speaking to him. He began with a commendation, followed it by a correction, added consolation, and at length he ended the letter with a promise. Even though I have something against you, you have something in common with me because *you hate the deeds of the Nicolaitans and I, too, hate them.*† †Rv 2:6

[4] Augustine, *Epistulae* 127.8; CSEL 44:28.

As to will and to not will the same thing pertains to friendship,[5] to love what the Lord loves is not enough unless you hate what he hates. As the zeal of the Lord does not leave his people, so he does not conceal what is acceptable to himself because he detects ingratitude in them.

†Ws 11:24 Moreover, because he hates none of the things he has made,† he takes this occasion to remind either [the angel], or perhaps himself, that he hates not them but their deeds. Works of this kind were their own, not his who is at work in his people both to will and to work
†Ph 2:13 for his good pleasure.† As he hates none of the things he has made, neither does he love anything he has not made, as the prophet says: 'By the Lord will a person's steps be directed, and he will choose
†Ps 37:23 his path'.† And so he hates, punishes, and pursues what he has not made in those things he has made.

†Rv 2:6 *The deeds*, he says, *of the Nicolaitans*.† Error alone, or rather the stubborn choice to continue to err in matters of faith, makes heretics. Some are deceived concerning the Trinity or the twofold nature of Christ, others regarding the church's sacraments. Some go astray over their behavior and actions, accepting norms that faith rejects or rejecting norms that faith accepts. In this way the Chaldeans
†Jb 1:17 made three columns† against the church, and the Nicolaitans seem to have arisen first or among the first. Thus it is that their deeds are called hateful, because especially in these sentences whose theme is deeds they were at variance with sincere faith.

The Nicolaitans are said to have taken from the word of a certain
†Ac 6:5 Nicolaus, who was one of the first seven deacons,† an occasion for overstepping the boundaries of lust and of using women with complete indifference. Nicolaus, who had a beautiful wife, came to have jealous suspicions. Aroused by a wrongheaded indignation he brought her into public and disrespectfully exposed her to all to use as they wished.[6] The name has come to mean vulgar folly; 'Nicolaus' means 'foolish people'.[7]

[5] Sallust, *Catalinae coniuratio* 20.4. Bernard of Clairvaux, *Sermones de diversis* 80.1; SBOp 6/1: 320.

[6] Isidore of Seville, *Etymologiarum libri XX* 8.4.5. Venerable Bede, *Explanatio Apocalypsis* 1.2; PL 93:138D–139A.

[7] Jerome, *Liber interpretationis hebraicorum nominum* 70.13; CCh 72:147.

The very make-up of the body shows how close gluttony is to lust.[8] The Nicolaitans went further, and began eating food sacrificed to idols, something they had possibly not learned from Nicolaus. Even though church history may excuse him his indiscreet relationships with women, it is hardly credible that in the presence of the apostles what we read was stated on account of his indignation had lost its effect by that time. We are, however, free to have whatever opinion we wish about his person.

And I, too, hate them.† We must understand this as causative: 'Because I too hate them'. Otherwise he would seem not to be pleased by hatred of this kind, which he did not cause. Yet this heresy of the Nicolaitans was long ago stamped out; no one today professes its foolishness. Would that no more adherents of impurity could be found than those professing this godless nonsense! Thus, let my hearers tremble, for God hates not only the words of such people but their deeds; he hates not only declared heresy but an offensive way of life. †Rv 2:6

Let anyone who has ears hear what the Spirit says to the churches.† Either in the body of each of these letters or at its end we find a sentence of this kind.[9] Yet the words which follow it in the first three letters, and the words which precede it in the last four, are not to be attributed to the Holy Spirit. So where we read, *in the paradise of my God,* anyone who wishes to refer these words to the Holy Spirit should search out where he has ever read anything similar. I do not recall having read it. †Rv 2:7

This idea would seem to indicate some relative greatness, which the catholic faith does not admit in its teaching on the unity of the Trinity. We are to believe that the Son calls the Father 'his' *God*, referring to him as greater than himself, only as a human being. If, however, someone were to hold that because they are from the Father, both persons, the Holy Spirit as well as the Son, can call him *my God*, he will find in what follows that he may not attribute this

[8] Gregory the Great, *Moralia in Job* 31.45; PL 76:622A.

[9] Attentive readers will notice that Geoffrey uses the singular and the plural (*aurem, aures*—ear, ears) apparently with complete indifference. In these letters to the churches the Vulgate always has the singular.

to the Holy Spirit. Nevertheless the Spirit speaks through Christ and in Christ what Christ speaks through and in that same Spirit.

†Mt 11:15, et al Because in the gospel the Lord has spoken about having ears† we know that this revelation is consonant with the gospel. He who does not receive it lacks ears of this kind, nor does he receive it unless it is granted him by the one from whom every perfect gift comes
†Jm 1:17 down.† As one of the saints says to him, 'Grant what you command, and command what you will'.[10] Those ears surely mean a readiness
†Rm 10:17 to believe and to obey, for faith comes from what is heard,† and the very word 'obey' is from the Latin, 'give ear to'.[11]

Let us analyze further: the left ear listens to the Spirit's dissuasion, the right ear to his persuasion. And woe to you, whoever you
†Ps 58:4–5 are, deaf adder who do not listen to the voice of the charmer† who chants wisely, for your good and not for your harm! Woe to you, whoever you are, deaf adder! You press one ear so hard to the ground below that you catch only what is low and earthy, and thus you sin against hope by stopping your other ear with your tail, arrogantly deluding yourself about the coming chastisement.

Grant to your servants, Lord, ears of your choosing, that we may hear what you suggest, what your Spirit is saying to the churches. For with him, equally with your Son, you are one God over all and blessed forever. Amen.

[10] Augustine, *Confessiones* 10.29.40.

[11] *obedientia ex obauditu*: Isidore of Seville, *Etymologiarum libri XX* 10.196.

Sermon Ten

TO THE ONE WHO CONQUERS *I will give permission to eat*
from the tree of life.† Our life here below is a warfare,* and †Rv 2:7
its outcome either our victory or our adversary's. Indeed *Jb 7:1
a perilous battle against the princes of this world and their many
minions, the spiritual forces of evil,† hangs over us, or, rather, draws †Ep 6:12
close. And yet, if we judge by faith, he who is among us is greater
than he who is in the world. Yes, if we but open our eyes with the
servant of Elisha we will see more for us than against us, more with
us than we have adversaries.† †2 K 6:16–17

The fight is serious, I grant; the battle is grave, but no one
who resists the adversary will succumb. 'Resist the devil, and he
will flee from you', says the Apostle.† 'Resist him, strong in the †Jm 4:7
faith'.† Our victory then is our faith,† not a dead faith, not a †1 P 5:9 †1 Jn 5:4
lukewarm faith, not a feigned faith, but a living, life-giving faith
working through love;† a faith vigorous and increased by the Lord, †Ga 5:6
as the apostles requested,† not a faith faltering in tribulation as did †Lk 17:5
Peter's when he grew frightened at the sight of the strong wind
and began to sink;† a faith that is true, the substance of things †Mt 14:30
hoped for and the conviction of things unseen;† otherwise, if it seeks †Heb 11:1
immediate, perishable goods it is feigned. Resist, he says, do not give
in; 'give no place to the devil'.† 'Resist him, and he will flee from †Ep 4:27

†Jm 4:7 you'.† His flight is your victory, his confounding your glory; your triumph is his despair.

Meanwhile your flight from him is more your victory than his. Certainly we are to flee fornication by getting away from the place, and to avoid persecution when lawful. By more important endeavors, or by physical exercise now and then, we must prevent useless thoughts lest they sneak up on us. The adversary is weighty, but he overcomes no one without that person's consent; anyone who refuses consent will benefit all the more. He does not attack unless God allows it, nor does he win unless we allow it.

†Rv 2:7 A careful study of *the tree of life*† in a recently published book of *Sentences* will yield much information. A statement of Augustine's which receives no little discussion in that book can be taken in a different sense. 'How was man created immortal', asks Augustine, 'when immortality was his as well from the tree of life, not from his nature?'[1] The author of the *Sentences* eventually answers: 'He clearly asserts that being able not to die came not from nature but from the tree of life'.[2]

I admit I would have preferred him to say that being able not to die came from the tree of life and not from his nature. For what could man have gotten from that tree that he did not already have? From the time of his first creation man was able not to die by gift of his Creator, but, for his necessary instruction, he kept this ability not to die by eating of the tree of life. As we understand it, man was then immortal by the immortality we are calling 'being able not to die'. Augustine claims that he possessed this possibility 'as well from the tree of life', meaning either that a longer and more active life than normal could be had by an occasional tasting of this tree's fruit, or that, eaten for a specified time, it would cause a passage over into complete immortality.

The remaining section discussing the tree itself seems ambiguous, since both of the above possibilities have their mystical fulfillment in the spiritual tree. For the time being we have its fruit in
†Rm 6:22 sanctification, but its end is eternal life.† *The tree of life* is a godliness

[1] Augustine, *De Genesi ad litteram* 6.25.36; CSEL 38:197.

[2] Peter Lombard, *Libri IV sententiarum* 2.19.4.

which is valuable in every way, holding promise for life now and in the age to come.† *The tree of life* is wisdom for those who grasp it, and it calls those who long for it to be filled with its fruit.† Twofold is its fruit and double its promise—a hundredfold now, and life eternal in the age to come.†

†1 Tm 4:8
†Si 24:19 (24:26 Vulgate)
†Mt 19:29

To the one who conquers I will give permission to eat from the tree of life† may likewise be understood in two ways: to the one who is struggling now victoriously, or to the one who is gloriously triumphing after victory. Thus one person sees it as food on the journey, another as his crown in his homeland; one as recompense in warfare, another as reward after victory is won.

†Rv 2:7

And how rightly does such a tree belong in *the paradise of*† his *God*. The paradise of diverse trees bearing various fruits is the church. So Wisdom says, 'My delight is to be with the human race'.† Christ, the power of God and the wisdom of God,* says to the church through his apostles: 'Behold I am with you even to the end of the age'.† It is meanwhile a paradise from which penitents are excluded at the beginning of Lent, to be mercifully admitted at the Lord's Supper.[3] It is a paradise outside of which we can never find the tree of life because no one can offer a true sacrifice outside the church.[4] It is a paradise where God plants and waters fruitful trees by the hands of his ministers, but where he alone gives the growth.†

†Rv 2:7
†Pr 8:31
*1 Co 1:24
†Mt 28:20
†1 Co 3:6

Yes, I say, trees are now walking, as the man in the gospel whose sight the Lord restored claimed he saw men [like trees] walking,† for trees walk while men live, but fall when they die. While they are still living, let them see where they are going; let them see what they are heading for before they fall; let them see where they are tending. Not everyone, in fact not many, can expect what once visibly happened to free blessed Martin, what occurred more miraculously to the thief confessing the Lord on the cross, namely, that the pine tree, about to fall on [Martin], changed direction to save him.[5]

†Mk 8:24

[3] Holy or Maundy Thursday.

[4] Gratian, *Decretum* C.l, q.1, c. 68, A. L. Richter-Aem, ed. (Fribourg-Graz, 1955).

[5] Sulpicius Severus, *Vita Martini* 13.1–8; SCh 133:280–282. To demonstrate the power of Christianity Martin agreed to stand under a sacred pine tree as sceptical pagans felled it. As the tree came toward him, Martin calmly lifted his hand to

†Qo 11:3 Wherever it falls, there it will be,† whether to the south at that
noontime when the bridegroom pastures [his flock] and has it lie
†Sg 1:6 down†—may he grant that we forever be there with him!—or to the
†Jr 1:14 north, from which every evil breaks forth and spreads out.† How
fortunate is the one who will be there where *the tree of life* is—indeed,
†Ezk 18:17 he shall surely live and shall not die!† This is truly and completely *the*
†Ps 16:11 *paradise of* our *God*, where pleasures last forever,† where the torrent
†Ps 36:9 of delight inebriates;† where *the tree of life* gives life without the
consumption of its fruit,[6] satisfies without satiety, refreshes without
fail, with a new food, a new type of existence, where seeing alone
blesses those who look upon it. In this paradise the bridegroom
†Sg 1:6 pastures [his flock] and has it lie down at a noontime† which does
†Ac 10:38 not pass away. There he is, who went about the world doing good,†
†Jn 1:36 while John saw him walk by and said, 'Behold the Lamb of God'.†

O happy thief,[7] who the Saviour promised would be with him
that day in paradise! O happy too that brother to whom Saint
Bernard, along with his abbot of happy memory, Dom Franco
of Liège,[8] deigned to appear with glistening face and garment as
he lay ill. And while that abbot, whose memory he had always
honored devoutly, was praying for him in these circumstances, the
brother spontaneously and warmly implored his help. Immediately
he replied with the Lord Jesus Christ's own words, words of faith we
†1 Tm 4:9 long to hear, a word sure and worthy of full acceptance:† 'Amen, I
†Lk 23:43 tell you, today you will be with me in paradise'.†

This vision happened about ten years ago in the region of Bourges, in a monastery called 'The House of God'.[9] To its truth the brother's previous commendable way of life gave absolutely credible testimony, as did his passing, which occurred that very day, even though an experienced physician who was there, along with

---

make the sign of the cross. The falling tree immediately changed directions, and the pagans converted to Christianity.

6 Bernard of Clairvaux, *Sermones de diversis* 42.7; SBOp 6/1:260. *Liber de diligendo Deo* 11.33; SBOp 3:147.

7 Bernard of Clairvaux, *Sermones de diversis* 40.2; SBOp 6/1:235.

8 Franco of Liège, the third abbot of Nerlac, in the diocese of Bourges, died in 1178 or shortly after.

9 Nerlac was named *Domus Dei de Nigro Lacu*, The House of God of the Black Lake.

several brothers who were carefully attending him, found in him that morning no sign of approaching death or terminal illness.

[This brother] never enjoyed the sight of you on earth, most holy Father, but he eagerly embraced your memory, followed your teaching, and imitated your life as far as he could. When shall we be with you, or shall we ever—unworthy compared to you, beloved Father now in paradise—be with you, we who walked with you in this world? But we must walk with all our exertions, if this be granted us, just as you walked,† we who long with all our prayers †1 Jn 2:6 to be both in paradise and with you. May [God] have pity on our weakness and mercifully spare our unworthiness, so that he who gives grace and glory may bring us to follow you manfully and to meet you happily, he who lives and reigns forever. Amen.

Sermon Eleven

And to the angel of the church at Smyrna write: These are the words of the first and the last, who was dead and who is alive. I know your affliction and your poverty, but you are rich. You are being blasphemed by those who say they are Jews and are not, but are a synagogue of Satan. Fear none of the things you are going to suffer. Behold, the devil is going to cast some of you into prison that you may be tested, and you will have affliction for ten days. Be faithful even to death, and I will give you the crown of life.† †Rv 2:8–10

TO THE ANGEL OF THE CHURCH AT SMYRNA WRITE.† 'Their song', the meaning of Smyrna,[1] may refer to the one hundred forty-four thousand in the third vision of this †Rv 2:8 Apocalypse, for no one else could say the new song that he heard.† It †Rv 14:1–3 can also refer to penitents, because among the angels of God there is joy over them,† breaking forth in a song of praise and thanksgiving. †Lk 15:10 It can also refer to those suffering wrong and bearing insults, as Jeremiah says: 'I have become a mockery to my people, their song all the day long'.† The condemned consider the life of the elect insane. †Lm 3:14 They do not recognize the honor of holy souls—more foolish than

[1]Jerome, *Liber interpretationis hebraicorum nominum* 81.4; CCh 72:160.

†Nm 23:10 Balaam who chose the death of the upright,† they consider that their
end will be without honor; but they will afterward hold them in
higher esteem than they once held them in derision. The song may
also suit the faithful who have freely and single-mindedly devoted
themselves to God, for God has given them, even now, gladness in
†Is 61:3 place of mourning, a song of praise in place of a spirit of grief.†
These have a song of their own, different from the songs of the
worldly. Though not yet in their homeland, they sing as they walk
†Ps 138:5 along the Lord's ways, 'Great is the glory of the Lord!'†

†Mt 26:75 Although some of the other angels of peace may weep bitterly,†
the angel of this church has nothing to weep over, with such
extraordinary people fortunately enrolled in it. It is for their angels
†Rv 2:22 to weep over those who sin and do not repent,† to weep for those
who weep for the wrong reason, to weep for those who laugh for
†Pr 2:14 the wrong reason and who rejoice in most wicked things.† No one
weeps for them more bitterly than do the angels of peace, as long
as they resist this peace, even when begged for Christ's sake to be
reconciled to God. Rightly do their angels, their servants, weep
†Rm 15:8 over them, just as Christ Jesus, the servant of the circumcision,†
†Lk 19:41 wept over Jerusalem.† But the angel of Smyrna has cause to rejoice,
not to weep, cause to sing rather than to mourn.

Another meaning of Smyrna is 'myrrh'.[2] Myrrh is bitter to the
taste but pleasant to the sense of smell; it tastes sharp but smells
sweet.[3] Thus Moses, looking forward to an eternal reward, chose
to be afflicted with God's people rather than to enjoy the fleeting
†Heb 11:25 pleasure of sin.† The church is like the myrrh of the saints, for it
sets the expectation of a blessed hope ahead of the experience of
this world's pleasures, preferring, as it were, the odor to the taste.

These are the words of the first and the last, who was dead and who
†Rv 2:8 *is alive.*† Thanks be to you, Lord Jesus, who disdain none of your
people, cast away none, receive and unite to yourself the last with the
†Ps 115:13 first, the little with the great,† impartially.†[a] You are the first and the
†[a]1 P 1:17 †[b]Is 41:4, 44:6, last†[b] because you are one Christ, head and body.†[c] You are among
48:12; Rv 1:17, 22:13 †[c]Ep 4:15, 5:23; Col 1:18, 2:17 †[d]Jr 14:9 us, we are called by your name; do not forsake us, O Lord†[d] our

[2] Venerable Bede, *Explanatio Apocalypsis* 1.2; PL 93:137D.

[3] *gravis sapore sed odore suavis.*

God. You are refreshed in your little ones,† you suffer persecution †Mt 10:42
in them,† you preside in leaders, and you are the same* in all, small †Ac 9:4–5
or great. Let none among the leaders fail to heed that saying of the *Ps 102:27
Apostle: 'I live, now not I, but Christ lives in me'.† Rather let all †Ga 2:20
of the leaders show themselves such that their subjects need not go seeking for the Christ who speaks in them.

Let no one look down on the last, for the anointing oil runs down from the head not only on to the beard but even to the hem of his robe.† Yes, let both types remember well, and the rest also †Ps 133:2
hear, that just as he *was dead* in his own person and *is alive*, so it shall be in the church, that one who dies with him also lives with him.† †2 Tm 2:11
Nor should it be desirable only to live with him, but sweet too to die with him. Even though they were unable to bring it to effect, the apostles were moved by deep affection to say, 'Let us also go, that we may die with him'.† Deep affection was there even if the †Jn 11:16
perfection of the deed was not.[4] How fortunate for him, O Lord, was the suffering of the thief that he shared with you! Not only did you remember him in your kingdom, as he asked; he was with you in paradise that very day, as you promised.† †Lk 23:42–43

Let us take care, brothers, lest it be said even now—let us take care lest it be said to us too, 'O foolish, and slow of heart to believe! Was it not necessary for Christ to suffer and rise from the dead and so enter into his glory?'† And what then? He entered the kingdom †Lk 24:25–26, 46
through pain and through suffering—are we going to enter through honor and pleasures? He entered by the cross and death—will we enter through this world's dignities and carnal pleasures? He entered by the strait way and the narrow gate—are we looking for the broad way and the wide gate?† Have mercy, O Lord, you who were *dead* †Mt 7:13–14
and are *alive*, have mercy, I pray, on the dead and on the living.

If some ungrateful Christian refuses to speak out, Christ cries out. If a Jew offers taunts, Christ preaches the gospel. If a heretic denies, Christ affirms. He *was dead*—consequently the text adds that he *is alive*. To recall the death he voluntarily underwent, so that we may confound those who disregard it, is no waste of time. The text tells what he bore, and why, so that the reader may tremble.

[4] *Etsi perfectio defuit, sed affectio pia fuit.*

It proclaims that he truly died, and after death he is alive. Thus a heretic on hearing it may be confuted, since a true death preceded, to which true life succeeded.

†Rv 2:9 *I know your affliction and your poverty.*† How is it he says in the
†Ps 18:44 psalm, 'A people I did not know has served me'?† He seems not to recognize those of his own whose suffering he does not relieve; he seems unaware of the harm to his own that he does not avenge; he seems to ignore those whose obedience he does not repay.

Antony, sorely beaten by evil spirits, recognized the Saviour's presence as a heavenly light fell on him. From the midst of his misery, he said: 'Where were you, good Jesus, where were you?' And a voice came to him, 'Antony, I was here, but I was waiting to see your fight'.[5]

How happily did blessed Bernard[6] used to tell us that the verse, 'A people I did not know served me', appears to have been spoken to the angels. The Lord is pointing out to them from heaven once delicate men now sworn recruits in his camp, and old men worn out by holy labors now chopping wood in the cold, and those who carried rocks in the snow now burned by the hot sun as they reap, now undergoing many fasts and vigils, and on top of this being harshly corrected for the least negligence. And he used to say,[7] 'In the kingdom of God, beloved, this song—"We have rejoiced for the
†Ps 90:15 days when you brought us low, for the years when we saw evils!"†—will belong to you, it will belong more to you than to the angels'. Let the timid not lose heart, nor those of lesser faith grow foolish. The Lord is clearly telling them not only that he knows, but that his care and concern is sufficient in all they do and all they endure.

And so he says to this angel, *I know your affliction and your*
†Rv 2:9 *poverty.*† Many are the afflictions of the righteous,* but if we look
*Ps 34:19 carefully, in the long run the afflictions of the unrighteous are far worse. Someone said, 'If I am righteous, I will not lift up my head, being filled with affliction and misery'. And what has gone
†Jb 10:15 immediately before? 'If I am a sinner, woe to me!'† If the righteous

[5] Athanasius, *Vita Beati Antonii* (Evagrius's version) 10; PL 73:132D.
[6] Bernard of Clairvaux, *Sermones de diversis* 77; SBOp 6/1:316–317.
[7] Ibid., 22.2; SBOp 6/1:171.

suffer afflictions for Christ, much more do their consolations abound through Christ.[8] The wicked derive no comfort from divine grace in their troubles; the godless are twice wounded, kicking against the goad,† but the righteous are freed in six afflictions,* lest evil touch them in the seventh, lest they be harmed by the second death,† as we read further on in this section [of the Apocalypse]. One who is not in affliction with them never rescues† them, for their sins are a barrier between themselves and God.† And therefore, lest they rest in the seventh, they are to be more greatly afflicted in an eighth. Now indeed they consider it a delight, not an affliction, to be wounded by concern, to burn with care, to be under the briars,† to lie on thorns—but how painfully shall the unrighteous experience those briars and be afflicted by those thorns!

†Ac 9:5 Vulgate
*Jb 5:19 Vulgate
†Rv 2:11
†Ps 91:15
†Is 59:2
†Jb 30:7 Vulgate

If you agree, I will distinguish and assign the six afflictions of the righteous. The first is the lash of a father's reproof. Is there a child whose father never administered discipline?† Consider what the Apostle says, that first comes sorrow, not joy.† The second are the sufferings we willingly take on ourselves in order to offer sacrifice to our Saviour in voluntary penances. The third arises from corrections and punishments by superiors, for they must sometimes visit us with the rod and not in a spirit of meekness. The fourth is from persecution by our enemies, a common occurrence to the good in these times when evil abounds, for the evil hate the good without cause.† The fifth comes from false friends who foolishly whisper harmful suggestions and connive at evil deeds. The sixth is caused by evil spirits. A certain writer[9] has said that these were once believed to incite people to vices through herbs and stones whose properties they knew by occult means; instead they tempt by unconscious suggestion, just as the holy angels help us by spiritual remedies and not by bodily medications.

†Heb 12:7
†Heb 12:11
†Pss 35:19, 69:4; Jn 15:25

Looked at in another way, the first of the six afflictions is the consciousness of our past sins; the second is fear of hell's torments; the third comes from the postponement of eternal joys. Of the first

[8] Ibid., 28.5; SBOp 6/1:207.

[9] Marbodus of Rennes, *Liber de gemmis* 1.3; PL 171:1737–1778. Isidore of Seville, *Etymologiarum libri XX* 17.9.42.

we read, 'I will recount my years to you in the bitterness of my
†Is 38:15 Vulgate soul';† of the second, 'Fear has to do with punishment';†[a] of the
†[a]1 Jn 4:18 third, 'Hope deferred afflicts the soul'.†[b] In these three emotions,
†[b]Pr 13:12 sorrow, fear, and heart's desire, are three types of affliction in this life.

Compassion with our neighbors brings the fourth affliction, as
the Apostle says, 'Who is weak and I am not weak? Who is made to
†2 Co 11:29 stumble and I am not indignant?'† The fifth arises from a glowing
displeasure with liars and those who defy God, as the psalm has
it: 'My zeal has consumed me, for my enemies have forgotten your
†Ps 119:139 words'.† They would not be enemies except that they have forgotten
†Jn 6:68 (6:69 Vulgate) your words. Your words are the words of eternal life;† your words
†Jn 6:63 (6:64 Vulgate) are spirit and life.† Our own need gives birth to the sixth affliction,
for we remain imperfect in the face of the many divine benefits
overwhelming us, and with no little anxiety we cry out, 'What shall
†Ps 116:12 I return to the Lord for all he has given me?'†

†Ac 1:1 And so he who began to do and to teach,† he who first
suffered in himself the affliction of death and the cross—as he now
lives in his own person, so too does he live in every one who
belongs to him, even to the least member of his body—tells the
angel of Smyrna that after their afflictions and deaths they will be
victorious forever.

†Rv 2:9 *I know your affliction.*† [He says], Even though I hesitate, even
though I defer consolation, I know it and keep it in mind; indeed, I
even suffer in you the affliction you suffer because of me. Although
†2 Co 8:9 I was rich, for your sake I became poor;† I know and I affirm
†Rv 2:9 *your poverty*.†

He is not speaking of universal poverty as did Tobias' father
†Tb 4:21 (4:23 Vulgate) when he reminded the boy, 'Remember, son, we lead a poor life'.†
He is not speaking of that mother of wretched anxiety which a
mendicant people bears under dire necessity. He has in mind that
poverty which by his counsel and grace the perfect embrace in
spiritual devotion. He once commended that poverty to his disciples
†Mt 5:1–2 as they were approaching him, when he opened his mouth† at
the beginning of his sermon, blessing the poor in spirit with the
promise, indeed the conferral, of a heavenly kingdom, just as he
commended those suffering persecution for righteousness' sake. Of
†Mt 5:3, 10 both he says, 'For theirs is the kingdom of heaven'.† They have no

regrets for having renounced the deceitful riches of this world, or for having been driven from their earthly dwellings by persecutors, for a kingdom is given them hereafter in heaven. And so, after commending poverty to this angel, he immediately adds that he is rich.

I know your affliction and your poverty, but, he says, *you are rich.*† Is the one who possesses the kingdom of heaven not rich? How much richer is he than if he possessed some earthly kingdom! Beloved, let us embrace the poverty that makes people rich. What wonder is it that plenty can at times make people poor, and opulence create paupers? Just as drink stimulates the thirst of dropsy victims,[10] so for the greedy, their love of gain increases as much as money itself increases.[11] Contempt for riches makes people rich just as yearning for it makes paupers. Perhaps we can now more easily understand why wisdom spurns riches first, and then poverty,† rather than poverty, then riches, choosing to grow rich out of poverty rather than to be impoverished from riches. Yet it is not out of their own poverty that the faithful grow rich, but out of the Lord's, as the Apostle says: 'Although he was rich, he became poor for our sakes, that by his poverty we may be enriched'.† No wonder we are enriched by his poverty, for we are filled by his self-emptying, and quickened by his death.

†Rv 2:9
†Pr 30:8
†2 Co 8:9

To this angel of Smyrna it is said, *You are being blasphemed by those who say they are Jews and are not.*† A blasphemous word, added to affliction and poverty, sears some people deeply as it passes quickly through already wavering hearts, especially as it is easier to counter injurious words with like words than deeds with deeds. The tongue is a small member yet it greatly exalts itself, and a small fire sets a great forest ablaze.† The prophetic spirit, in speaking of the Saviour, praises the fact that 'like a lamb before the shearer, led to the slaughter, he was dumb'.† The apostle Peter says of him, 'When he suffered he uttered no threats'.† And the Jews, when they had no further means of raging against the crucified one, did not cease to increase the pain of the cross's nails with their blasphemous jeers.

†Rv 2:9
†Jm 3:5
†Is 53:7; Ac 8:32
†1 P 2:23

[10] Alcuin, *De virtutibus et vitiis liber ad Widonem comitem* 30; PL 101:634B.
[11] Juvenal, *Saturae* 14.139.

To the angel of Smyrna then the Lord says, *You are being blasphemed by those who say they are Jews and are not.*† Grammarians teach that words used as nouns have the qualities of substantives.[12] Frequently people seem to themselves and to others to be what they are called. We, my brothers, we above all must attentively consider and carefully attend to this fact: our Judge, to whom we speak, considers and attends not to what we are called but to what we are. How does it benefit us to be labeled monks if there is no true unity among us, to be called 'converted' and found rather to be perverted?[13] What does it matter to us, beloved, to be named 'human' by humans, and have the true Judge reckon us malicious dogs, filthy swine, greedy ravens, cunning foxes,[14] pompous fowl? What does it benefit us to be called Christians if, like so many now, we are antichrists instead?

†Rv 2:9

I beg you, let us exert ourselves in pondering who we are by nature rather than what we are called or what we seem to be.[15] But who is up to this?[16] 'Know yourself', someone says, 'came down from heaven.'[17] If only the gift of accomplishing it would come from the place from which the commandment itself came! As a great teacher used to pray, 'O God, may I know myself, may I know you!'[18] How does some half-educated person think he can easily know himself? He does not know his own bodily appearance, and does he think he is capable of perceiving his character, or of penetrating the intimate recesses of his own heart, which is far more complex in construction than that building called the labyrinth was

[12] Peter Abelard, *Dialectica, I Antipraedicamenta* 92; *III Postpraedicamenta* 134; ed. L. M. De Rijk, *Dialectica* (Assen, 1956).

[13] *conversos et perversos*. *Conversus* meant someone 'converted' from the world to monastic life; among Cistercians a *conversus* was a laybrother.

[14] Bernard of Clairvaux, *Sermones super Cantica Canticorum* 66.1; SBOp 2:178; CF 31:191.

[15] Bernard of Clairvaux, *Sermones de diversis* 2.1; SBOp 6/1:80.

[16] Ibid., 22.7; SBOp 6/1:175. *Sermones super Cantica Canticorum* 12.11; SBOp 1:67; CF 4:86.

[17] Juvenal, *Saturae* 11.27. Bernard of Clairvaux, *Sermones de diversis* 40.3; SBOp 6/1:236. Note that where Juvenal has the Greek gñothi seautov, Geoffrey has the strange word *ostiselitos* followed by *quod est scito te ipsum*.

[18] Augustine, *Soliloquia* 2.1; PL 32:885. Bernard of Clairvaux, *Sermones de diversis* 2.1; SBOp 6/1:80.

or ever could be? Who remains always in the same state? And who, by his own efforts, can understand who he really is?

They *say they are Jews and are not*.† We are on dangerous ground †Rv 2:9 if others say we are better than we are. How much worse is it if we ourselves, who know what is advantageous, say we are not such as we are? Blessed Job recalls that neither when he looked at the moon moving in splendor, nor at the sun when it shone,† did his †Jb 31:26–27 heart secretly rejoice as he gave heed to the testimony of his own thoughts and actions. How much more dangerous was it for these false and lying witnesses to have mendaciously blasphemed others and praised themselves than for this angel and his church to be blasphemed by them?

'Judah' means 'confession';[19] hence the Jews are 'confessors'.[20] Thus these who said that they knew God but denied him by their deeds and disavowed him by their works were not Jews, although they were said to be. They would exist more authentically, and be more truly called Jews, if they desisted from implicating themselves in crimes, and insisted instead on confessing their own sins. They were neither true Jews, nor were they called so by those who speak the truth, as long as they prided themselves on attacking the just with false blasphemies instead of honestly praising the Lord—for he is good,† for they themselves are evil.* †Ps 106:1, et al *Mt 7:11, 12:34 Truth himself said, 'For if you, who are evil, know how to give good gifts to your children, how much more will your Father', your good Father, 'give the good Spirit'.† And again, 'No one †Lk 11:13 is good but God alone'.† There is no human goodness except †Lk 18:19 from him who gives the good Spirit, no goodness except in him, just as 'no one has ascended into heaven except the one who descended from heaven'.† This is surely the twofold confession we †Jn 3:13 sing to him in the psalm, 'We will praise you, O God, we will praise you!'† †Ps 75:1

Both aspects deeply affected the man we mentioned above: 'O God, may I know myself, may I know you!'† May I know myself †Augustine, see note 8 in order to hate myself, lest I be found among those who love

[19] Jerome, *Liber interpretationis hebraicorum nominum* 7.19; CCh 72:67.
[20] Ibid., 75.22; CCh 72:154.

themselves because they do not know themselves. May I know you
in order to love you, whom no one can know without loving. May
I know you, whom to know is to live.[21] May I love you, who love
†Pr 8:17 those who love you,† and show yourself to them when they are pure
of heart through faith, hope, and love. From my self-knowledge
arises a confession of my own wickedness, so that when I hate and
admit it, when I am cursed and persecuted without pretense, you
may expiate it. Confession of your goodness goes hand in hand with
knowing you, so that you can communicate to me, unworthy as I
am, what it is I love; what I ask for in every prayer as you grant
†Jn 15:5 me the ability to ask, for apart from you I can do nothing;† what I
desire with my whole heart; what I strive to glorify by my actions
and preach by my words.

But what of them? They *say they are Jews and are not, but are a*
†Rv 2:9 *synagogue of Satan*.† A synagogue means a 'gathering';[22] Satan is 'the
adversary'.[23] Satan gathers them adversely to the Lord, not with
the Lord. This 'gathering' is a scattering, as is said: 'Whoever does
†Lk 11:23 not gather with me scatters'.† Satan insidiously scatters them where
they will deservedly lie scattered. Our Lord and protector will scatter
†Ps 59:11 them by his power and bring them down† as they deserve. Satan
gathers them now before the harvest, collecting them as bundles
†Mt 13:30 to be burned,† so that their sins may be made manifest before the
judgment lest the weeds somehow take on the appearance of wheat.
He gathers the godless, and draws up their battle line to attack the
just, that the just may be mindful how closely they must gather
to resist.

How miserable to fight under such a prince! Those who imitate
†Rv 2:9 him, who belong to the *synagogue of Satan*,† deserve to hear: 'Go, you
accursed, into the eternal fire which has been prepared for the devil
†Mt 25:41 and his angels'.† And as they not only blaspheme but also actively
†Rv 2:10 persecute, the Lord says, *fear none of the things you are going to suffer*,†
surely from Satan and his synagogue, so that an arrow foreseen may

[21] *Gelasian sacramentary*, n. 1476.

[22] Isidore of Seville, *Etymologiarum libri XX* 8.1.7.

[23] Jerome, *Liber interpretationis hebraicorum nominum* 43.13; CCh 72:112. Isidore of Seville, *Etymologiarum libri XX* 8.11.19.

inflict less injury.[24] Do not grieve over the past—these things are laid up and held for you in the treasury of my memory. Do not be afraid of the future—because these things are set aside to be held in the same way.

Behold, the devil is going to cast some of you into prison.† Clearly †Rv 2:10
this is spoken not just to the leader but also to the church from which some are going to be imprisoned. Clearly the devil is the agent for what will happen to God's servants at the hands of the wicked. Those godless servants are meant to tremble with fear at the realization of who is dwelling and working in them, who is placing the weapons of iniquity in their hands. As once the Lord
gave Satan power over Job's possessions,† so Satan has brought about †Jb 1:12
more harm through human beings than by himself.

That you may be tested,† he says. This is the reason why the devil †Rv 2:10
is going to cast you into prison, and why God is going to allow it. The devil is not appeased by our bodily afflictions, nor is God pleased. The devil is eager to test you so that you may succumb; the Lord allows you to be tested so that you may conquer.

And you will have affliction for ten days.† We can take this in a †Rv 2:10
straightforward way, so that a day stands for a year. The term *day* suggests how quickly the years pass by.

In another sense, the affliction of the elect is of the day, and that of the condemned is of the night. A just person who falls by
day is said to rise stronger;† the writer does not add that the godless †Pr 24:16
person who falls in the night rises at all. The just person walks as a
child of light† even when afflicted, because his life is day. He is in †Ep 5:8
the day even when he stumbles, saying, 'If I have been mistaken,
my mistake is with me'.† Anyone suffering for righteousness' sake, †Jb 19:4
for the faith, as a Christian and not as a thief or a murderer,† is said †1 P 4:15–16
to have affliction for days, not for nights.

In that *ten days*† are specified, perhaps a definite number is set †Rv 2:10
down for an indefinite one, as if 'many days' was meant. Although in the light of the decalogue[25] we can take ten days to mean obedience

[24] Gregory the Great, *Homiliae in Evangelia* 35.1; PL 76:1259C; CS 123: 301.

[25] Haymo of Auxerre, *Expositionis in Apocalypsin Beati Iohannis libri septem* 1.1; PL 117:970D. Richard of Saint Victor, *In Apocalypsim Iohannis libri septem* 1.6; PL 196:720C.

to divine precepts. Someone who embraces with a quiet conscience
†RB 7:35 the difficulties and contradictions he meets† in obedience to divine law suffers *affliction for ten days*. Our teacher used to construct a bridge for us from the two tablets of obedience and patience[26] in case one may not be enough to span the perilous stream. Once, I recall, we referred the Lord's own words, 'Let not your left hand
†Mt 6:3 know what your right hand is doing',† to this same topic, so that we may suffer no harm when giving alms, as happens to some when an awareness of obedience becomes an occasion for impatience.[27] Twofold is the merit and twofold the virtue in doing good manfully while peacefully suffering evils. 'Where is it grace', says Peter, 'if you endure when you sin and are beaten? But if you endure patiently
†1 P 2:20 when you do right, this is grace before God'.†

†Rv 2:10 *Be faithful even to death*.† These words have two meanings: to the hour, and to endurance of death. 'To the hour' means that no ear—because you are faithful—or tail—because you persevere to the end of life and the hour of death—is missing from your
†Lv 22:23 Vulgate sacrificial victim.† As to the rest, things neither commanded of us, nor forever demanded from us as victims lacking ear and tail, can become voluntary sacrifices, but cannot be used to pay vows. Perhaps he is warning his faithful servant, who we believe is to be crowned among the martyrs, not only about perseverance in his faith, but also about the acceptance of suffering, when he straightway promises him *the crown of life*.

†Rv 2:10 Why does it say, *Be faithful*,† but not add to whom? Not to himself, for no one who is not faithful to the Lord his God can be faithful to anyone else. To be faithful to earthly lords and magistrates is not enough if one is not faithful to the heavenly Lord. These things
†Mt 23:23; Lk 11:42 you must do, and not neglect what is greater.† A person pledging fidelity by his profession to humans is responsible for these things, but he cannot keep his word unless he is faithful to the one granting and guarding faith. Rightly is it required, especially of stewards, that
†1 Co 4:2 a person be found trustworthy† to the one whose servant he is. He

[26] Bernard of Clairvaux, *Sermones de diversis* 2; SBOp 61:80–85.
[27] Gregory the Great, *Moralia in Iob* 32.20; PL 76:658A.

must seek not his own glory but the other's; he must demand that his subjects accomplish not his will but his lord's.

Be faithful,† not only you who are in charge, but you who are subject as well. Give back faithfully to Caesar the things that are Caesar's, and to God the things that are God's.† They act very foolishly who at an opportunity for fidelity either demand of their subjects something contrary to the greater lord or allow it to be done. They err no less who think themselves obliged by fidelity or faith to be controlled by people in opposition to God. Whoever dissembles errs no less, for we have to obey God rather than humans.†

†Rv 2:10

†Mt 22:21; Mk 12:17; Lk 20:25

†Ac 5:29

Be faithful even to death,† that glory may immediately follow virtue, that blessedness may replace goodness, that joy may join fidelity. At whatever time you begin, see that you do not turn away before you die. Judas walked with the Lord among the apostles for no short time, but, when death was already imminent, at that last hour bordering on the life to come, it went better for the thief than for him.

†Rv 2:10

In view of this, the person who is *faithful even to death*† never ceases to be afraid, remembering what the Apostle says: 'Let one who is standing see to it he does not fall'.† *Even to death* he does not know whether he will be faithful *even to death*, and so receive *the crown of life*. It is not a crown of life which—as we read in Ecclesiasticus—is given from generation to generation;† it is not a lifegiving but a mortal glory which ends with death. A crown of life is promised to the victor who remains victorious so that, *faithful even to death*, he will not later be injured by the second death.† May he who makes us faithful and gives us perseverance in fidelity, who lives and reigns without end, deliver us from that injury. Amen.

†Rv 2:10

†1 Co 10:12

†Pr 27:24

†Rv 2:11

Sermon Twelve

Let anyone who has ears hear what the Spirit says to the churches. Whoever conquers will not be harmed by the second death.† †Rv 2:11

SPEAK, LORD, FOR YOUR SERVANTS are listening.† They desire you, they wait for you, that your Spirit, rather than we ourselves, may speak graciously in us, unworthy as we are. Not even Moses, if he were here, would be worth listening to apart from you, Lord, although people told him: 'You speak to us, and we will listen; let not the Lord speak to us lest we die'.† Beyond question 'you have the words of eternal life';† people recognized that [his words] had life in them. Their ears are open and alert to hear what you say, what your Spirit says—two ears, one to hear what he commands and one to hear what he promises. Far less are his commands, greater are his promises. It may be that we see angels announce the commands as being very small matters, but archangels announce the promises as being very great.

†1 S 3:9, 10

†Ex 20:19

†Jn 6:68 (6:69 Vulgate)

What does he demand that is so far from us, or too much for us? 'Be faithful even to death',† he says. Whatever has an end is brief, but it seems great if it exemplifies fidelity to the Lord even to accepting death. Many people earn our respect by bravely facing life's hazards

†Rv 2:10

and death's perils in the service of earthly lords. And these worthy people, what return is made to them after death? Perhaps their lords are obliged to pay back what is fair—if a dead man has been snatched away is an eye to be plucked out? They sometimes promise that they will pay back a farm for a farm—do they also promise a life for a life?

Our being faithful to the Lord even to accepting death is a great thing because we have nothing more; there is no greater proof of love than acceptance of suffering. This is the greatest witness, and we call martyrs 'witnesses' in that they provide it. How truly great was it for the human being who did not deserve to die, who alone was unable die, to die on behalf of humans! That he died sinless was even more marvelous—for death is sin's penalty—than if he had not tasted a death he did not deserve, if he had not restored what he did
†Ps 69:4 not steal.†

What is so exceptional in our submitting ourselves a little more quickly to a death which we can by no means evade or long turn aside, and to do so for the sake of his grace and our everlasting glory? Briefly put, we gain a great return for a small price. By accepting this transitory death we avoid the peril of a second and eternal one. We know full well how little is demanded of us if we consider how great is our hope. There is no comparison between such littleness and an unlimited measure, pressed down, shaken together, running
†Lk 6:38 over,† no more than between a brief moment and eternity.

Let those who wish to be 'faithful even to death' listen to the
†Rv 2:10 promise: 'I will give you the crown of life'.† How long, O Lord?*
*Ps 13:1, et al From the time of the first death onwards there will be no end to the second life and its crown. The one who deserves the crown of life
†Rv 2:11 *will not be harmed by the second death*.† 'I will give the crown; no one will come to take it away. I will crown him; no one will lay it aside. I will raise him up; never will he die. I will bring him to life; no
†Ps 58:4 one will slay him'. The unfortunate deaf adder† presses its inferior ear to the ground so that it can hear what the flesh desires and what the world offers, not what the Spirit wills and commands.[1] Its tail stops its superior ear, and it mistrusts and denies the everlasting

[1] Bernard of Clairvaux, *Sermones in psalmum 'Qui habitat'* 13.3; SBOp 4:465.

recompense promised to both the good and the wicked by the divine Judge.

Let us listen to what the Spirit says, my brothers. Let us listen with our inferior ear to what the Spirit demands and with the superior one to what he promises: *Whoever conquers will not be harmed by the second death.*† Among all the things seen to befall human beings on earth, and ourselves in particular—although we see it more frequently in others—nothing is more fearful than death and coming face-to-face with our Judge. No change in human affairs is so wretched, no hopelessness so deep. Then perish all the thoughts of those whose days pass more swiftly than a weaver cuts a web and are consumed without any hope.† At this point especially our Saviour's marvelous grace and faith's great strength appear, for they make the recollection of death festive—not funereal or mournful, but delightful.

†Rv 2:11

†Jb 7:6

Happy was the day when blessed Benedict, not from his own experience but struck by a salutary fear as he saw ruin come upon others, drew back from entering the world in order to withdraw 'knowingly ignorant and wisely unlearned'.[2] Happy was the day when he comforted his nurse by restoring to her the sieve for cleansing grain in one piece,[3] but happier still the time when he wrote his Rule of monastic life to cleanse the wheat of the chosen, and to renew a holy Order on the verge of decay with this special word of advice, that we not be left upon the table again if we do not wish to be broken. Happy those days when he broke the pitcher of poisoned drink by blessing it from a distance;[4] when as Maur was running he snatched up Placid, covered by his own mantle, out of the water;[5] when he saw things far off and hidden, and foresaw the future; when, as the Lord said, he healed the sick, cast out demons, cleansed a leper, raised a dead man.[6]

[2] Gregory the Great, *Dialogi* 2 prol.; ed. Moricca.

[3] Ibid., 2.1.74. The whole of Geoffrey's sentence has to do with the sieve, which fell from the table and was broken.

[4] Ibid., 2.3.81.

[5] Ibid., 2.7.90.

[6] Ibid., 2. 27 (the sick), 16 and 30 (demons), 26 (the leper), 11 and 32 (the dead).

The memory of all these deeds is helpful for us. Happier still, for you and for us, holy Father, is this great festive day of your holy passing! You ran to it faithfully, and on this day you trustingly entered eternal life. You fought courageously, and today you were triumphantly crowned in heaven. Long ago now you conquered sin while remaining in the flesh by altering the fire;[7] by preferring to endure the evils of this world rather than its praises you conquered the world. Even the evil one recognized that he was conquered, although unwillingly, when he burst out in furious blasphemies: 'Benedict, Benedict—not blessed, but cursed!'[8] While yet in part you chastised your body, the world stood against you and the evil one laid snares for you; and all the while your life on this earth could
†Jb 7:1 not but be a warfare.† But all at once there was no more warfare, no poor life, and with no reason or occasion henceforth to fight, then your victory was complete.

In the first vision of the apostle John people are commanded to listen to a victory and its reward of this kind, which the Spirit tells to the churches. To the angel of Smyrna, the second in the series, a promise of the same kind is made: *Whoever conquers will not be harmed*
†Rv 2:11 *by the second death.*† Let us then say: *Let anyone who has ears hear what*
†Rv 2:11 *the Spirit says to the churches.*† Of an ear of this kind the prophet says: 'My ear', that is, my faith, 'will hear [the downfall] of the wicked
†Ps 92:11 who are rising up against me'.† 'Faith is the victory that overcomes
†1 Jn 5:4 the world',† that brings forward a twofold battle line and does not succumb to the world's blandishments and scandals.

What are 'the wicked who are rising up' to hear? 'The righteous
†Ps 92:12 will flourish like a palm tree'.† The authority of the Holy Spirit who speaks[9] makes us attentive and well-disposed, because no one is kept from listening provided he is willing. Let anyone who has ears of faith and obedience hear what the Spirit says, not only when he commands but also when he promises. A person with faith cannot lack hope. Anyone who shows obedience can be sure of its good

[7] Ibid., 2.10.

[8] The name 'Benedict' means 'blessed', hence the pun. Ibid., 2.8.96.

[9] *Glossa ordinaria* Ap 1; PL 114:710C. Augustine, *De doctrina christiana* 4.2; CCh 32:117.

outcome and reward. Let him hear what the Spirit of truth says, and not doubt the truth of his promise.

What [the Spirit] says to the churches.† Evidently this does not pertain only to the bishops but also to the churches named; it is to be made known by them to the churches. The Lord gathers the churches through his angels, as is fitting, for the serpent led the man into the sin of lying by means of the woman. When the Spirit speaks to the churches he is indicating to all the faithful who listen, without exception and without partiality, what he is promising and to whom. He makes his promise 'to the one who conquers', and 'listen' is one of the things he commanded the first angel to write.†

†Rv 2:11

†Rv 2:7

But the promise is made 'to the one who conquers', *whoever* already *conquers*,† as is plain from other letters, especially the fourth. This [angel] is in the middle, and what is written to him is common to the earlier and later letters. 'Whoever conquers and keeps my works until the end'.† Perseverance alone will receive the crown; only to perseverance will victory be attributed.† The explanation of 'whoever conquers' is in the following clause: 'who keeps my works until the end'. It is not enough for a sacrifice to have an ear if it lacks a tail.† Both faith and obedience are necessary. God accepts no works apart from faith; he refuses to consider them his own, for the life of faith is tested and proven by works.† We can take the works of God to be those things pleasing and acceptable to him, but also the works he himself performs in his faithful people, as the prophet says: 'O Lord, you will give us peace, for you have done all our works for us'.† And the Apostle says: 'It is God who is at work in you, not only to will but also to accomplish for his good pleasure'.†

†Rv 2:11

†Rv 2:26

†Mt 10:22, 24:13

†Lv 22:23 Vulgate

†Jm 2:14, 20

†Is 26:12

†Ph 2:13

Our text, *whoever conquers will not be harmed by the second death*,† may well refer to the death of the body, for the first death occurred to the soul when it sinned.[10] Fortunate then is the victory by which the second death is overcome—not only is it not harmful then, but it is precious in the Lord's sight† and in the judgment of Truth. It does not harm the victor, but it delivers him from his labors. The Spirit says that now he may rest from his labors,† from cares and all perils, and that from now on he may be secure, no longer leading a

†Rv 2:11

†Ps 116:15

†Rv 14:13

[10] *Glossa ordinaria* Ap 2; PL 114:715A.

life of poverty. When sleep is given to his beloved, he receives the
†Ps 127:2–3 Lord's inheritance.†

Therefore, as those who judged rightly when they were alive kept the eyes of their hearts ever focused on the day of death, so the memorials of the saints are celebrated especially on the anniversaries of their deaths. Their memory is celebrated when their presence is taken from us; they are transformed into human memories when they pass to the joys of the angels. Not only are those crowned whose death the cause, not the penalty, enlightens when he makes them martyrs, but also those in whom God's victorious care of all their works persists to the end. Blessed are the dead, not only those
†Rv 14:13 who die for the Lord, but those who die in the Lord.†

The life and death of this most holy Father of ours deserves a solemn remembrance, for perhaps no one since the apostles drew so many spiritual fish out of the great sea. No one upon reaching shore
†Mt 13:48 put more fish into vessels,† and rarely will there be one who chooses better. Rightly did such a life end in a joyous death, and rightly did so marvelous and miraculous a death conclude such a life. This joyous death deserved to be foreshown, foretold, and revealed in such a way by worthy witnesses. It is altogether clear that it did not harm him, but that it glorified the one who stood before the sacred altar, supporting his weak limbs with the help of his disciples, with his hands raised to heaven, and who breathed his last amid words of prayer.[11]

†Rv 2:11 But we can also take *the second death*† as eternal death. Happy is the one who is not harmed by it, not touched by it, who does not experience it. Its harm is intolerable; no resurrection follows; no consolation comes but rather unending despair. Beloved, I ask that we honor the victors by striving as hard as we can to attain the palm of victory. Let us keep the works of God lest—which God forbid!—we lose them through intemperance and disfigure them through injustice, or they be snatched from us by our imprudence or our timid inertia. And let us keep them even to the end, that we may be reckoned victors and avoid harm from the second death which will have no end. May he grant it whose reign will never end. Amen.

[11] Gregory the Great, *Dialogi* 2.37.132.

Sermon Thirteen

And to the angel of the church at Pergamum write: These are the words of the one who has the sharp two-edged sword: I know where you live, where Satan's throne is. Yet you hold fast to my name, and have not denied my faith even in the days of Antipas, my faithful witness, who was killed among you where Satan dwells. But I have a few things against you, because you have there people holding the teaching of Balaam who taught Balak to put a stumbling block before the children of Israel, to eat, and to fornicate. You also have people who hold to the teaching of the Nicolaitans. In like manner repent. If not I will come to you quickly and I will fight against them with the sword of my mouth. Let anyone who has an ear hear what the Spirit says to the churches. To the one who conquers I will give the hidden manna and I will give him a white stone, and on the stone a new name written, that no one knows except the one who receives it.† †Rv 2:12–17

YOU ONCE WERE STRAYING like sheep, but now you have returned to the shepherd and guardian of your souls'.† Paul, †1 P 2:25
his fellow apostle, uses words similar to Peter's: 'Once you were darkness, but now in the Lord you are light.'† They were †Ep 5:8

darkness because they were straying; they are light because they have returned to the shepherd and guardian of souls. You were straying by your earlier way of life, and are sheep by divine predestination. At present the sheep are mixed in with goats, and are unsettled and anxious among them, but they differ now by divine design, just as they will be separated in the final judgment.

The book of Wisdom shows us the reason for their straying.
At the end the condemned will say, 'We have strayed from the
†Ws 5:6 way of truth, and the sun of righteousness did not rise upon us'.†
†Ps 12:8 Those who walk in a circle† stray, turning a natural desire for the
highest good into seeking to obtain first the lowest and least. As our teacher often used to suggest to us, if a person could first attain all the other goods, he would then be drawn on by the highest desire to that highest good which alone he lacked. But it is impossible to complete this circle, impossible for one person to obtain all the other things first so as at last to desire the highest good alone. This good can be grasped not by assembling the lesser goods but by leaping over them.

'Look, we have left everything', Peter says, 'and have followed
†Mt 19:27 you'.† They received everything because, after they left everything,
†Lk 5:28 they followed him.† The godless walk in a circle,* and happy is the
*Ps 12:8 †Ps 1:1 one who does not follow the counsel of these ungodly ones.† The
godless walk in a circle, and the angel of bad counsel, knowing
what he has himself suggested (as you have heard just now) 'circles,
†1 P 5:8 seeking someone to devour'† in order to catch those circling.

Would that our faithful shepherd would call us back, would lay
†Lk 15:5 us on those holy shoulders† that bore the wood of the cross, so
that he may make us who share in his blessed passion sharers in his redemption. Would that anyone borne on those shoulders may be overcome with amazement at such an honor, as is only fitting, may be filled with awe, may, as such a deed requires, be humble and modest, disciplined and quiet. Would that no madman may dare to harm, to strike, or to throw down, a little sheep borne on such shoulders! Would that the kindness of the shepherd who pastures
†Sg 1:6 his flock and makes it lie down at midday† may call us wretched
wanderers back to that blessed company from which we have been cut off. Would that he would seek us and find us; would that he

may bring it about that the watchmen of that city through which we journey may find us, and we also find our beloved.† †Sg 3:3

These are intercessors, these are mediators for those hastening to him who is seated above the cherubim. These chose not to be matched with beasts grown senseless† through excess, with those experienced in sensuality, stupidity, and stubbornness, and with those unable to enjoy life because of infidelity. For the just person lives by faith,† discerns by loving-kindness, and assents to understanding and distinguishing by sobriety. †Ps 48:13, 21 Vulgate †Rm 1:17

Brothers this is the way that stretches eastward in a straight line from the cell of blessed Benedict to heaven.[1] This is the way; walk in it; turn aside neither to the right nor to the left.† One who turns away to either side is straying, either losing hope from awareness of his sins, or rashly presuming on his own merits. The way is secure; stumbling blocks are set along side it.† At midday Joseph's brothers dined with him;† at midday the bridegroom lies down and pastures his flock.† The way of life lies down the middle, and one who changes course to right or left is straying. †Dt 17:1 †Ps 140:5 †Gn 43:25 †Sg 1:6

Here we see why blessed John, at the beginning of the vision, is commanded to write to the angel of Pergamum what *the one who has the sharp two-edged sword*† in his mouth says. What are each of its two edges, so sharp and penetrating, if not the Judge's right and left hands? No one at the present time should dare to assure himself of entrance into the kingdom of heaven until he hears, 'Come, you blessed, possess the kingdom'.† No one should say he is departing, no one should so cruelly condemn himself, when he has not yet heard, 'Depart, you accursed, into everlasting fire'.† Thus the prudent man should separate the edges so as to hold to the middle way, that he may avoid the sword's two sharp edges that penetrate deeply into those who rashly turn to either side in this life. †Rv 2:12 †Mt 25:34 †Mt 25:41

In this connection, the Spirit, who made them, described the wheels as 'whirling' in the prophet's hearing.† 'Whirling' is neither to the left nor to the right, which means neither presuming nor despairing of salvation. These people remain on course until he is present who distinguishes—as the Apostle says, 'Who distinguishes †Ezk 10:13

[1] Gregory the Great, *Dialogi* 2.37.132–133; ed. Moricca.

†1 Co 4:7 *Mt 25:32 you?'†—until he is present who separates the sheep from the goats,*
who discerns between those worthy of love and those meriting
hatred. They turn around with perfect ease by his judgment. The
wheels were large enough for motion straight ahead, for they were
†Ezk 1:18 lacking neither the height of hope nor the awesome aspect of fear.†

A ship's course is directed straight on by oars on either side,
by one who stands between them, so that it never turns aside.
Simeon was a righteous man, for he was devoutly looking forward
†Lk 2:25 to the consolation of Israel.† We strayed then, and were going astray
†1 P 2:25 like sheep;† we left the middle way for one of the sides; but we
were recalled by him who graciously cries out, 'Return, return,
†Sg 6:13 O Shulammite!'† We have returned to the shepherd and guardian
†1 P 2:25 of our souls;† we have returned to him who loves souls* and who
*Ws 11:26 watches over them—as the name 'guardian' or 'bishop' signifies.[2]
He cares for us, as we have heard, and we should confidently cast
†1 P 5:7 all our anxiety on him.†

What then does he order written to the angel of Pergamum,
he who has in his mouth *a sharp two-edged sword*? *I know where you*
†Rv 2:12–13 *live, where Satan's throne is. Yet you hold fast to my name.*† Truly he
knows, truly he who directs his attention on us notices what we do
and where. He knows because he causes it, he knows, who grants
†Ph 2:13 us not only to will but also to accomplish for his good pleasure.†
He approves the good wherever we accomplish it, and he does not
forget unless—which God forbid!—by a change for the worse we
turn from righteousness to iniquity. By his great grace he grants
us to hold to the faith among the godless,[3] to be acknowledged a
follower of righteousness among the godless by divine judgment.
We find it a burden, but God a pleasure, when we are peaceable
†Ps 120:7 with those who hate peace.†

On the other hand, for a person to be treacherous with the faithful, boisterous with the undisciplined, to do what is wrong in the land of the saints and hence not to see the Lord's glory, is burdensome. To be lax with the devout, immoderate with the sober, a liar among the truthful, negligent with the zealous, cruel

[2] Isidore of Seville, *Etymologiarum libri XX* 7.12.11.

[3] Bernard of Clairvaux, *Sermones super Cantica Canticorum* 48.1.2; SBOp 2:68.

among the meek, arrogant among the humble, is burdensome. Satan has fallen from heaven, never to rise again. The fault committed in paradise was not punished by death only in our first parents, but it is still being punished in their posterity. Under the Saviour's instruction avarice turned Judas from an apostle into a devil.† Be aware, beloved, how fortunate is the necessity that forces you to do better.[4] Be aware that your sublime profession, your worthy dwelling place, your holy community, amplify the fault you commit there; it does not excuse it. †Jn 6:70–71

The Lord says, *I know where you live, where Satan's throne is. Yet you hold fast to my name, and have not denied my faith.*† What this church is presently, and was in the past, receives high commendation. Otherwise it would not find grace with God, nor merit a reward, for it would have been faithful once but be unfaithful now. Better for it to have once been unfaithful, and to be faithful now, to have been straying earlier and now to have returned to the shepherd and guardian of souls,† better indeed not to know the way of truth than to go backward when it is known.[5] †Rv 2:13 †1 P 2:25

He commends them by asserting that this church holds fast to his name, and gives as proof of this that they have not denied the faith, the confession of their lips, even though some are denying it in practice. The Lord's name is Jesus, the name given by the angel before he was conceived in the womb.† The meaning of his name was explained to the husband of his virgin mother, that he would save his people from their sins.† We can understand and desire to be saved in two ways: from past sins, that they be forgiven, and from future ones, that they not be committed. Thus it seems that someone holds fast to the Saviour's name with both hands by acknowledging in both ways the power of that name to reach true salvation. †Lk 2:21 †Mt 1:21

And have not denied my faith.† Satan strives to cause us to cling to sin and to distance ourselves from faith. If he is blocked in one direction he works on the other, for he knows that faith without works is reckoned dead† and that works without faith are not pleasing to God. †Rv 2:13 †Jm 2:17, 26

[4] Augustine, *Epistulae* 127.8; CSEL 44:28.

[5] Richard of Saint Victor, *In Apocalypsim Iohannis libri septem* 1.2; PL 196:695B.

Even in the days of Antipas, my faithful witness, those days when †Rv 2:13 you *have not denied my faith.*† Antipas remained my faithful witness, *who was killed among you* for confessing the faith. When he says *among you* he means that his words are not directed to the priest alone but to the whole church. He praises their constant and persevering faith for, when one of their own suffered a violent death under their very eyes, they would have turned aside in fear had they been cowardly. By mentioning the example of Antipas he is encouraging others to accept suffering. His witness, his martyr, 'faithful' to himself 'even †Rv 2:10 to death' as he said to the angel of Smyrna,† he recalls as having appeared out of their own congregation and among them.

†Rv 2:13 And lest anyone conjecture that *Satan's throne*† refers to where he once sat, although he is no longer sitting there—as today the Pantheon, once a temple dedicated to all the demons, is a church in honor of the blessed virgin Mary and all the martyrs[6]—he says again *where Satan dwells.* He means that as Satan stirred up his followers to murder Antipas then, so now he is stirring up those persecuting and afflicting you.

†Rv 2:14 *But I have a few things against you.*† Consider here 'the division of horns', which is what we said the name Pergamum means.[7] There was in that church a division of horns, some firmly holding the catholic faith, and others no less hardened in error. Some were holding fast to the name of the Saviour, as he said, but others held the teachings of the tempter.

I have a few things against you. He is gently warning that he will censure a few things while commending them in many. A few things, but not little ones. Gluttony and fornication are related vices, as the very nearness of the organs concerned shows.[8] Our first parents presumed to eat the forbidden food, and immediately shame and confusion followed. The plain phrase *to eat* seems usually to refer to gluttony; fornication follows it because gluttony overwhelms and suffocates chastity. Thus the apostolic prohibition associates rioting †Rm 13:13 and drunkenness with debauchery and lewdness.† Likewise among

[6] In 609 the Pantheon in Rome was consecrated as a christian church under the title Santa Maria ad Martyres.

[7] Jerome, *Liber interpretationis hebraicorum nominum* 81.1; CCh 72:160.

[8] Gregory the Great, *Moralia in Iob* 31.45; PL 76:622A.

the high priest's vestments an undergirdle of abstinence was added to the girdle of continence, because, as the proverb from Wisdom has it, a man will have a stubborn servant if he nourishes him on delicacies from his youth.† †Pr 29:21

Here, however, *to eat* seems to apply especially to food offered to idols. This is the *stumbling block* which, by Balaam's teaching, Balak put *before the children of Israel*.† Lured by the love of Midianite †Rv 2:14 women, they began to worship idols at their suggestion, and their lust led them to the sin of idolatry.† This offence, as the ancient †Nb 25:1–2, 6 history tells, caused a great slaughter among God's people,† for the †Nb 25:9 Lord in anger withdrew his help from those who abandoned their Creator in order to serve creatures. Thus he shattered them, in accord with Balak's name, which means 'the one who shatters'.[9]

That women caused even the wise to fall away† was nothing †Si 19:2 new. At the beginning Satan shattered a man through a woman, overthrowing and casting away one whom he never dared approach himself. Balaam was minister of this advice; his name means 'an empty people'.[10] It not only signifies his own emptiness, but it censures a multitude of heretics and demons who lead humans astray through the allurements of pleasure.

And so, he says, *you have there people holding the teaching of Balaam*.† What does he mean by this? The Lord does not disapprove †Rv 2:14 of this angel's living *where Satan's throne is* and *where Satan dwells*, but instead he commends him because he has not denied the faith. The Lord holds against him that he has *there people holding the teaching of Balaam, the teaching of the Nicolaitans*.† The fault lies in his sharing †Rv 2:15 with those fallen into heresy, in his restoring to life people who were not living because they were alienated from God, whom he still has as his own.

He reminds this angel that he has a few things against him, while signifying that he finds many things in him that please him. The angel must therefore correct the few displeasing matters, and he suggests and urges him to work more faithfully and zealously. Perhaps he was charging only a few of his people with holding this

[9] Jerome, *Liber interpretationis hebraicorum nominum*16:19; CCh 72:79.
[10] Ibid., 16.20; CCh 72:79.

pernicious teaching. Yet the Lord holds against him that he has those few among his own, holding other teachings in place of his, and does not cut off the followers of such faults from himself and his people. Fortunate is the one the Lord censures only for the faults of others, prepared, if he does penance, to spare his servant for them too.† And if the angel of Pergamum is exhorted to repent of those of others, which are perhaps less deserving of censure, what are we to do, I ask, concerning our own?

†Ps 18:13 Vulgate

In like manner repent† for the uncorrected evildoing of your subjects, just as I warned the angel of Ephesus about his abandoned love.† We said something about the Nicolaitans when we treated of that letter,† and we will not repeat it here. *Repent* is sure and worthy of full acceptance.† Buy something great at a small price. Perform a light, short, useful penance in this world lest you have to perform a useless, intolerable, and endless one in the life to come. This can also mean that the warning is addressed not only to the angel but to those as well whom he threatens with a more serious punishment unless they repent.

†Rv 2:15
†Rv 2:4
†See Sermon 9
†1 Tm 1:15

If not I will come to you quickly, and I will fight against them with the sword of my mouth.† He threatens him and them equally, in accord with the words, 'He will die in his wickedness, but his blood I will require at your hand'.† This *sword of* his *mouth* is the *sharp two-edged sword*, both seen and said to be in his mouth. Indeed he accomplishes everything by his word. He restores life to the chosen and destroys the condemned by his word, as the Apostle says of the wicked leader of all wickedness, 'whom the Lord will destroy with the breath of his mouth'.†

†Rv 2:15
†Ezk 33:8
†1 Th 2:8

And as nothing is easier than to say a word,[11] nothing is stronger than its blow. In this word we are not to understand the sound of his voice but only the result of his will. How sharp is the sword with which he cuts off the breath of princes and inspires fear in the kings of the earth!† He alone is rightly to be feared who after he has killed the body has power to destroy soul and body in hell. 'Yes', Truth says, 'I tell you, fear this one'.† He *has the sharp two-edged sword*;*

†Ps 76:12
†Lk 12:5
*Rv 1:16

[11] *Nil est dictu facilius*. Terence, *Phormio* 300. Bernard of Clairvaux, *In nativitate Sancti Ioannis Baptistae* 12; SBOp 5:184.

there is nowhere anyone can flee, can hide, can turn away. Whether John is saying that he will come quickly in his own person and fight against godless people of this kind with the sword of his own mouth I leave to your judgment.

Would that today our priests may contend with tongues afire rather than with rigid iron swords! Would that they found armaments and shields fit for burning intolerable, and would prefer the dalmatic to the breastplate, the miter to the helmet, the pastoral staff to the military banner! The servants of God are to fight for God with
spiritually powerful weapons, not with material and physical ones,† †2 Co 10:4
contending with prayer, preaching, supplication, and reproof.† Is †1 Tm 2:1
there any wonder that unclean demons and wicked people have so little fear of the sword of their mouths when they put their confidence in material arms?

But here let us remain silent, especially since among some of them the sword of their mouths is blunt and useless, nor have they perhaps ears open enough to hear what the Spirit is saying to the churches. Would that the Spirit may open our ears to hear by the same goodness that causes him to speak! The twofold promise of godliness demands two ears, as the Apostle says: 'Godliness is
valuable in every way, holding promise of life now and to come'.† †1 Tm 4:8

And what does the Spirit say? *To the one who conquers I will
give the hidden manna,*† and so on. Manna is a marvelous, miraculous †Rv 2:17
refreshment that the Saviour promised to those who came to him, to
those who labor and are burdened,† those laboring for the king of †Mt 11:28
Egypt, for the ruler of this world,† those given to earthly labors, †Jn 14:30, 16:11
subject to lust and greed. They are not laboring simply in the present, but for the past too, because they are burdened by their many grave sins. Solomon says of them, 'Heavy is the stone' of each fault and 'weighty the sand' of many offenses, 'but a fool's anger is
heavier than both'† in the rage of despair. †Pr 27:3

The *hidden manna*† is the secret pleasure of the inner self. The †Rv 2:17
prophet speaks of this *hidden manna* in the psalm, 'How abundant is your goodness, Lord, which you have hidden for those who fear
you!'† Manna is called 'the bread of angels'* not because angels eat †Ps 31:19
it but because it was served to the children of Israel through the *Ps 78:24–25
ministry of angels.

He distinguishes this manna as *hidden* because it was found in a
†Ex 16:25 field.† In a spiritual sense we can compare the *hidden manna* to the
†Mt 13:44 treasure hidden in a field.† Concealed in the labor of our duties here
below is the secret refreshment of divine consolation, having in it
†Ws 16:20 everything delicious to the taste.† It is called a 'treasure' because it
is precious and useful; food because it is sweet and brings joy. But
this manna melted in the sun's heat and, by God's dispensation, the
gift of consolation is sometimes taken from the chosen for a violent
temptation. We are warned to anticipate the time carefully, and to
†Jn 6:12 gather up† and store something with which to refresh ourselves in a
time of necessity. Likewise too, since we sometimes allow ourselves
leisure in accord with the text, 'One who has little to do perceives
†Si 38:24 (38:25 Vulgate) wisdom',† we are not to seek manna of this kind for ourselves,
†Ex 16:25 because it will not be found in the fields† on the Sabbath, but we
must lay it up beforehand if we are to be refreshed.

†Rv 2:17 *And I will give him a white stone.*† Because manna is sweet rather
than firm, a promise of eternal life follows in the stone. Another
translation has 'pearl' in place of 'stone',[12] that fine pearl for the
sake of which the wise merchant joyfully gave all he had when
†Mt 13:45–46 he found it.† In a stone of this kind, costliness and firmness are
commended, that it may be indestructible and remain always in its
integrity. Its brightness signifies joy and purity. As we await this
stone, nothing should be more important for us, we should judge
nothing more desirable, than that Christ present to himself a glorious
†Ep 5:27 church having neither spot nor wrinkle.†

What should we find more irksome among all the miseries of
this life's journey than that nothing is done without sin, because
†Jm 3:2 while we live here we all make many mistakes.† Since our sins are
†Is 59:2 a barrier between ourselves and God,† what is more unfortunate
than that we eagerly tear it down only to have it instantly grow up
and sprout, so that it has to be torn down again if we want to cleave
to him.

Would that, were it possible, the strength of the Almighty would
grant to a wretch like me a purity altogether immune from sins and

[12] Primasius, *Commentariorum super Apocalypsim Beati Iohannis libri quinque* 1.2; PL 68:807A.

perils, or to acquire a fear of sinning even amid the troubles of the present life. Beloved, our supreme happiness ought to be the anticipation of that most genuine and shining purity, and of that freedom from danger that the prophet describes: 'Return, my soul, to your rest, for the Lord has been bountiful to you; he has delivered my soul from death, my eyes from tears, my feet from stumbling'.† †Ps 116:7–8 He is describing security from sin, from punishment, from the danger of offending and falling back into sin, or punishment, or both.

We are promised a *new name written on* that *stone*,† †Rv 2:17 written by God's finger and deeply carved, written in letters that will never henceforth be obliterated or forgotten. It will be a great name, not by earth's reckoning, but by heaven's. A *new name* is the sign of a new dignity, a new glory, a new elevation, a new adoption and inheritance. Do not trouble to seek what it will be, of what sort. It appears when Truth says in the gospel, 'Blessed are the peacemakers, for they will be called children of God'.† †Mt 5:9 Meanwhile he relieves you of any hope of finding out, and us of the labor of inquiry, by adding, *that no one knows except the one who receives it*.† †Rv 2:17 No one should presume to want to teach another, and no one presume to be taught by another. When they receive it they will all be taught by God,† †Jn 6:45 and no person will stand before any other in this regard.

As for us, beloved, let us try, as the divine gift and divine assistance enable us, to faithfully fight a good fight for him, and happily end in a glorious victory. Meanwhile let us sample the promised sweetness of this spiritual sustenance as our military pay, but much more, let us wait expectantly in every prayer for the Lord's promised good things which eye has not seen, nor ear heard, nor the thought of the heart attained,† †Is 64:4; 1 Co 2:9 which no one can know until he receives them. May he grant us by his mercy a share in the knowledge and experience of these things, who has graciously promised them, Jesus Christ our Lord. Amen.

Sermon Fourteen

And to the angel of the church at Thyatira write: These are the words of the Son of God, who has eyes like a flame of fire, and whose feet are like fine brass. I know your works, your faith, and love, and ministry, and patience; and your last works are more than your former ones. But I have this against you, that you permit the woman Jezabel, who calls herself a prophet, to teach and lead my servants astray to fornicate and to eat food sacrificed to idols. I gave her time to repent, but she is not willing to repent of her fornication. And behold, I will cast her on a bed, and those who commit adultery with her will be in very great distress unless they repent of their deeds. And I shall put her children to death, and all the churches will know that I am the one who searches loins and hearts, and I shall give to each of you as your works deserve. But to the rest of you at Thyatira I say: Those who do not hold this teaching, who have not known what some call the 'deep things of Satan', I will not lay any other burden upon you. Only hold fast to what you have until I come. And to the one who conquers and keeps my works until the end, I will give authority over the nations, and he will rule them with an iron rod, and they will be broken like a potter's jar, even as I have received from my Father,

and I will give him the morning star. Let anyone who has an ear
†Rv 2:18–29 *hear what the Spirit says to the churches.*†

And to the angel of the church *at Thyatira write.*†
Beloved, this brotherhood of yours ought to keep in mind
†Rv 2:18 that we said that Thyatira is interpreted 'enlightened'[1] or
'living sacrifice'.[2] We should notice that from the many things
that blessed John saw as foretold of each, he told different things
to different angels, but to each one of them he told what was
appropriate. Thus to the angel of Thyatira he makes special mention
of the *eyes* and *feet*, comparing them to *a flame of fire* and, as before,
†Rv 1:15 to *fine brass.*† From those eyes we have enlightenment, and we can
also liken those feet to a living sacrifice.

No one can doubt that he is writing of 'the one like the Son of
†Rv 1:13 Man' who appeared in the midst of the lampstands† when he says
to this angel: *These are the words of the Son of God, who has eyes like a*
†Rv 2:18 *flame of fire, and whose feet are like fine brass.*† The Son of God not only
condescended to appear as Son of Man for people's edification, but
genuinely to become so, that he may give to those who received
†Jn 1:12 him power to share his sonship.† He did not refuse a humble form
and to live among humans as a human when he deigned to be seen
on earth, so that those who are only human may fear to be raised
above him by their own presumption and arrogance. For the same
reason the Lord of majesty shows the likeness of truth itself, and the
truth of that likeness, to his faithful people, to whom, and when,
and how he wishes. To edify them, and through them a multitude
of others, as in the present case, he tells them he is the Son of God,
and orders it believed and written.

And what then, my brothers? Will we ignore what the only-
†Jn 1:18 begotten Son of God, who is close to the Father's heart,† tells us?
Will we ignore what the Spirit, who knows what is God's, who
†1 Co 2:10–11 searches even the depths of God,† says to the churches? As Scripture
testifies, the Son of God is also the Lamb of God, having seven eyes
†Rv 5:6 which are the seven spirits of God.†

[1] Jerome, *Liber interpretationis hebraicorum nominum* 72.8; CCh 72:149.
[2] Venerable Bede, *Explanatio Apocalypsis* 1.2; PL 93:139B.

I know your works.† He commends their way of life, which is self-controlled, upright, and godly,† because faith is working through love† in them. Therefore he adds, *your faith and love*. Works without faith, and faith without works,† are unacceptable to God, nor is he pleased by either faith or works apart from love. Work is the effect, faith the root, and love the life and the strength of both. †Rv 2:19 †Tt 2:12 †Ga 5:6 †Jm 2:20

The words that follow, *and ministry*,† some experts[3] take to mean almsgiving, in light of the Apostle's words, 'concerning the ministry being accomplished for the saints'.† As included among these works, however, ministry seems to pertain more properly to a prelate's office, in which one who ministers well gains a good standing.† Deservedly does he recall that he knows and confirms this ministry after works, and faith, and especially after love, the greatest of all. Examples of works are required for the dull and hard-hearted, so that whatever the Lord's minister teaches his disciples is inopportune he will show by his deeds is not to be done.† He not only needs faith to believe with his heart unto justification,† but an increase of faith, a fullness of faith, that he may be ready to give an account of his work† to the One who is all-demanding.[4] He needs faithfulness, as it says, 'Now it is required of stewards that one be found faithful'.† Especially is no ordinary love needed by one about to undertake the ministry of pastoral care, in accord with what the Lord said to Peter, 'Do you love me more than these? Feed my sheep'.† †Rv 2:19 †2 Co 9:1 †1 Tm 3:13 †RB 2:12–13 †Rm 10:10 †RB 2:37 †1 Co 4:2 †Jn 21:15, 17

In carrying this out, patience is needed in many different circumstances. That a person's learning is known by his patience† is not hidden from those who have tried it. How arduous and difficult a task it is to serve a variety of temperaments!† What soothes one increases the irritation of another. Certainly if everyone who wants to live a godly life† will have to endure persecution, how much more will those whose duty it is to teach many others to live in a godly way sometimes urge and even compel some. In truth, Paul, the Lord showed you, as he had promised Ananias, how much you †Pr 19:11 †RB 2:31 †2 Tm 3:12

[3] Pseudo-Alcuin, *Commentariorum in Apocalypsin libri quinque* 2.1; PL 100:1106C. Richard of Saint Victor, *In Apocalypsim Iohannis libri septem* 1.8; PL 196:725C.

[4] *Omniposcenti*.

†Ac 9:16 had to suffer for the sake of his name† while you were becoming
†1 Co 9:22 patient in all things to all people.† As you said, 'Who is weak, and I
†2 Co 11:29 am not weak? Who is made to stumble, and I am not indignant?'†

Moreover, the one to whom what follows applies is most
†Rv 2:19 fortunate: *and your last works are more than your former ones*.† Nowadays
not all of those holding a prelate's office—I wish there were more!—
move beyond their former good works, especially when the scandals
current now are tolerated.

†Rv 2:20 *But I have this against you*.† O most kind God, why do you stand
in the adversary position? Why have something against one whose
works please you, whose faith you approve, whose love you accept?
Do you approve his ministry, yet still have something against him?
†Lk 21:19 By patience he is in possession of his soul,† and do you still have a
†Col 3:13 complaint against him?† Is he judged not to be going forward lest
he later be found wanting? Are you saying that his *last works are more*
†Rv 2:19 *than* his *former ones*,† and yet not keeping silent, not holding back,
that you have something against him?

A life where there is no freedom from care, where no matter
how hard a person works to avoid faults of his own he still has to fear
†Ps 18:13 Vulgate the faults of others,† is a wretched life! And yet we love this poor
life, a Delilah to our Samson. Do we want to escape this miserable
life? Do we weep as life comes to a close, poor in all that is good,
but rich in hurts, in dangers, even in crimes?

Listen to the statement against this priest of Thyatira made by
†Rv 2:18 the one to whose eyes as to *a flame of fire*† all things are naked and
†Heb 4:13 open.† *You permit the woman Jezabel, who calls herself a prophet, to*
†Rv 2:20 *teach and lead my servants astray.*† I doubt that the false prophet was
named Jezabel; rather she deserved the name of Israel's worst queen
for imitating her evil ways. The first Jezabel punished the Lord's
prophets by physical death, but this one was doing all in her power to
lead his servants astray by pernicious examples and reasonings. Since
the name Jezabel means 'pouring blood and dung',[5] this prophet is
called that because of her abounding iniquity and impurity.

He is said to permit her presence doubtless because he could
†Ps 19:12 have prohibited it. Beloved, who can understand offenses?† He

[5] Jerome, *Liber interpretationis hebraicorum nominum* 80:20; CCh 72:160.

indeed whose *eyes are like a flame of fire*.† We are not to believe that this priest, whose *works*, and *faith*, and *love* are commended, would have approved such depravity. We are not to believe that he hesitated to give correction, for his *ministry* is applauded. But perhaps his *patience*, rightly praised in the case of other afflictions, led him to oppose this one less strongly, and, fearing excessive severity, he fell into the fault of too great lenience. Thus Eli,† once the Lord's priest, perished when he spared his own sinful sons. Although he rebuked them verbally, he never punished them by depriving them of their priestly earnings, barring them from the altar, or removing them from office.

†Rv 2:18

†1 S 2:12, 4:18; RB 2:26

Some have thought that this woman was the priest's wife.[6] If true, the rebuke would have been stronger and the language clearer. For how could such a man have knowingly kept an adulteress, much less a blasphemer and heretic? Would she not have been warned once and twice, and then been avoided by all the faithful?† Wisely does Paul prohibit women from speaking in the churches when he says, 'Let them ask their own husbands at home'.† 'At home', not in public; 'let them ask', not presume to teach; ask 'their husbands', not themselves; 'their own', not any husband at all.

†1 Co 5:11

†1 Co 14:35

And what of you, O illustrious region of Gaul? Why have you of late spurned and despised your ancient privileged reputation: 'Gaul alone had no monsters'?[7] The principal see of the Gauls, Lyons, created new apostles, and has not blushed to bring women into that circle. These vixens[8] went forth to ravage the Lord's vineyard. Contemptible and worthless, they usurped the preacher's office. They are altogether or almost without education, or rather without the Spirit, in accord with the text, 'Natural beings, not having the Spirit'.† They go around cities and villages pretending poverty and looking for opportunities to preach, impudently eating others' bread without working with their own hands. They sharpen their

†Jude 19

[6] Isidore of Seville, *Etymologiarum libri XX* 8.5.5. Haymo of Auxerre, *Expositionis in Apocalypsin Beati Iohannis libri septem* 1.2; PL 117:978B. Richard of Saint Victor, *In Apocalysim Iohannis libri septem* 1.8; PL 196:726A.

[7] Jerome, *Contra Vigiliantum liber unus* 1; PL 23:339.

[8] *Vulpeculae*. Bernard of Clairvaux, *Sermones super Cantica Canticorum* 64.3.8; SBOp 2:170.

†Ps 140:3 tongues† with exquisitely composed words; they are novel parrots, unaware of what they are saying and declaring. The hellebore they use to color, or rather discolor, their words, is insult and railing against the clergy.

The founder, Wandesius (from his birthplace), abjured the sect at the Council of Lyons in the presence of our venerable lord and father, Henry, bishop of Aubagne, then serving as legate of the Apostolic See, and Wiscardus of holy memory, archbishop of that church. I myself was present, along with a great multitude of honorable people, mostly priests. For obvious reasons he was
†2 P 2:22 convicted of sacrilegious presumption, but he returned to his vomit† and did not stop recruiting and sending out disciples. Among them are even wretched women burdened with sins, who make their way
†2 Tm 3:6 into others' households,† busybodies and gossips,* shameless, bold,
*1 Tm 5:13 and impudent.

Almost five years ago two of them, with a troop of wicked lackeys, attacked the venerable bishop of Arvenica on his travels with all the vituperation they could muster—as he afterwards told many—insulting him because he had once discovered them preaching in his diocese and forced them to renounce this sect by threats and arguments. And so, blaspheming him shamelessly, they shouted at him, and publicly declared, 'Each day after we preached we feasted elegantly; almost every night we chose new lovers for ourselves. We were responsible to no one, and went through life without cares, without work, without danger. Now, as servant girls we are in daily danger of death, and are miserable, suffering all kinds of hardships'.

What remains to be said, my brothers? Who has raised up this young Jezabel after a thousand years, to run through the streets and
†Sg 3:2 the squares† as a preacher-whore? Although this sect has now been excommunicated by bishops, by archbishops, and by the Roman church, for this reason it is the more warmly welcomed and attentively heard by people who find stolen waters sweeter and hidden
†Pr 9:17 bread more tasty.† For the female sex rather than the male to be convicted of talkativeness and poor choice of words is cheap and common. No wonder that, if on account of its first destructive suggestions the snake was altogether deprived of speech, the woman was in some measure restrained.

I believe that some of our brothers can still be found alive today who listened with me to our blessed father and teacher[9] praise the nobility of silence, one of her greatest gifts, in Mary, mother of God and greatest of all women. In all the holy gospels we find her words a mere seven times. Many times did she ponder in her heart,† but seldom did she speak. Certainly more than these few words would have been written had she said more, especially because her frequent recollection could have brought only the most salutary and important words from such a fullness of the Spirit. We read that she spoke twice to the angel, twice to Elizabeth, twice to her son, and once to the servants at the wedding. †Lk 2:19

Perplexed and wondering at Gabriel's extraordinary and fitting greeting, she did not immediately speak. She thought, she deliberated, she waited until the angel, proceeding with the mission he had begun, added more important things to what he had first said. At length, answering him with a reverent question, she asked, 'How can this be?'† She was asserting that what he was promising regarding conception and childbirth could not happen to her as it happens to other women. When she had attentively heard, faithfully believed, and accepted with fitting desire how it could be, she answered without any further hesitation, 'Behold the handmaid of the Lord. Be it done to me according to your word',† according, that is, to the way you have told me, and I have found pleasing. †Lk 1:34 †Lk 1:38

Then, ascending into the hill country, she greeted Elizabeth. At her voice, John, enclosed in the womb, rejoiced with a novel joy.† And although she could have been carried away with the great news, she burst out in a song of thanksgiving and praise,† magnifying the Lord,† and rendering thanks to him as the source of benefits. †Lk 1:41, 44 †Ps 42:4; Jon 2:9 †Lk 1:46

Then she sought her son in Jerusalem. He was twelve years old in his humanity, for according to his divinity his years neither pass nor pass away.† In testimony to his real incarnation she used appropriate maternal authority and said, 'Child, why have you treated †Ps 102:27

[9] Bernard of Clairvaux, *Sermones de diversis* 52.3–4; PL 183:675CD. *Dominica infra octavum Assumptionis* 10; SBOp 5:270.

us like this? Behold, your father and I have been seeking you in
†Lk 2:48 sorrow'.† And although he spoke of a far different Father,* for his is a
*Lk 2:49 †Lk 2:51 two-fold nature, the Lord showed himself obedient† to his servants,
the Creator to his creatures.

As the mother of mercy at a wedding in Galilee, she pitied
the couple's embarrassment and simply suggested to her son, 'They
†Jn 2:3 have no wine'.† She was content to mention the need for kindness
†Ps 41:1 to the One who understands the needy and the poor.† The last
words of the Virgin in the gospels were addressed to the servants at
the wedding. She advised them to keep and to do whatever the
†Jn 2:5 Lord might tell them,† if he should say something. Excuse me
from further explanation, [she said,] because he of whom it was
written, 'The voice of the Lord is over the waters, the God of
†Ps 29:3 †Mt 17:5 majesty thunders',† meets every need. 'Listen to him!'† That word
had its effect among those servants. When they drew water at the
Saviour's command, those who were complaining of the lack of
wine filled water jars in place of wine jars, preparing baths in place
of drinks. Yet they had not yet tested the power of the one giving
†Jn 2:11 the command, for this was the first of his signs.†

Perhaps it is not inappropriate to draw a parallel between the
seven words of the most holy Virgin and the equal number of gifts
†Is 11:2–3 Vulgate of the Holy Spirit.† The spirit of the fear of the Lord seems to
parallel what she said to the servants: 'Whatever he says to you, keep
and do'. As Wisdom teaches, 'One who fears the Lord neglects
†Qo 7:19 Vulgate nothing'.† That she interceded mercifully for what the suffering
needed corresponds to the spirit of godliness. That she asked with
an appropriately motherly voice, 'Son, why have you treated us
like this?' and so forth, can perhaps be attributed to the spirit
of knowledge, which deals rather with human than with divine
matters. In the spirit of might and magnanimity she indicated to
Gabriel, who was promising an inviolable conception, her resolve
to preserve her virginity: 'How can this be, since I know not man?'
She answered him deliberately, then, in the spirit of counsel: 'Behold
the handmaid of the Lord'. Her word of greeting was filled with
the spirit of understanding, for on hearing it the unborn forerunner
recognized the Lord's presence, and his mother the joy of her
exultant son. [Elizabeth] understood both Gabriel's announcement

and the mystery of the Lord's incarnation. The virgin mother's response to her was to exult in God her Jesus,† whose name had already been spoken by the angel.† In the fullness of the spirit of wisdom, she burst forth in a song to his glory, magnifying him of whom she had heard that 'he will be great',† who is truly one with the Father and the Holy Spirit, God, over all and blessed forever. Amen.

†Hab 3:18 Vulgate
†Lk 2:21
†Lk 1:15

Sermon Fifteen

THE PRIEST OF THE CHURCH AT THYATIRA deserved his rebuke because he permitted a woman with no right to teach in public to instruct the servants of God and even to lead them astray. We see how she led them astray alluded to in the words *to fornicate and to eat food sacrificed to idols.*† This is what †Rv 2:20
the children of Israel did in the desert, and, what is sadder and more alarming, Solomon fell into idol worship in his own kingdom through women's charms.† This Jezabel too was leading God's †1 K 11:4
servants astray to sin in lower and higher ways: by fornication against their bodies, and by idolatry against their Creator. How detestable is each part of the filthy mixture, the spiritual as well as the carnal fornication; how every creature endowed with reason should curse them when they are found in the faithful! Rightly are like causes found for each. Perhaps it would be more tolerable for humans—if only they did not both lead to such human wretchedness—for demons, also called incubi, to unite with them in lust, than for humans to have no fear of communicating with demons in idolatry. Nature made demons neither male nor female, but, despite their original condition, they love involvement in base physical pleasures, and are said to be dishonored by unnatural desire for intercourse with both sexes. We do not know whether their pleasure comes solely

from the ruin of the people who consent to them, or whether they can themselves experience carnal pleasure.

We know a priest, for many years dean over other priests, whose good reputation is attested by neighbors and officials. When the Duke of Burgundy's sister was engaged to Roger the Magnificent, King of Sicily, this priest was living for a time in Sicily, and discovered there with perfect certainty what he still tells today.

A young man, a strong and skillful swimmer, was bathing in the sea with some companions of his own age about dusk of an evening when the moon was shining brightly. He heard some commotion near him, and supposed one of his friends was going to dunk him as swimmers do in sport. Strong and quick, he fell on him—and caught hold of a woman's hair! Holding what he believed was a woman, he plunged into the waves and drew her after him to the shore. He spoke to her and asked her certain things, but could not get a single word from her. He covered her with his cloak and took her home, and his mother gave her suitable clothes to wear.

She sat silently among them, but otherwise was grateful and obliging enough. After a while she responded to signs and nods, but never indicated her nationality, homeland, or the reason why she had come. She was among them eating and drinking,† apparently comfortable in all things, just as if she were visiting neighbors, relatives, and friends.† When asked if she believed in God and was a Christian, she nodded in the affirmative. Asked whether she wished to marry the young man, who had fallen deeply in love with her, she gratefully bowed her head and gave him her hand.

†Mt 11:19; Lk 7:34

†Lk 2:44

And what then? After a few days the mother gave in to her son's desire, and his friends agreed. The priest was summoned, and the betrothal was contracted, without a dowry, at the groom's word and the bride's silent assent. Then the party went to the church, and the wedding was celebrated in the usual manner. Love grew daily, and the newlyweds seemed more and more happy with each other. The woman conceived, and at length she bore a son. She was so affectionate with him that she never allowed the baby away from her lap or her bosom. She nursed him, washed and diapered and dressed him. As the days passed and the boy grew, her love for him seemed to grow too.

Meanwhile it happened that the young man on his way to work with a friend began to converse with him as he usually did. The friend told him that such a marriage was wrong, and that he was living with a phantasm and not a woman. Although the bishop, when they had presented themselves before him and he had inquired as carefully as he could into the details, had prudently agreed that this was not an unfortunate marriage, the young man's heart began to be more than usually moved at his friend's words, and to grow anxious over his marriage. Finally they agreed that he would return home to the privacy of their bedroom, and with words, eyes and threats—even at sword's point—demand that the woman with the child confess on the spot who she was. If she hesitated he would pretend that he was going to kill the boy, for he was sure she loved the child with all her heart.

He returned home, and carried out without delay what he had decided, what his friend had suggested. She trembled to see the sword hanging over her son's head, and immediately burst out: 'Woe to you, wretched man! You are losing a good wife since you force me to speak. I could be with you, and it could go well for you as long as you let me keep the silence enjoined on me. Now I am speaking to you, as you demand, but after I have spoken you will never see me again'. With this the woman vanished. The boy she left grew, and lived like the rest of them. He began to bathe often in the sea where once his mother had been found, until one day the fantasy woman seized the boy as he was swimming in the same waves, as many present witnessed. From that time on neither was seen again.

I wish this Jezabel were less harmful and would remain silent, or would likewise disappear while speaking her poisonous words. A demon seems to have appeared in a woman's form with the command not to speak in order to show the baleful talkativeness of women. It seems impossible that fantasies of this kind could produce real offspring. Hence the dead body of this boy was not washed up by the sea nor buried in the earth as would happen in accord with reason and nature if he had been a true human being. Although the fact that we heard this story told some time ago would seem to be against it, many agree to its truth.

In the diocese of Cologne a very famous and vast castle called the Nimmaium rises above the Rhine. Once when many princes were gathered there, and, some say, in the presence of the Emperor, a silver swan came pulling a little boat by a chain around its neck, and put into the shore. Everyone was astonished by so strange a thing, and rose up at the sight. A young unknown soldier sprang out, and the swan drew the boat away by the chain, just as it had brought it.

The soldier was found to be a good fighter, a thoughtful counselor, and an effective businessman; he was obedient to his commander, fierce against his enemies, liked by his companions, and happy among his friends. He married a noble wife, was enriched by her dowry and secured by her kindred. At length children were born, and after a long time spent residing in that same castle he caught a distant glimpse of his swan gliding toward him with the little boat and the chain. Without delay he got up and ran to the boat, got in, and was never seen again.

Many of his descendants went on to become nobles, and even today his large family remains and continues to grow. Our own diocese of Langres even now is said to have noblemen and lords of this military camp who are like a brood of vipers,† descendants of that serpent's stock. The father of their great-great-great-grandfather, or an even more remote ancestor, when he had penetrated into the remote places of the forest, met [the serpent] in the guise of a beautiful, well-dressed woman. He fell in love with her at first sight, seized her and took her with him, content with that dowry. He was betrothed by the church's ministers, since no one could object that they were related by blood or marriage. He had children by her, and for many days and years his great love made him forget that he did not know of his wife's parents or homeland.

†Mt 23:33; Lk 3:7

The woman loved bathing, and frequented the bath. She never allowed herself to be seen naked even by servant girls, but, when everything was ready, she would send them away in order to remain alone in the room with the door bolted from inside. At last it happened that one of her servant girls, looking curiously through a hole in the wall, saw not a woman but a serpent twisting sinuously through the water. When the servant girl had seen her in such a state many times, in her great astonishment she revealed the mystery of iniquity† to her lord. †2 Th 2:7

The husband grew afraid when he heard the word serpent, and was easily persuaded to believe that something was wrong, for he did not know his wife's origins. He waited for the right moment, and when he saw with his own eyes what he had heard with his ears, he was astounded. Knowing the old enmity between woman and serpent, he was aghast that a new covenant had been formed. He could not hide what he saw, but loudly burst in to destroy that room. But she disappeared, never to appear to him again; she did not remain, for she had been discovered in the form of a serpent.

Let no one complain or charge that I tell these tales for curiosity's sake or to offer examples worth following. The careful and faithful hearer should notice where our prayer is heading, and what our intention demands. I admit that I want to render lust hateful—for in such uncleanness the angels of Satan rejoice—and this to the end that the Christian may flee the lasciviousness so dear to demons, and detest the alliance with idolatry.

Perhaps the Jezabel of whom we were speaking did not persuade the servants of God to idolatry but to the eating of food sacrificed to idols. She cleverly led them into iniquity unaware, getting them accustomed to eating sacrificed foods, so that as they became more used to the idols, they could not profitably share the Lord's cup together with the cup of demons.† †1 Co 10:21

I gave her time to repent, but she is not willing to repent of her fornication.† Here we are given to understand that among the benefits †Rv 2:21 of the divine loving-kindness we are to reckon a time of waiting, a capacity for repenting, and a postponement of chastisement. This grace is seen most starkly when it is taken away. A man breathing his last loudly begs for a delay, just until morning; he receives it, considers it to be nothing, and then goes on day and night as before, until the end suddenly comes. If we recall that each of our days could be our last, if we are apprehensive that each may be our last day, we come to realize how great is the gift of the Judge we await, and the capacity he gives us to do penance before he arrives. We also realize that we must take this opportunity seriously, neither neglecting it nor treating it as of little account. Once it is taken from us, no eagerness, or prayer, or argument, can bring it back.

How dear would that brief hour be to a wretched person whose existence is worthless and whom a long delay would not benefit. They claim that they will do serious penance, but the claim, though constant, is ineffective. No delay, no rebuke or correction can bring them to perform the penance which is in reality light,
†Ws 5:3 brief, and salutary. Groaning in anguish of spirit,† they will one day say of the elect: 'These are people we once held in derision—
†Ws 5:4 fools that we were! We thought their lives were madness'.† The second gift is rebuke, the third is correction, and we will take that up now.

But she is not willing to repent of her fornication. And behold, I will cast
†Rv 2:21–22 *her on a bed*,† and so on. The merciful Lord is patient with sinners, reproves the negligent, and punishes the unrepentant. He pretends to punish the faults of sinners to lead them to repentance. He reproves those who leave their offenses and his patience unnoticed in order to bring them to consider both things. As a last resort he brings physical pain on them to make them realize their state. We read in the second book of Maccabees: 'In the case of other nations the Lord waits patiently, that when the day of judgment comes he may punish them in the fullness of their sins. Not so with us, that with our sins reaching their height he may take vengeance on us. And so he never withdraws his mercy from us; and although he chastises
†2 M 6:14–16 his people, he does not forsake them'.†

These gifts are neither good nor evil, not less dangerous to the condemned than they are salutary to the elect. From the same gifts some are led to repentance and others to store up wrath for
†Rm 2:5; Jm 5:3 Vulgate themselves.† Thus we should be zealous for the greater gifts,* we
*1 Co 12:31 should eagerly long for and pursue those gifts that bring a more sure hope of salvation. We should also notice in how many and
†Heb 1:1 various ways† people are chastised here below, in themselves or in what belongs to them in equal measure. So the Lord says about this
†Rv 2:22 fornicating woman, *I will cast her on a bed*,† a bed of pain in place of unchaste couches, that an hour's evil may make her forget her great wantonness. Or, as another translation has it, 'I will cast her into

mourning'.[1] The bed of pain suggests great affliction; mourning suggests grief of heart.

And those who commit adultery with her will be in very great distress unless they repent of their deeds. And I shall put her children to death.† Some of the impenitent learn nothing from punishment, †Rv 2:22–23 but for others, who are more aware, it works together for salvation.† †Rm 8:28 *And all the churches will know that I am the one who searches loins and hearts*, the one from whom no bodily pleasure or thought remains hidden.

And I shall give to each of you as your works deserve.† By these works †Rv 2:23 and by their punishment he is making known to others that 'No matter how long I seem not to notice, I will leave no good deed unrewarded nor any evil deed unpunished'.

But to the rest of you at Thyatira I say.† Those whom the nefar- †Rv 2:24 ious woman led astray into committing adultery and eating food sacrificed to idols with her, although they seemed to be at Thyatira, were not; they were destitute of true enlightenment, nor did they offer themselves a living sacrifice† to the Lord. †Rm 12:1

Those who do not hold this teaching,† the teaching of that impure †Rv 2:24 and impious woman, a teaching filled with seduction and completely foreign to the truth. *Who have not known*, that is, favored, *what some call the 'deep things of Satan'*. This does not mean that there really are *deep things* but that some claim there are, that, as they talk among themselves or reflect on their doctrine alone, they magnify and extol them.

I will not lay any other burden upon you. Only hold fast to what you have until I come.† If we take all these things as spoken by the Son †Rv 2:25 of God, perhaps he is promising to come at their final call, because then he will be present to his own when he calls them out of this world into his presence and the beatific vision. Nor is he placing a further burden on them, as when he called Peter to bear a cross and to imitate his own passion. When Peter inquired about this in reference to John and asked, 'What about him?' Jesus replied, 'So it is my wish that he remain until I come'.† †Jn 21:21–22

[1] *luctum* in place of *lectum*. Primasius, *Commentariorum super Apocalypsim beati Ioannis libri quinque* 1.1; PL 68:808C.

†Rv 2:24 But *the rest of you at Thyatira*† can also be taken as spoken by
John himself. In order that they may separate themselves from the
wrong doctrines of the faithless, he is warning them to be content
with what he previously taught until he should return. In the Spirit
he foresaw that the gospel he would write would contain none of
their teachings.

†Rv 2:26 *And to the one who conquers,*† and so on. While in visions of this
sort there may be a variety of speakers, these words can only be
attributed to the Son. Only one who conquers is crowned, and
no one will obtain the triumph of victory unless he competes
†2 Tm 2:5 according to the rules.† Yet it seems that something further is
promised one who *keeps* his *works until the end*, one not only working
out his own salvation but zealous for perfection, who imitates the
Saviour as well as he can. Salvation, victory, and life lie in the
divine commandments; perfection lies in the counsels and examples.
Those following them, and keeping them *until the end*, are promised
not only victory, which is for all the elect, but judiciary rank and
authority as well. The Lord promised his followers, that is those
†Mt 19:28 keeping his works, 'You also will sit on twelve thrones, judging'.†

*I will give him authority over the nations, and he will rule them with
an iron rod*, that is, with inflexible justice, *and they will be broken like*
†Rv 2:26, 28 *a potter's jar.*† The potter has power to make from the same lump
†Rm 9:21 one vessel for noble and one for ignoble use.† Those who must
be broken *will be broken* irreparably. In the present age he sets him
over his church, that with his inviolable power—like a straight rod
made of iron, which is stronger than any other metal—he may rule
over the elect and break the condemned. Some people indeed are
neither victors nor keepers of divine works, yet he tolerates them
even though he does not move them forward. Of such people the
prophet said, 'They have reigned but not through me; they set up
†Ho 8:4 princes, but I have not called them'.†

†Rv 2:27 What follows, *even as I have received from my Father,*† shows that he
proclaims the Father's glory in everything, and equals him in honor.

†Rv 2:28 *And I will give him the morning star.*† He is speaking of himself,
†1 Co 15:20, 23 the first-fruits† of those who have risen. This *morning star* can also be
taken as faith, and as chastity. Faith is the conviction of things unseen
†Heb 11:1 and the substance of things hoped for.† Chastity belongs rather to

the future than to the present life, and anticipates the day of the Lord by its likeness to the children of the resurrection; chastity stands in opposition to the idolatry and fornication that the false prophet and seducer Jezabel counseled.

And since what the Son of God says to this Angel his Spirit says to his churches in the other letters, he adds, *Let anyone who has ears hear what the Spirit says to the churches.*† He is speaking not only of his commandments but also of counsels. That person has two ears who sings in mind and spirit, 'My heart is ready, O God, my heart is ready!'†—ready not only to obey your precepts but to follow your counsels as well. And may the eternal Father grant us both through his only begotten Son, in their common Spirit, with whom he lives and reigns without end. Amen.

†Rv 2:29

†Pss 57:7, 108:1

Sermon Sixteen

And to the angel of the church at Sardis write: These are the words of the one who has the seven spirits of God and the seven stars. I know your works, that you have the name of being alive and you are dead. Be watchful, and strengthen what remains and is on the point of death. I do not find your works perfect before my God. Keep in mind then in what manner you received and heard; and obey and repent. If you are not watchful I will come to you like a thief, and you will not know at what hour I will come to you. Yet you have a few names in Sardis who have not soiled their garments, and who walk with me in white because they are worthy. Whoever conquers will be clothed like them, and I will not blot his name out of the book of life. And I will confess his name before my Father and before his angels. Let anyone who has an ear hear what the Spirit says to the churches.† †Rv 3:1–6

A*ND TO THE ANGEL OF THE CHURCH at Sardis write: These are the words of the one who has the seven spirits of God and the seven stars.*† The name Sardis, as mentioned before, means †Rv 3:1

'the commencement of beauty'.[1] In reference to this church it means that the comeliness begun in some parts was not yet perfected in the rest, as it ought to have been, and as was hoped for. Hence it is like a single body that had apparently begun to live in some of its members but was not alive in others. Its faithful and hard-working
†Tb 8:2 minister is counseled to apply the burning coals, the live embers,†
†Ps 119:4 Vulgate the coals that lay waste,† that they may be enkindled and vivified
by them.

In another sense, a beginning of beauty is found in a person even though it lacks perfection. Thus the name is empty without the reality, and a false appearance brings no truth to onlookers. However, the verse probably refers to the church, because the church is said to have certain names, while the only reference to individuals is that they have not soiled their garments.

That the one who railed at fornication in the fourth letter should preach and praise modesty in the fifth, and the one who earlier reproved their wrong deeds now encourages them to greater zeal, is not strange. 'The holy spirit of discipline flees from the deceitful,
†Ws 1:5, 4 nor does it dwell in a body subject to sin'.†

That he is speaking *who has the seven spirits of God and the seven*
†Rv 3:1 *stars*† is appropriately stated at the start of this letter. Upon him
†Is 11:2–3 Vulgate the sevenfold Spirit rested;† he *has seven spirits* in his own people,
†Jn 1:16 who receive from his fullness† as well. He also has *stars* in works of
light, to illuminate his faithful people by his own example. When
†Ac 1:1 [Christ] began to do and to teach,† he taught what we are to do by
first doing what he was to teach. He has *stars* which he hands out in abundance to the children of light when he causes them to do what glorifies him. And as Christ had *the seven spirits of God*, those seven charismatic gifts, through which the Holy Spirit promised and foretold by Isaiah was to rest on him and fill him, and which
†Jn 1:32 John saw and declared had descended and remained on him,† so too
his daily presence declares itself by the same number of stars, the same number of words and works.

His heavenly teaching is related to the spirit of wisdom and understanding, for the inner eyes of the Jewish police were struck

[1] Jerome, *Liber interpretationis hebraicorum nominum* 81.5; CCh 72:160.

by the light of interior stars when, sent to apprehend the One who cannot be apprehended, they reported that 'never has any person spoken as this one speaks'.† That he was endowed with a spirit of counsel was made known when he put forth counsels of perfection, preserving chastity and following voluntary poverty, superior to the precepts. The star of might shone forth in the suffering of the passion and the glory of the resurrection.

†Jn 7:46

The star of knowledge is evident, for he revealed secret things such as the integrity of Nathanael who was without guile,† the thoughts of the Pharisees,† and the deeds of the Samaritan woman who said, 'See the man who told me everything I have done'.† He also foretold events to come, for example that 'we are going up to Jerusalem, and everything said about the Son of Man will be accomplished',† that 'one of you will betray me',†[a] that Peter would deny him three times,†[b] that he would go before his disciples into Galilee,†[c] and other similar things.

†Jn 1:47
†Lk 6:8, et al
†Jn 4:29
†Lk 18:31
†[a]Mt 26:21; Mk 14:18; Jn 13:21
†[b]Mt 26:34; Mk 14:30; Lk 22:34; Jn 13:38
†[c]Mt 26:32; Mk 14:28

The star of his wonderful loving-kindness, glowing brighter than the others, shone in the miracle of the few loaves with which he mercifully fed a crowd lest they faint on the way,† and in the other good deeds in which he cured the paralyzed, gave sight to the blind, cleansed lepers, raised the dead, made the deaf hear and the dumb speak,† and forgave those ensnared in various offences.

†Mt 15:32; Mk 8:2–3
†Mk 7:37

In his complete obedience to the Father, to whom he submitted his own will in everything, the star of the fear of the Lord, a filial and not a servile fear, radiated powerfully. For the Son took the form of a servant† but not the mentality of a servant. This star of fear glowed most evidently at the very hour of his passion, when he prayed that the Father's will and not his own would be done.†

†Ph 2:7
†Lk 22:42

We may also take the seven stars to mean various members of the faithful, for when Elijah claimed that he alone was left, he heard, 'I will leave for myself seven thousand men who have not bent their knees to Baal'.†

†1 K 19:14, 18

And so Christ the Lord *has the seven spirits of God* and he has *the seven stars of heaven*† which he illumines. He also has with him the many graces he distributes and the many people he distributes them to. Both correspond to him and properly dwell with him because he has both and both are his. But, 'Anyone who does not have the Spirit

†Rv 3:1

†Rm 8:9 of Christ does not belong to Christ',† and, 'Happy is the nation
†Ps 33:12 whose God is the Lord, the people he has chosen as his inheritance'.†

So if anyone needs wisdom, or understanding, or any of the other gifts, let him ask it from the one who has them, and who gives them to all in abundance. If anyone desires to have the Lord, or to be possessed by the one *who has the seven stars*, let him notice carefully
†Jude 19 that 'natural beings, not having the Spirit',† are never numbered among his stars, those stars especially that are mentioned in Daniel's prophecy: 'Those who are learned will be like the brightness of the sky, and those who teach many righteousness, like the stars for
†Dn 12:3 endless ages'.† A like insight is found in the book of blessed Job: God
†Jb 28:23 understands the way to wisdom and knows its place.† The place of wisdom is one of the faithful, one who is instructed and taught righteousness, who will be like the brightness of the sky. The way of wisdom, the way leading to the city, is one who teaches many righteousness, who will have his own splendor among the stars.

†1 Co 15:41 For, if 'star differs from star in glory',† the full light of the entire sky must be much brighter. He alone has the stars who alone knows
†Ps 147:4 them, who alone determines their number,† who alone distinguishes them from the sky and from each other, he who says to this angel
†Rv 3:1 of the church of Sardis: *I know your works.*† As I said before, in this vision the seven stars are the angels of the seven churches. The
†1 Jn 3:20 Lord knows the works of each, he knows everything† fully, not only superficially but in the depth and hidden intention of the heart.[2] He knows what, why, and how they have performed their works, and he fully comprehends the works of them all.

Let us not reckon as *works* only what is done with the hands, but whatever is done by word, deed, or thought, whatever its merit may be. 'We must all stand before the tribunal of Christ, for each
†2 Co 5:10 to receive as he has done in the body',† says the Apostle. That is, he will receive according to what he merited while in the body. Now is the time of meriting, the time of sowing; the future life is the time of receiving and of reaping. Both quality and quantity are important now to the sower, for harvest time brings a return for both.

[2] Augustine, *Psal* 65.20: *non . . . in superficie, in medullis meis . . . diligo te* (Blaise, s.v. *medulla*).

He knows both, to whose eyes all things are naked and open,† †Heb 4:13
just as he orders written to this angel, *I know your works.* † He knows †Rv 3:1
'the commencement of beauty', and is not ignorant of its progress or lack of progress. He knows what is within and what is on the skin,[3] who has both the seven spirits and the seven stars. Hence he had regard for Abel and his offerings by accepting them, while
he had no regard for Cain and his offerings.† To Cain he says, *I* †Gn 4:4–5
know your works, that you have the name of being alive and you are dead. Words used as nouns in conjunction with 'name' have the quality of substantives but are never entirely similar to them.[4] Sometimes they are not such as they are called. And the church at Sardis, on account of 'the commencement of beauty' which seems to be present in certain deeds and perhaps in some persons, is said to be alive while in many it is dead. What is written to the angel refers to the church.

Are we surprised that a dead person is said to be alive? I believe that many have heard how, in the east, the city of Tripoli ignorantly supported one such person for many years, and, not surprisingly, was shocked to discover the fact. Such a person had been ordained a cleric as a child. His uncle, with difficulty, persuaded his mother to allow him to take the boy along to another city to live. After a short time the boy fell sick, and after a few days he died in bed. The funeral was held, and the corpse lay in the middle, washed and shrouded.

The uncle, unable to bear the sight, went out. Thinking rather of the mother's grief than the boy's death, he was consumed by sorrow. An old woman, abandoned rather than accustomed to witchcraft, barely able to extort from him the reason for his great sorrow, persuaded him to hand the boy over to her for a moment, with the promise to return him not only alive but perfectly well. Grief and pain convinced the man to agree to what she promised. Everyone left, and she remained alone with the corpse. No one knows what she said or did, but subsequent events proved that she cut the skin of his arm, and in the little opening she inserted certain written marks. Then she closed the wound.

[3] Persius, *Saturae* 3.30.

[4] Peter Abelard, *Dialectica. I Antipraedicamenta* 92; *III Postpraedicamenta* 134, L. M. Rijk, ed., *Dialectica* (Assen, 1956).

The boy immediately sprang up as if from sleep, and called his uncle. He appeared healthy, and the uncle's tears were turned to joy. A few days later he returned to his mother in Tripoli, and was seen in its church for many years. His appearance, his voice and body, were not changed. He sang with the choir as he had been accustomed to doing, and there was nothing unusual about him except that he never grew, nor did any sign of increasing age appear on him.

At length a cause arose that brought many people to that city from all around, and among them was a certain clergyman. Whether from his knowledge of the sacrilegious art or from a spirit's revelation is not known, but he heard the boy's voice and recognized a deception unnoticed by others. Hearing him in church singing the verse of a responsory during mass, and wonder-struck, he said to the bystanders: 'I hear the voice not of a living man but of one already dead'. He called the boy's relatives together and said, 'The boy's soul is not in him'. All who heard were astounded, but he continued, 'If you agree, I will demonstrate here and now what I am saying'. They agreed, and he set the naked boy on a rug and carefully felt his body in their presence. Under the skin of the arm he felt the little piece of paper which the wicked old woman had inserted. Without delay he opened the skin and took out the paper. Skin and flesh turned immediately to powder, and the bones fell apart from one another in a heap. Thus he showed that this was only a fantasy life that fooled onlookers, and that the boy was dead while he seemed to be alive.

Thus do the demons fool unfortunate souls by making them appear to themselves and to others to be alive even though they are dead in sin. Some hearers may perhaps find it difficult to believe the story, for it seems impossible for a body no longer animated by its spirit to perform its usual activities. It seems impossible that after a soul departs a strange spirit may henceforth animate a dead body. It is impossible for a body to immediately dissolve if it has been animated for so long a time, so that the spirit may depart. But we know that the lives of the fathers contain something similar, and this is the tale.

The evil one envied a religious man who applied himself assiduously to hospitality along with his other pious works. Dreaming up a novel sort of malice, the evil one occupied the corpse of an unfortunate woman who had died without confession and viaticum. Dressed as a man, he entered the monk's cell, and accepted for an annual wage the necessary service of receiving guests. For a while he showed himself diligent, quick, and ready, seeking an opportunity to upset him with the malign sting of carnal desires.

But divine loving-kindness was ahead of his cunning. A holy bishop endowed with a prophetic spirit arrived to visit his parishes. Observing the hired servant at work, he perceived the hidden intent of the evil spirit. In private he anxiously asked his host who he was and where he came from. When the monk responded openly and unsuspectingly, the priest began to ask whether he ever saw him enter the oratory or participate in the divine mysteries. He answered that, when he himself arose for vigils, the man remained asleep outside with the rest of the seculars, but beyond this he had noticed nothing. The bishop called the man, and commanded him by authority of the divine name and of his episcopal office to tell who he was, what he was called, and why he came. But, gnashing his teeth and melting away,† he replied, 'Truly, is what concerns you so well †Ps 112:10
finished—or perhaps so neglected—that you have come to inquire about my affairs, which are none of your business? If you had delayed your prying visit a few days, I would have gotten what I came for'.

But, O great power of the divine name, and episcopal authority, so effective against us! At the bishop's command this creation of diabolical fraud vanished, and the corpse fell into dust and dry bones. The power of malignant spirits to simulate this visible and bodily life is so great—yet only with God's leave—that they craftily try many things, and sometimes they succeed in the measure that God's just judgment permits. With every form of malice they try to bring it about that those reputed by themselves and others to be living in spirit and truth may be condemned as dead before God. May the merciful and gracious Lord† protect us always from this,[5] for he †Ps 86:15
alone truly gives life who lives and reigns without end, true God over all and blessed forever. Amen.

[5] *Verona sacramentary* n. 1282.

Sermon Seventeen

THE LORD COMMANDS BLESSED JOHN to write to the angel of the church at Sardis, *Be watchful, and strengthen what remains.*† Sleep is a powerful image of death, just as awak- †Rv 3:2
ening is of resurrection. We say that the dead are sleeping, and that people rise from the dead as if from sleep. *Be watchful*, he says, be careful, diligent, assiduous. No longer be heedless of your life, nor careless and uninterested in your neighbor's salvation. *Strengthen what remains and is on the point of death.* This may refer to each one's works that are not yet lost, but that possess a certain 'commencement of beauty' because they are not without brightness and value, but which will be speedily condemned from their own development unless they are amended. Or it may refer to the healthy members in the body of the church. They will be quickly corrupted by contact with sick members of the flock unless these are either cured or eliminated.

I do not find your works perfect before my God.† What advantage †Rv 3:2
is there to appear before humans but not to be found before God? Why do you value an empty reputation and not true inner identity? Fortunate the one who stands in the Lord's sight and has no desire for human judgment. Fortunate the one who counts human judgment a small thing† because he knows it is the Lord who judges. †1 Co 4:3

Keep in mind then in what manner you received and heard.† [Rv 3:3] Be a clean animal, ruminating†[a] [Gn 7:2; Lv 11:3] and pondering in your heart†[b] [Lk 2:19] what you received through faith†[c] [Ga 3:14] for faith comes from what is heard.†[d] [Rm 10:17] *And obey*, he says, warning about the future; *and repent*, that is, for the past, for a past fault is not forgiven without a promise to avoid it for the future.

If you are not watchful with regard to care and repentance *I will come to you like a thief, and you will not know at what hour I will come to you.*† [Rv 3:3] Every simile makes a point by comparing two things. The two terms, although dissimilar in other respects, are alike in one aspect. He who loves souls† [Ws 11:26] and is zealous for their salvation says that he is coming *like a thief* to the drowsy and negligent to render them careful and diligent.

The comparison to the thief here in the Apocalypse and in the gospel† [Lk 12:39] does not refer to any kind of injustice or fraud but simply to an unforeseen coming. So great is the Saviour's love for us that he willingly compares himself to base things for our instruction. What the thief takes with him when he hastily disappears the owner loses; so, when the Lord, the avenger, comes, one who has fallen asleep will find in his hands none of the things he has loved. In the commandments in the decalogue and the plagues of Egypt, theft is compared to a hailstorm that destroys everything when it bursts out. Let a wicked servant not say, 'My lord is delayed'.† [Mt 24:48; Lk 12:45] He will come on a day when he does not expect him, and at an hour he does not know.† [Mt 24:50; Lk 12:46] Since we do not know the hour of his coming, let us consider every hour the one. He will come to the watchful and ready, but not like a thief. He will never come unaware upon such a one, and will never find him unaware. One who is constantly aware is always fearful.

Yet you have a few names in Sardis who have not soiled their garments.† [Rv 3:4] In the three earlier letters the Lord commended the church before he spoke of matters to be corrected, perhaps because in those churches good things abounded. But here he finds only a few people with whom he is pleased. Perhaps the name Sardis pertains to them, because modesty leads to 'the commencement of beauty'. The foretaste of the first-fruits is above all in modesty, as the Apostle wrote to the Philippians of the Saviour: 'He will transform the body of our lowliness, made like the body of his glory'.† How seriously †Ph 3:21 does that person sin against his own body who is not afraid, or grief-stricken, or ashamed, to defraud his body of desirable glory and honor for the sake of base pleasure?

Names here means persons of name, not of shame, whose names are written in the book of life.† These *names* are far different from †Ph 4:3; Rv 17:8 the one who has *the name of being alive and* is *dead*.† We can take the †Rv 3:1 limbs of the body to be the garments of the soul. Fortunate is the one who does not corrupt any of these garments with the filth of licentiousness, but who keeps them spotless forever. Fortunate those to whom it has been given to turn aside from past uncleanness, and to propose and promise so for the future, that grace upon grace† may †Jn 1:16 follow. Since their sins have not separated them from the Lord, they are worthy to walk about modestly in uncorrupted bodies clothed in white garments.

They receive names, dignities which they exercise, and the privilege of never henceforth being blotted *out of the book of life*,† †Rv 3:5 the book of divine election. Thus the Lord says to his disciples in the gospel, 'Rejoice and be glad that your names are written in heaven'.† *Whoever conquers* immodesty *will be clothed like them* in the †Lk 10:20 future; this one will have no stain, but wear the whitest garment, shining henceforth with never-fading brightness, just as his name can no more be blotted *out of the book of life*. Meanwhile, a person's name appears to be blotted out when it no longer stands where it has appeared up to now.

Moses, who is rightly acclaimed for the favor he found in God's sight, and who burned with love for the people entrusted to him, was not afraid to ask God to forgive his sin or to blot out his name from the book he had written.† The radiance of white is the sign †Ex 32:32 of modest purity just as the ruddiness of blood signifies a martyr's suffering. When asked to describe her beloved, the bride calls him both radiant and ruddy;† so among the members of his body, the †Sg 5:10 church,† the choir of virgins and the army of martyrs take first place. †Col 1:24 Indeed, they are rightly first, since we are pleased when flower beds contain both roses and lilies.

My sermon must end, since speaking tires me and listening tires you. However, one instance of a name not being blotted out comes to mind. Perhaps it will be of some profit to you.

When the divine loving-kindness laid the original foundations of our Cistercian Order, there was a noble and honorable cleric in the church at Lyons whose name was John.† Struck by a report of so many recruits for this revived observance of blessed Benedict's Rule, he thought it over by himself, and decided to join their number. After a few days, however, another thought came to him, and he changed his intention. He was afraid of judgment by the one who sees in secret because of a violation of his promise, even though it was hidden, and so as satisfaction he undertook the pilgrimage of blessed James, which he faithfully completed. On his return his household and friends received him with great joy. Wearied, as people are, by the journey, he went to his room and gave his limbs rest.[1]

†Jn 1:6

Without delay the Lord Jesus Christ appeared to him in a vision, along with his blessed disciples Peter and James, standing at a distance. Blessed Peter held a book in his hand, and opened it at the Lord's command. When the apostle came to John's name in the book the Lord said, 'Remove it. Remove it. Blot out his name, because he promised to be mine and retreated from his promise'. Then blessed James approached and begged him eagerly, 'Lord, he is my pilgrim. I beseech you not to blot out his name!' The Lord replied, 'One who is mine must be a citizen, not a pilgrim'. The apostle continued begging, 'Most merciful Lord, do not blot out the name of my pilgrim; do not blot it out of your book. I guarantee it, Lord, he will do what he intended'. The Lord said to him, 'When will he do it?' 'Within fifteen days', replied the apostle.

Frightened at these words, John threw himself on the ground. With an outburst of tears he gave wholehearted thanks to his kind guarantor, and said, 'Holy Apostle, I will do it immediately and without question, for you compassionately made the promise for me unasked when I was in such straits'. With these and other words of thanks, promise, and prayer, by God's gift he fell asleep again.

[1] Vergil, *Aeneid* 4.5; 10.217.

Once again he saw the Lord with the two apostles, and again the Lord ordered the book opened. He heard blessed Peter reading in it this verse from the Song of Songs: 'We will make you a golden necklace inlaid with silver'.† Waiting no longer, but anticipating the day set, he joyfully and faithfully fulfilled the promise made for him by the apostle. †Sg 1:11

That you may realize how worthy and believable this revelation is, I would like you to know that this was the John who was first abbot of the well-known monastery of Bonneval, good by grace and in name.[2] He later became bishop of Valentina. His life was worthy of such a calling, and was renowned for merits and miracles. His precious death† shone with many signs of virtue, and his tomb is frequented by those who live nearby. His name is recorded in the Lord's book among the holy bishops. †Ps 116:15

This story instructs attentive listeners, and gives them a warning lest any one of them be neglectful or heedless about fulfilling the purpose he has fixed by wholesome deliberation in his heart, unless something more worthy is offered. We must fulfill our resolutions before the Lord our God. The true lover of souls is zealous for their salvation, and charges with inconstancy and ingratitude those who are not afraid of drawing back from their better decisions. He is not limited to what is visible, so as to regard as of little importance those secrets decisions that people keep hidden.

Do not be surprised when the Israelites were imposed upon because they returned in heart to Egypt if this man John deserved to be convicted because, after going in heart to the Cistercians, he turned back. For a transgression of his secret intention, the one who was aware of his secrets ordered that his name be wiped out of his book and from the list of those who belong to him. Nevertheless, let the faithful consider how devotedly the saints supported him; let them as trustingly rest on the holy prayers of those who lovingly support those devoted to them, and who effectively intercede for them.

[2] *gratia simul et nomine Bonaevallis*. The name means 'good valley'. The first antiphon on the feast of Saintt Benedict includes the words, *gratia Benedictus et nomine*, 'blessed by grace and in name'.

The Lord says, *I will confess his name before my Father and before*
†Rv 3:5 *his angels*,† that is, among those belonging to me. As belonging to
me, he too is given the kingdom by the God and Father; he will
reign forever with me among the saints and angels. Woe to those
blaspheming for any reason the name of the Lord in their hearts,
or faithlessly complaining of his judgments, which are sometimes
secret but never unjust. Woe to those falling away in persecution
and denying the name of him who will never deny them in the
†Mt 10:33; Lk 12:9 presence of God the Father and his angels.† Woe to those who
†Tt 1:16 deny in their actions what they profess by their words.[3]† Woe to
those, not only by whom, but those through whom the name of
the Lord is blasphemed. Woe to those wretches ruled and dominated
by every iniquity!

†Rv 3:5 For *whoever conquers*,† whoever is strong in faith and not in
himself, whoever stands firm, not consenting to any wrong but
†Lk 3:8 pursuing fruits worthy of repentance,† rises stronger after a fall. The
One who allows his own name to be confessed, not only in word
†1 Jn 3:18 but in action and truth,† will confess this name in the time to come.
Let him who is a servant worthy of his Lord confess the Lord. Let
him who has feared the Lord confess the Lord, for it is written:
†Ml 1:6 'If I am the Lord, where is fear of me?'† What a great exchange
is promised to a confessor like this, for he not only deigned to say
but ordered written that he *will confess* him *before* his *Father and his*
†1 Ch 29:11 *angels.* Yours is the power, yours the victory, Lord,† as he says: 'Take
†Jn 16:33 courage, I have overcome the world'.† You will graciously confess
him who fought by your grace and won by your strength. You will
graciously honor, repay, and crown this victor.

†Rv 3:5 *I will confess*,† he says, and I add, 'Come, blessed of my Father!'*
*Mt 25:34 †Mt 25:35 *I will confess* because I was the one hungry to whom they gave food,†
I was the one with other needs to whom they ministered. I will not
only confess them all in common, but each one individually, and by
name. I will mention and repay each one of their merits, for their
merits are nothing else but my gifts.

Joyful is your promise, and happy this hope of your victors,
Lord. And rightly does this letter end: *Let anyone who has an ear hear*

[3] Bernard of Clairvaux, *Sermones super Cantica Canticorum* 24.8; SBOp 1:161.

what the Spirit says to the churches.† For the Spirit speaks of spiritual things; the Spirit of truth speaks the truth. He speaks to each, he speaks to many, he speaks to the churches of our Lord Jesus Christ, who with the Father and the same Holy Spirit is one God over all and blessed forever. Amen. †Rv 3:6

Sermon Eighteen

And to the angel of the church at Philadelphia write: These are the words of the holy and true one, who has the key of David, who opens and no one closes, who closes and no one opens. I know your works. Behold, I put before you an open door that no one is able to shut. You have little power, but you have kept my word and have not denied my name. Behold, I will give those of the synagogue of Satan into your power, those who say they are Jews and are not, but are lying. Behold, I will make them come and bow down before your feet, and they will know that I have loved you because you have kept my word of patient endurance. And I will keep you from the hour of trial that is going to come over the whole world, to try the earth's inhabitants. Behold, I come quickly. Hold on to what you have, that no one can seize your crown. Whoever conquers I will make a column in the temple of my God, and he shall nevermore depart from it. And I shall write on him the name of my God and the name of the city of my God, the new Jerusalem that comes down out of heaven from my God, and my own new name. Let anyone who has an ear hear what the Spirit is saying to the churches.†

†Rv 3:7–13

AND TO THE ANGEL OF THE CHURCH *at Philadelphia write.*† Philadelphia takes its name from love of a brother, we are told.[1] Nothing is more true than that the love of a brother calls the church into being, and nothing more befits a society than love causing brothers to dwell in unity.† This is love of a brother, love of any neighbor whatsoever—but we are especially to love that one neighbor who took pity on the man wounded and left half dead by robbers.† That love with which he loves our souls* binds them like glue with threats and promises; it joins them solidly with nails and ties of every kind.

†Rv 3:7
†Ps 133:1
†Lk 10:30
*Ws 11:26

The lower border of the priest's vestment, the chasuble, which gets its name from the 'casual' and capricious way it flows round about, represents the fullness and inclusiveness of a love that embraces every neighbor without any exceptions. The upper border surrounds only the head and refers to him who is our head, to whom the whole body is bound by its ligaments and joints.† Doubtless as his love for us comes first so is it better, more powerful, stronger, and more effective, not only in calling, justifying, and ennobling those he loves, but also in calling them together and uniting them in justice and nobility.

†Col 2:19; Ep 4:16

Fortunate is the angel of this church that the love of this brother calls together to become a single communion of all. Thus in him and through him they are united not only to him but with one another. Some people[2] wonder whether, since Peter seemed to love the Lord more, and John was loved more by him, one of these two states is more desirable, whether one is to be preferred to the other? Perhaps loving should be judged greater in merit, and being loved greater in recompense. But this is an external difference, and does not signify the heart's inner love. Peter gave greater evidence of love for the Lord, but the Lord showed greater evidence of love for John than for Peter. Moreover, as he who is first to love everyone loves those who love him, so that those who watch for him early in the morning† find one who loves them there already, so also, although

†Pr 8:17 Vulgate

[1] Venerable Bede, *Explanatio Apocalypsis* 1.3; PL 93:140B.

[2] Augustine, *In Iohannis Evangelium tractus* 124.4; CCh 36:683. Bruno of Segni, *Commentaria in Iohannem* 3.21; PL 165:601B.

there may be an increase or decrease in human love, since the Lord's love is predestined to remain steady and eternal it seems incredible that a person loving him less would be loved by him more.

Now let us listen to what the Lord orders written to the angel of this church: *These are the words of the holy and true one.*† The Lord mentions his own holiness, his own truthfulness, and does so graciously for our edification. Let no one doubt what the holy and true one says; let no one hesitate to submit to his holiness and to his truth. †Rv 3:7

These are the words of the holy and true one, with whom there is no deceit and no iniquity.† Woe to you, ancient serpent, woe to you, evil Satan, you liar from the beginning,† who came in serpent guise. Woe to you, woman, whom he wickedly and mendaciously persuaded, as if your Creator was a wicked liar in his prohibition of one tree. [Satan] was a liar when he said that death would not follow, wicked and envious when he claimed that you would gain a great advantage from this food. And to you, Adam, woe to you as well, for you were enticed by the woman who had been led astray, to obey her voice rather than God's. Hence from then on she appeared to be inextricably wrapped in the sinews of Leviathan's testicles,† so that a judge would have to be reckoned a liar if he did not punish, and wicked if he did not spare. But wisdom conquered malice, and there was no counsel against the Lord.† †2 Ch 19:7 †Jn 8:44 †Jb 40:12 Vulgate †Pr 21:30

In the Saviour's death and resurrection mercy and truth fortunately met.† People die in order that the truth of the Lord may remain forever,† and nevertheless his mercy may be established over those rising to life. *The holy and true one*† speaks; he speaks and he teaches, because truth pertains to faith, and holiness to character and actions. *The holy and true one* speaks to free his own from evil lips and a lying tongue,† lest error steal their faith, or some suggestion attract or impel them to sin. He is the holy one in his divinity, along with the Father and the Holy Spirit, and the angelic multitudes endlessly call out, 'Holy, holy, holy, Lord God of hosts!'[3] He is also the holy one in his human nature, as Gabriel said to Mary, 'The holy one to be born of you will be called Son of God'.† †Ps 85:10 †Ps 117:2 †Rv 3:7 †Ps 120:2 †Lk 1:35

[3] Canon of the Roman Mass. Cf. Is 6:3, Rv 4:8.

†Rv 3:7 *These are the words of the true one*,† true in both natures, true God and a true human being. He is true God, truly born of the Father, not made or fashioned as a certain heretic[4] once blasphemously claimed. In his sacrilegious voice he burst out, 'I do not envy Christ made God; I too can become God just as he did'. He is truly a human being as well, truly conceived, truly borne in a virginal womb, truly fed at her virginal breasts, truly living among human beings; in truth suffering, dying, and rising; carried up into
†Ac 1:9 heaven, out of the sight of the apostles;† and to come at last in judgment, according to the promise of the angels present at his
†Ac 1:11 ascension.† He was not found a small child* as if he had fallen into a
*See pp. 163–64 above strange body different from ours, with everything afterwards done and spoken being false. He is a true human being, true head of
†Ep 5:23 the church,† one Lord with the church, one Christ. He is true and speaks the truth in all his mysteries and teachings. Is it any wonder, my brothers, that a false and lying doctrine prefers appearance, and denies the power of holiness and piety? Whatever heretics may represent or misrepresent, there is no true holiness or doctrine among them.

Let us now say something about our own little foxes of these
†Sg 2:15 times, who continue to wickedly destroy the vineyard† of the Lord and of his bride. We know of two arch-heretics sunk in malice,
†2 Tm 2:17 whose talk spread like a canker† and led to great impiety. They were caught a few years ago around Toulouse, in a town called Valence, by a zealous band of the faithful, and were brought before our venerable father and lord Henry, bishop of Alba, then legate of the Apostolic See in Aquitaine. They stood there while the bishop delivered a sermon against their heresy to a great multitude from
†Ac 2:4 every walk of life, as the Holy Spirit gave him the ability.†

By the Lord's inspiration the arch-heretics were struck with sorrow at the gracious words coming from his mouth. Immediately, in the hearing of all, they confessed with tears the secret blasphemies and cursed abominations of this heresy. In their confession they made public certain extremely harmful teachings that they reveal only to the perfect, and hide from their patrons and newly initiated

[4] Unidentified.

followers. The first is that Lucifer himself, who from the beginning dared to proudly oppose God, was the creator of all things, visible and corporeal, in heaven and on earth. The second is that whatever is read about Christ is altogether false and fictitious, for a body created by the devil could not be united to the Lord's Word. So this corrupt and worst of all heresies undermines the truth of the Old Testament in its first teaching, and of the New Testament in its second.

Passing to moral corruption, they condemn marriage in order to use every woman indifferently. Thus a brother need not keep away from his sister, nor a son from his mother, nor anyone from any woman whatsoever. And because they assert that all flesh is the devil's work, they teach that children conceived and brought forth must be destroyed by maternal parricides—would that this had been done to all such demented preachers by their own mothers! This foul and evil sect turns aside from no disgrace, no outrage, yet they are not afraid to promise their followers expiation for their sins while condemning the chaste and the innocent. They alone know the truth hidden from the rest!

They altogether deny the holy Eucharist and infant baptism—this they claim is of no profit to adults either, until they receive the imposition of hands from their own elect. They disparage almsgiving unless shown to their own people, and claim that the devil's work must on no account be encouraged before their own forgiveness. They preach that penances for the dying and prayers for the dead were invented by the clergy for base gain.

We must not keep silent concerning the aforesaid former arch-heretics who confessed all these things publicly, accusing themselves as severely as they could, and the countless souls they destroyed. They gave sure testimony to the truth of their confession and conversion by persevering penance and amendment. Six or seven years have already gone by since they cried out these things. They now live religiously in the city of Toulouse, and bring forth fruits worthy of repentance† among the Canons Regular. †Lk 3:8

The holy and true one says of himself in the Apocalypse, *who has the key of David, who opens and no one closes, who closes and*

†Rv 3:7 *no one opens.*† The holy commentators[5] refer this key and this
opening to the power of granting and denying an understanding
of scripture. After the resurrection Christ opened the minds of
his disciples to understand scripture with this key. Rightly does
the one who understands himself better than all teachers say, 'You
†Ps 50:8 Vulgate have shown me the unknown and hidden things of your wisdom'.†
†Ps 50:8 Vulgate He prefaced this with, 'Behold you have loved truth',† to make
himself known as *the holy and true one.* As truth manifests the
true one, so does the love of truth prove that he is the holy
one. For the hidden things of wisdom to be truly and effectively
shown us, and for knowledge of the Saviour to be present equally
with good zeal, truth must illumine reason and love enkindle
the will.

Our forebears seem to have taken the key of David, which
opens not so much to him as to others, and his psalms, which
are filled with sacred mysteries, as the words of him whom the
One who truly knows and sanctifies hearts found to be 'after his
†Ac 13:22 own heart'.† And perhaps the Lord kept silent about the other
prophets, and merely recalls that he has the key of *David*, to specially
commend a less familiar book of Scripture. From this book he
taught that the Lord called him in the Spirit; not from that psalm
alone, but from other words of David's as well, 'I have said, you are
†Ps 82:6 gods',† he refuted his adversaries; at the hour of death he used the
beginning of the twenty-first psalm, 'O God, my God, why have
†Ps 22:1 you abandoned me?'†

†Rv 3:7 Another *key of David*† can, I think, be understood as the means
by which he opened the gate of mercy, and his soul to repentance.
†Qo 4:12 He mercifully forgave David the threefold cord† of shame, outrage,
and sacrilege. He could not be excused from sacrilege because he
killed by the sword of the sons of Amon one who faithfully trusted
†2 S 11:14 him, and he did this by the letter he gave him,† a fact the prophet
†2 S 12:9 later charged him with.†

[5] Pseudo-Alcuin, *Commentariorum in Apocalypsin libri quinque* 2.1; PL 100:1111C. Berengaudus, *Exposition super septem visiones libri Apocalypsis* 1.3; PL 17:869B. Richard of Saint Victor, *In Apocalypsim Iohannis libri septem* 1.10; PL 196:733BC.

Would that none of us, beloved, may henceforth sin in hope, trusting foolishly in a power he lacks and a key he does not possess, so as to think he can turn to repentance whenever he wishes. No one can open when the one who has the key has shut against him, whom the Lord disregards in his fearful judgment. No one can correct such a person, not another human being, not even himself. He not only has the key, he is the key. With this key—the name *David* means 'strong hand'[6]—he penetrated the bounds of hell, and with might he led forth the prisoners out of prison, and those sitting in darkness and shadow of death.† He opened and no one closed, †Is 42:7; Lk 1:79
no one resisted him, and the greatest of the wicked rulers scarcely believed he would escape. Woe to the wretches against whom it is closed in such a way that henceforth no one will be strong enough to open, absorbed as they will be in an abyss of damnation and complete hopelessness.

With the *key of David*† he opened to the thief the beautiful †Rv 3:7
paradise closed by the first man, and he presented to those rejoicing in the heavenly kingdom the glory of victorious flesh. From that time on the heavens stand open for those striving for eternal glory; they will not be closed until all good is accomplished and all good people are present. And now beloved, I beseech you, let us wholeheartedly run the race lest—may God avert it!—at the end we find the gate closed. None can be more wretched than those for whom, when he closes, there will no longer be anyone to open.

He has the key, and the opening and closing can be taken in four ways. He opens to understanding by manifesting to some the unknown and hidden things of wisdom;† he closes to others over †Ps 50:8 Vulgate
whose hearts he draws a veil. He opens to repentance by answering those who ask how many are their iniquities and their sins, and by showing them their evil deeds; he closes to those who harden their hearts against the voice of reproach and, like whitened sepulchers,† †Mt 23:27
have only foulness inside because they prefer an empty external comeliness. They rejoice when they do evil;† none of them says †Pr 2:14
what is good; no one stops and asks, 'What have I done?'† †Jr 8:6

[6]Jerome, *Liber interpretationis hebraicorum nominum* 35.11; CCh 72:103.

In another sense, he opens to those whose conversation is in
†Ph 3:20 heaven,† who seek what they have set their minds on, the things
†Col 3:1–2 that are above and not on earth,† who by thought and desire spend
†Sg 2:14 their lives in clefts of the rock and cavities in the wall.† He closes to
†Dt 28:23 those for whom the heavens are bronze and the earth iron,† so that
†Jos 15:19 they deserve no share in either the upper or the lower springs,† nor the joy that comes from the fruitfulness of good works. Yet most fortunately he will open the gate of the kingdom, the gate of life, the gate of eternal blessedness, to those to whom he says, 'Come, you blessed of my Father, receive the kingdom prepared for you
†Mt 25:34 from the foundation of the world'.† To such as these no one closes, no angel, no human being; and no person whatever will reproach
†Ac 10:15, 28; 11:9 Vulgate them for their former sins or call common† what God has sanctified.

'On that day', the Lord says to his church, 'you shall not be put to
†Zp 3:11 shame for all the ways by which you have transgressed against me',† however many, however hateful, however worthy of condemnation they may be. The woes of the damned are many and immense—more than I can say, than I can imagine, than I can guess at or fear! The sentence of condemnation excludes those who hear, 'Go, you
†Mt 25:41 accursed, into eternal fire',† from every good thing and every good person; it includes them with the fire that is not quenched and the
†Is 66:24 worms that do not die,† with total darkness, unbreakable chains, and inconsolable torments, so that no one can open for them anymore and no one can lead them out.

Listen now to what the true and holy one says to the angel of
†Rv 3:8 Philadelphia: *I know your works. Behold, I put before you an open door.*† This opening refers to the understanding, as we said before, because it opens the hearts of those who hear it to this leader who has the key. It is greatly desirable for the angel of Philadelphia and those associated with him that Christ's love bring them together as one[7] so that they may no longer fear but may love Christ their God.

Indeed it is as desirable as it is necessary that one who desires remember that he who has the key and holds open the door considers works more meritorious than any studies. *I know your*

[7] Antiphon at the washing of the feet on Holy Thursday. *Graduale Romanum* (Solesmes, 1979) 168.

works. I consider them, I approve them. I am pleased with them, and because of them I am putting before you an open door, and not only for you to enter, but that you can bring in your hearers as well. *I put before you an open door,* that the hearts of many may be laid bare before you, that their hearts may be open and receptive when they hear your voice. Nothing can close this door, not their own stubbornness, not tyrannical persecution, not heretical seduction, not any diabolical temptation.

You have little power, but you have kept my word and have not denied
my name.† The Saviour's kindness, looking for opportunities to repay †Rv 3:8
his followers so that the merits of the weak and the works of the little ones may be more acceptable to himself, takes their *little power* into consideration. The small and the weak-souled have much to bear, and they trust not in their own good spirits but in divine assistance.

But why is it, then, that the giver of the talents is said to distribute them according to each one's power? We read in the gospel: 'To one was given five talents, to another two, to another
one, to each according to his own power'.† What is this 'own power' †Mt 25:15
according to which something is given to each? Or does it come from the talents? Whether inborn or acquired, it is not the response to the Apostle's question, 'What do you have that you have not
received?'† Truly the power does not come from the talents, but †1 Co 4:7
grace is added to grace, and this is the meaning of the gospel, 'To each according to his own power'. Therefore one possessing *little power* by nature is more acceptable when his great-souled patience is tested in affliction.

Behold, I will give those of the synagogue of Satan into your power.† †Rv 3:9
'Our struggle is not against flesh and blood but against the spiritual
forces of evil'.† Most unfortunate are those who rejoice over the fall †Ep 6:12
of their adversaries, as from the region of the blessed there is joy over
their conversion among the angels of God,† not only the earthborn †Lk 15:10
preachers and ministers, but those who continually see the Father's
face in heaven.† The adversary circles, seeking someone to devour,* †Mt 18:10 *1 P 5:8
but the hook pierces his jaw,† and God compels him to vomit up †Jb 40:26
the riches he has gathered, and draws them out of his belly.† †Jb 20:15

Who say they are Jews and are not,† because they deny by their †Rv 3:9
actions the Lord they confess by their words.† They are not Jews who †Tt 1:16

†Jn 19:15 once cried out in their ancestors, 'We have no king but Caesar!'† Upon them the terrible curse remains, 'His blood be on us and †Mt 27:25 on our children!'† Thus they have been satisfied with children, and †Ps 17:14 they have left the rest to their little ones.†

The two meanings of 'confession' find expression in the psalm †Ps 75:1 verse, 'We will confess to you, O God, we will confess to you!'† Both are necessary for Jews who are true and truthful, who are †Rv 3:9 really Jews, not *those who say they are Jews but are lying.*† The greatest number of the elect are found in the rank of confessors. Judah means 'confession';[8] a Jew is a confessor.[9] The former confession pertains to what is our own, the latter to what is divine. The former concerns our sins, which are washed away by humble confession, as is said: †Is 43:26 'Tell your iniquities yourself, that you may be justified'.† The latter concerns the divine benefits we must recall in devout confession, that his mercies may confess the Lord, and his wonderful works †Ps 107:8 among humankind.†

Impenitence and ingratitude stand opposed to this twofold confession. Neither spring feeds it, as Caleb's daughter complained, †Jos 15:19 Vulgate having received a southern and dry land.† The former confession is made in fear and sorrow, the latter in desire and rejoicing; the former in a spirit of compunction, and the latter in devout thanks and praise.[10]

The man who prayed, 'O God, may I know myself, may I know you!'[11] wanted to be given from heaven ground for both confessions. Knowledge of ourselves makes us humble and reverent; knowledge of God makes us prompt in obedience and faithful in love. A soul unaware of itself goes after the flocks of its companions, not only associating with irrational beasts through wanton craving, but is later, when it has put aside reason, reckoned one of them. Neglecting its own reflections, it goes out in love of its own will. †2 Tm 3:2 People of this sort are lovers of themselves† simply because they do not know themselves. The more the elect love God, the more aware

[8]Jerome, *Liber interpretationis hebraicorum nominum* 7.19; CCh 72:67.

[9]Ibid., 75.22; CCh 72:154.

[10]Bernard of Clairvaux, *Sermones in psalmum 'Qui habitat'* 14.3; SBOp 4:16–17.

[11]Augustine, *Soliloquia* 2.1; PL 32:885.

they are. The more they set their minds only on what is lovable, the more truly they discover and understand in themselves things to hate. The Lord promises that he will give this angel the members of that synagogue because they are being converted from error and vice through his grace and mercy.

Behold, I will make them come and bow down before your feet.† When he said above, *I will give into your power,* he means that he will pour grace into their hearts in order that, by his inspiration, he may *make them come*, and, progressing by free will, they may go from strength to strength,† *and bow down before your feet.* They will prostrate themselves in humble penance, and from then on live in justice and patience. One must first depart from evil,† and then diligently do the works of righteousness, ready to bear whatever affliction may come from it. This 'bowing down' refers to reverence and humility, and not to the worship we are to show to God alone, of which it is said, 'Bow down before the Lord our God and serve only him'.†

†Rv 3:9
†Ps 84:7
†Ps 37:27
†Mt 4:10 (Dt 6:13)

And they will know that I have loved you because you have kept my word of patient endurance.† There are two ways to understand this: *they will know that I have loved you* because of the *word of patient endurance* you have kept, or, the way *they will know that I have loved you* is because you have kept my word of patient endurance.

†Rv 3:9–10

And I will keep you.† Love precedes and follows patience; he grants patience to his beloved as a gift when they request it, and he rewards them for it. *You have kept my word of patient endurance* is equivalent to the earlier verse, *you have kept my word and have not denied my name.* Through patience endurance a man's teaching is recognized,† and he possesses his soul.*

†Rv 3:10
†Pr 19:11
*Lk 21:19

And I will keep you from the hour of trial that is going to come over the whole world.† You give grace upon grace,* and reward your own gifts in us, good Jesus. At the end you crown your own gifts, because we have nothing except what we have received from you. The devotion of your own people offers you what your generosity bestows on them, as it is written, 'My beloved is mine and I am his'.†

†Rv 3:10
*Jn 1:16
†Sg 2:16

After Domitian's death, when blessed John, as we know, was recalled from exile, the church enjoyed a brief time of peace. After

the blessed evangelist's death, however, a more severe persecution
†Rv 3:11 arose, the one he says will come *to try the earth's inhabitants.*†

Commentators[12] say that, as in the following visions the sixth place contains material distributed throughout the other seven, so here in the letter written to the sixth angel the last and greatest of antichrist's persecutions is spoken of. Yet the preservation promised to this angel can less easily be understood in the hour of this trial, unless perhaps we refer what is said concerning him to the faithful of that time.

†Rv 3:11 *Behold, I come quickly.*† No trial is worse than one that come,
from delay of a promise or an extended period of waiting. Hope
†Pr 13:12 deferred afflicts the soul.† The greater and more desirable is the
thing hoped for, the greater is the affliction.

I can recall hearing our blessed father counseling clerics about
conversion.[13] He was well on his discourse when he added something like the following: I know what keeps you back, what makes
you hesitate. Were I to tell you to abandon these empty and pernicious things of sense and immediately take up eternal goods, to
embrace heavenly happiness without delay, not one of you, if not
clearly mad, if he firmly believed, would refuse your acquiescence.
But your faces fall, your hearts fill with fear, and your desires cool,
when I ask you to abandon what is earthly and wait for what is
heavenly. O that you would fall asleep among the middling clerics
and your soul would sing of your beloved, 'His left hand is under
my head' where riches and glory are, 'and his right hand' which
†Pr 3:16 contains length of days,† 'would embrace me'.* O if it would be
*Sg 26:6, 8:3 granted us not to fall between these two, but to sleep, as the psalmist
†Ps 4:8 says, and rest, singularly settled in hope†—or rather to rejoice in
hope, for when the time comes to experience the salvation that
now you desire with the hope you have acquired, you will see that
†Pr 10:28 the expectation of the righteous is a joy.†

Delay pains us, but the pain that comes from love has a joy of its own. And besides, when we consider eternity, how long is this

[12] Venerable Bede, *Explanatio Apocalypsis* 1.3; PL 93:141B. *Glossa ordinaria*, Ap 3; PL 114:716D.

[13] Not found in any extant edition of Bernard of Clairvaux's works.

delay? The Apostle did not err when he said, 'Our momentary and slight affliction is working in us an eternal weight of glory, sublime beyond all measure'.† †2 Co 4:17

The Lord's words are apropos here: *Behold, I come quickly. Hold on to what you have, that no one can seize your crown.*† Hold on to the pledge of the kingdom, for, by keeping always before you and faithfully displaying what has been commended, you will attain an everlasting crown. *That no one can seize* means for all to be certain that anyone can be excluded on his own deserts. Nevertheless as the wedding banquet will be filled,† and the Lord's house will be filled with glory, so will it be filled with people. The number of the elect will be filled, and nothing will be lacking from the fullness of the rewards. The individual crowns will complete the universal crown made by the great and unique Artist. *Hold on to what you have,* hold on to the first fruits, hold on to the hundred-fold of this interim age, that you may afterwards receive the fullness of eternal life. †Rv 3:11 †Lk 14:23

Whoever conquers I will make a column.† This exhortation and promise does not seem to refer to the common victory of all the elect. Just as the columns of a temple receive greater notice than the rest of the stones, so in the afflictions of that time the victors are assured of something more than the rest. For not all will be columns, just as here not all are. Would that here merits could be taken into consideration in making and raising up columns in the way it will happen there! A person must acquire here what can be repaid there. Firmness and exactness, uprightness and balance are required for columns. In them an equal number of virtues is recommended, strength and prudence, justice and temperance. Its base is fear of the Lord, its capital the expectation of everlasting life. One who clings firmly to these neither falls nor wavers. †Rv 3:12

Now we must seek and investigate the makeup of the heavenly columns which the matchless Craftsman promises to make for his temple. It may be enough to mention that in the temple the supreme Architect is building from living stones he has some special glory to show to the columns. All the stars light up the sky, yet among them star differs from star in glory.† †1 Co 15:41

And he shall nevermore depart from it.† Those living in the temple of the Lord will be embraced by the greatest joy, the certainty that †Rv 3:12

they will dwell there forever. Meanwhile, although we may go to the
†Ps 43:4 Lord's altar† many times, may go about it, and offer in his sanctuary
†Ps 27:6 a sacrifice of jubilation,† and although we cannot yet stay in it, still it
†Heb 13:14 is that lasting city that we are looking for.† There is silence in heaven
†Rv 8:1 *Ps 21:3 for about half an hour,† and one who enters its blessed sweetness*
†Jb 4:12 Vulgate perceives the veins of the divine whisper.†

†Rv 3:12 *And I shall write on him the name of my God.*† Just as Isaiah began
†Is 11:2 his list of the Holy Spirit's gifts from the greater ones,† so here these
names are inscribed in an order different from the way we now
perceive them and invoke them upon ourselves. The Lord's new
name is Jesus, and the bride in the Song says of it, 'Your name is
†Sg 1:3 oil poured out'.† It is a new name because it belongs to the new
†Jr 14:9 Vulgate mystery of his incarnation. This name is called upon† any of the
elect when he is absolved and cleansed from all sin by its power in
baptism, or confession and penance. He is called Jesus because he
†Mt 1:21 saves his people from their sins.†

†Ps 48:8 *The name of the city* of the Lord of hosts,† the new city *that comes*
†Rv 3:12 *down out of heaven*† by emulation and conformation, is invoked upon
him. And all the while he perseveres faithfully in communion with
holy church by pursuing sanctity as a citizen with the saints and a
†Ep 2:19 member of the household of God.† The name of God the Father is
invoked when [Christ] receives the spirit of adoption in which he
†Rm 8:15 too cries out, 'Abba, Father'.† God's only begotten son has given
†Jn 1:12 to those who receive him power to become children of God† that
†Rm 8:29 he may be the firstborn among many brothers.† Moreover these
names will then appear clearly written on the elect, making known
certainly and clearly the efficacy of the merits and the reward of
those shining gloriously in God's temple, persevering in happiness
†Dn 12:3 forever and ever.† These names will remain forever, never to be
effaced or blotted out.

Commentators[14] on this book refer the column and the names to the present state of the church. The Saviour makes those victorious in the trial to be columns in God's temple for, while others

[14] Pseudo-Alcuin, *Commentariorum in Apocalypsin libri quinque* 2.3; PL 100:1112C. Berengaudus, *Exposition super septem visiones libri Apocalypsis* 1.3; PL 17:870C. Haymo of Auxerre, *Expositionis in Apocalypsin Beati Iohannis libri septem* 1.3; PL 117:992B. Anselm of Laon, *Enarrationes in Apocalypsim* 3; PL 162:1514D.

become weak and succumb, he stands firm. Although he does not make others fall, he tolerates this, and keeps his own counsel. He uses his own resources, and even uses well the evils of others.

And he shall not depart,† that is, he will not hear the dogs outside,* †Rv 3:12
nor be thrown on the dungheap like salt that has lost its savor and *Rv 22:15
is good for nothing.† *And I shall write on him the name of my God*, as †Lk 14:35; Mt 5:13
Moses was promised that he would become a god to Pharaoh.† *And* †Ex 7:1
the name of the city, the new Jerusalem. Not just the church, but also the soul made perfect by many virtues and contemplation of true peace, deserves to be called the devout city Jerusalem. *That comes down out of heaven,* having received there a new comeliness from imitation of the angels, ascending with them by a longing for happiness and
warm devotion, but also descending† by the practice of power, and †Gn 28:12; Jn 1:51
by a way of life made perfect.

From my God,† he says, from the Father of lights, from whom †Rv 3:12
every best and perfect gift comes down.† *And my own new name.* †Jm 1:17
I was once promised through the prophet that I would call my
servants by another name,† so that Christians receive their name †Is 62:2
from Christ.† To write upon the elect names like these is to cause †Ac 11:26
them to show forth certain signs in their actions and way of life, and to give clear proof that they are true Christians, true imitators of the citizens on high, true children of God the Father. One who is called a Christian and who claims to abide in Christ ought to
walk just as he walked.† The city coming down form heaven ought †1 Jn 2:6
to live angelically, ought to render angelic obedience, and maintain angelic celibacy. Children of God ought to seek the glory of the Father in and through everything, as it is written: 'If I am a father,
where is my honor?'† †Ml 1:6

Let anyone who has ears hear what the Spirit is saying to the churches.† †Rv 3:13
The Spirit speaks of spiritual things to those he gathers into himself by his gift and his work. May his inspiration make us sharers with them, and may our Lord Jesus Christ grant it, who with the Father and the same Spirit is one God, blessed over all forever. Amen.

Sermon Nineteen

And to the angel of the church at Laodicea write: These are the words of the Amen, the faithful and true witness, who is the beginning of God's creation. I know your works, that you are neither cold nor hot. Would that you were cold or hot. But because you are lukewarm, and neither cold nor hot, I will begin to vomit you out of my mouth. You say, I am rich, and well-provided for, and need nothing, and you do not know that you are wretched and miserable, poor, blind, and naked. And so I urge you to buy from me gold refined by fire, that you may become rich; and may put on white garments, that the shame of your nakedness may not be seen; and anoint your eyes with ointment that you may see. Those I love I reprove and chastise. Therefore be zealous and repent.† †Rv 3:14–19

AND TO THE ANGEL OF THE CHURCH *at Laodicea write.*† We read two explanations of this name. Laodicea can mean 'vomit' or 'a lovable people'.[1] These not only differ from †Rv 3:14 one another, but seem to be opposed if given to the same church, though not if given to the same people. Although if we take into

[1] Jerome, *Liber interpretationis hebraicorum nominum* 80.23; CCh 72:160.

account the line near the end of the letter, *those I love I reprove and chastise,*† we can perhaps take it that the warning about vomiting proceeds from love rather than from indignation.[2] The Lord said to Peter, who was stubbornly reluctant, 'If I do not wash you, you will have no share with me'.† What could be more dreadful for an intensely loving disciple than to have no share with the Lord? And what could be more grievous for 'a lovable people' than to be vomited out of his mouth? Fortunate is the one whom the whale that has swallowed him vomits up at the Lord's command;† exceedingly unfortunate is the one whom Christ vomits out of the bowels of his mercy.

†Rv 3:19
†Jn 13:8
†Jon 2:10

These are the words of the Amen, the faithful and true witness.† Amen, a Hebrew verb or adverb significative of truth,[3] is rightly given to the one who is the way, the truth, and the life.† We can take it not only as the Lord's name, but adverbially, because the faithful witness says these things *amen*, that is, with absolute truthfulness—as in the gospel, 'Amen, I say to you'.† He is indeed the faithful and true witness who always speaks faithfully and truly, never testifying out of ignorance. Let us avoid conjectures, my brothers, let us shun the serious vice of asserting incorrectly whatever is uncertain, not only referring to what is past and present, but especially to future contingencies.

†Rv 3:14
†Jn 14:6
†Mt 6:2, and often

One person accepts slight evidence, and affirms as certain doubtful things he receives from others or about others, adding and exaggerating as he passes them along. Rumor, swiftest of evils, gathers strength as she goes.[4] The faithful witness testifies to what he has seen and heard, what he sees done or not done by another, what he hears said by another. Note carefully that I did not say 'about' another but 'by' another. Of course, if there are faults they ought not to be covered over. At an opportune time they ought to be brought to the attention of the one whose job it is to reprove and punish. But some more simple souls want to include what another tells them about a brother, along with what they have actually seen

[2] Bernard of Clairvaux, *Sermones de diversis* 5.4; PL 183:555C.

[3] Jerome, *Liber interpretationis hebraicorum nominum* 60.14, 80.10; CCh 72:134, 159.

[4] Vergil, *Aeneid* 4.174–175.

and heard, in their accusation of him. Let us be the more afraid, beloved, of sinning against that witness before whose judgment seat we must all stand;† it is a fearful thing to fall into his hands.* The common proverb says that the forest has ears and the field has eyes.[5] 'The ear of jealousy hears all things',† and everything is naked and open† to the one who says through the prophet, 'I am the judge and the witness'.†

†Rm 14:10 *Heb 10:31 †Ws 1:10 †Heb 4:13 †Jr 29:23 Vulgate

He is *the faithful and true witness*† who has spoken faithfully in this world what he heard from the Father† and saw with the Father. He has spoken faithfully for our own good; he has spoken truly, mixing no falsehood with his warnings, threats, and promises. And so certain of the saints have not been afraid to say in confrontation with heretics that the Lord threatened the wicked with eternal torments not because he was going to afflict some of them with them, but in order to frighten them away from their evil deeds by so serious a threat. 'If therefore he threatened something worse than he was going to do in order to frighten them away from their vices, we must also believe that he has promised more than he is going to give in order to incite us to the virtues'.[6]

†Rv 3:14 †Jn 15:15

But the Almighty has absolutely no need of lies. He declares nothing false or doubtful, for he has the power to do anything whenever he wills.† Perseverance in good, and sinful impenitence, may at different times change or relax the judgment he makes, from either direction. *The faithful and true witness*† has promised this as well. A promise that can be changed does not show his lack of foreknowledge, but shows that a change in their deserts is answered by a change in him, without changing his plan.

†Ws 12:18 †Rv 3:14

Woe, woe to those wretches who do not care, or who refuse to be faithful, to his great majesty, even though they can neither hide nor flee, while he shows himself pleased to be faithful to them.

'I have called you friends', the Lord says to his disciples, 'because everything I have heard from my Father', everything that needs to be told you, 'I have made known to you'.† Beyond doubt he is *the faithful and true witness,* he *who is the beginning of God's creation.*† He

†Jn 15:15 †Rv 3:14

[5] Bernard of Clairvaux, *De moribus et officio episcoporum tractus* 6.21; PL 182:823A.

[6] Gregory the Great, *Dialogi* 4.46.303.

created all things when they did not exist, that they may exist, for
their sake for whom he had everything written, as it says, 'everything
†2 Tm 2:10 for the sake of the elect'.† Never was *the faithful witness* known to
have foretold to his own rational creatures anything that was not or
would not be. He sent them forth only to engender faith in those
who were to follow, out of the vomit of the tepid, and all the others.

But let us now listen to what he orders written to the angel of
†Rv 3:15 Laodicea. *I know your works, that you are neither cold nor hot*,† taking
into account especially the fruit of your works in their relationship
to their root. As the early teachers explained, this heat refers to the
fervor of spiritual devotion, according to the Apostle's words, 'Be
†Rm 12:11 fervent in spirit, serving the Lord'.† We believe that what is written
here pertains not only to the leader but to his church as well, as
we said before when discussing the first letter. The word cold is
not used absolutely, but was chosen in reference to tepidity. Those
same teachers attributed coldness to those deprived of spiritual grace
by an evident ignorance of God. They take the tepid to be those
in whom faith's devotion has grown weak. Better for them not to
have acknowledged the way of truth than to have turned back after
acknowledging it.[7] For the cold to come to their senses is easier
than for the tepid, and doubtless if neither come to their senses, the
tepid will be more severely punished than the cold. Judas was more
severely judged than the thieves, not only the one who confessed,
†Lk 23:39, 42 but even the one who blasphemed.† Judas, already rejected from his
†Jn 6:70–71 first call, was a devil;† Satan entered into him after he received the
†Jn 13:27 bread that [the Lord] dipped† which he deceitfully received. The
†Jn 12:6 thief† perished outside the law for he sinned outside the law.

But to move our discussion further and avoid scrupulous discussion, we can say clearly that the Lord ascribes coldness to this angel. Although the more wicked tepidity is more perilous, yet there is no salvation without it. Our holy father of blessed memory, Bernard, was accustomed to interpret these words whenever he spoke of them by saying that God rightly prefers and accepts heat and cold, but finds tepidity hateful and condemns it alone. He used to say that the hot were on fire with spiritual desires, while the cold were held

[7] Richard of Saint Victor, *In Apocalypsim Iohannis libri septem* 1.1; PL 196:695B.

in check by dread of his threats and by fear of eternal damnation. The tepid, as can be easily understood, are clearly negligent and committed to neither. They are devoid of both holy desire and fear, and are the kind of people the Lord described in the gospel as children playing in the marketplace and saying, 'We sang to you and you did not dance, we wailed and you did not weep'.† Neither the austere life of John the Baptist, nor the welcome gift of his own worthy presence, could move the children of that generation to which the Lord directed his remarks. †Lk 7:32

Wretched are those whom sinners are waiting to destroy, and whom the righteous are waiting to have as companions in their reward,† but who are careless, neglectful, and unconcerned, and who refuse to watch so that their house may not be broken into, even though they do not know the hour when the thief may come.† Even more wretched are those who are, as blessed Thaddeus† the apostle says, 'trees without fruit, twice-dead'.† Thus it is that no peals of thunder, no matter how terrifying, awaken them to fear the threat of damnation, whose intensity and uninterrupted continuance the prophet refers to: 'Which of you can live with the devouring fire? Or which of you will live with the everlasting flames?'† Nor do they hear the sweet melody of the divine whisper,† at whose sound the dead are raised.† †Ps 141:8 Vulgate †Lk 12:39 †Mk 3:18 †Jude 12 †Is 33:14 †Jb 4:12 †1 Co 15:52

Consequently the Lord wants to find us hot or cold, for he loves souls† and wants them converted to himself rather than lost. This conversion is true wisdom, whose beginning is fear of the Lord,† and whose fullness is love.† And although the heat of the moving sun is a more effective cause of a person's removing his cloak than the harsh blast of the north wind,[8] as we read eagerly when we were boys, learning the arguments along with the stories, the north wind is not ineffective, although the sun's power is greater. †Ws 11:26 †Ps 111:10 †Rm 13:10

Both the grace of love and the impetuous force of fear are useful in destroying those baleful loincloths of leaves† that we used in our folly to cover the disorder of our sins. The Lord wants either one or the other from us, and he who more willingly accepts a heart widened by love† does not despise a heart contrite and †Gn 3:7 †2 Co 6:13

[8] Avianus, *Fabulae* 5.4.37–38, A Baehrens, ed. (Leipzig, 1883).

†Ps 51:17 humbled† by fear. Perhaps this is why he calls both winds in the Song
†Sg 4:16 of Songs: 'Arise, O north wind, and come, O south wind!'† The
frigidity and rigidity of the one is summoned to rise; the mildness
of the other is summoned to come. The source of trembling is in
the depth and arises out of us, while love comes down from above,
making known to us how guilty we are and how lovable God is.

This is the same twofold spring Caleb is said to have given to his
†Jos 15:19 daughter when she asked.† The good Father gives one or the other
†Lk 11:13 spirit to those who ask him,† because although one is better than
the other, both are good. This may be the double spirit of Elijah that
†2 K 2:9 Elisha prayed may come over him.† Would that we could effectively
remind ourselves of what we sing, 'Let us fear and love Christ our
†Lk 10:1 God'.[9] That Christ sent his disciples out ahead of him in pairs† refers
again to this twofold quality. What we read in the Apocalypse, that
†Rv 12:4 the dragon's tail drew a third part of the stars,† refers to those who
are neither hot nor cold, who will sit neither at his right nor at his
left in the kingdom for they will never enter it. The Lord denied
†Mt 20:23 these seats to Zebedee's sons: 'It is not mine to grant you',† that is,
to give you as you are now.

This twofold quality is seen in the blessings and curses that we
read that Joshua was ordered to declare to the tribes of Israel on
the mountains of Ebal and Gerizim, as Moses had commanded him
†Jos 8:33–35 by the Lord's word.† And although he deputed the more important
tribes to proclaim the blessings—those standing on Mount Ebal
[were to be blessed by] those on Mount Gerizim—nevertheless the
two groups were in agreement, so that one could answer 'Amen' to
†Dt 27:11–26 each judgment of the other.†

Ebal means 'abyss' or 'heap of stones'.[10] The abyss or stoneheap
gathers to itself those whom God has not changed into children
†Mt 3:9; Lk 3:8 of Abraham.† Up this mountain [of Ebal] climbs the man who
has become familiar with the great sorrows of hell by reflection,
self-judgment, and mental dread, imitating Hezekiah who said in
†Is 38:10 the midst of his days, 'I will go to the gates of hell',† perhaps
reckoning that in the other half of life he would be approaching

9 Antiphon at the washing of the feet on Holy Thursday. *Graduale Romanum*, 168.

10 Jerome, *Liber interpretationis hebraicorum nominum* 6.6, 22.14; CCh 72:66, 87.

the gates of heaven. On this mountain the lesser tribes pronounce the numberless curses† the damned are to hear at the judgment: †Dt 27:13
'Go, you cursed, into everlasting fire'.† †Mt 25:41

On Gerizim, which means 'a cutting off',[11] the stronger tribes joyfully pronounce rich blessings on those the Lord comes to meet,† †Ps 21:3
those he has cut off from the 'lump of ruin'[12] by his almighty loving-kindness. They now picture themselves standing at his right hand, and hearing those most delightful words, 'Come, you blessed, receive the kingdom'.† †Mt 25:34
Those on one mountain are in agreement with those on the other, although the former wait less confidently. The latter are in full accord with them, even if they have less fear of the torments prepared for the condemned.

He who wrote, 'Behold, he comes, leaping on the mountains, bounding over the hills',† saw the Lord leaping on these mountains. †Sg 2:8
While he leaps on those steep mountains, Ebal and Gerizim, he causes us to leap on the low hills of this life's adversity and prosperity, which the faint-hearted and profligate exaggerate and enlarge in their thoughts. He leaps across them in order to cause us to leap across, to consider them as nothing, and to hold them in contempt. Both feelings move us strongly ahead; one leads us to turn away from evil, the other to do good.† †Ps 37:27

Rightly is the negligence of the lukewarm condemned, so that they will be vomited out of Christ's mouth. The sword coming out of his mouth enters them from either side since both sides are so sharp. Our forebears[13] took being vomited out of God's mouth to mean being excommunicated and cut off from his body. This is done by those we call 'God's mouth' since he speaks through them, and says to them, 'Whoever listens to you listens to me'.† †Lk 10:16
Would that those mouths could always successfully and wisely distinguish among foods which among them is sweet and which bitter, which insipid and which tasteless—and not only distinguish, but

[11] Ibid., 35.27; CCh 72:104.

[12] *massa perditionis.* Augustine, *De gratia Christi et de peccato originali liber secundus* 29.34; PL 44:933, and often. Bernard of Clairvaux, *In nativitate Domini* 2.4; SBOp 4:254.

[13] *Glossa ordinaria*, Ap 3; PL 114:717B. Anselm of Laon, *Enarrationes in Apocalypsim* 3; PL 162:1515D.

distinguish with care, with penetrating deliberation, with trouble and hesitation.

†Rv 3:15 *Because you are lukewarm,* the Lord says, *and neither cold nor hot.*†
By repeating the words he is urging us to take the easier road if we cannot take the other one.

†Rv 3:16 *I will begin to vomit you out.*† What will they say to this, those
who vomit before they *begin,* who bring to birth before they
are in travail, who excommunicate before they give warning? Let
one excommunicated be afraid, but let the one bringing a hasty
†1 Jn 3:20 excommunication not be secure. If one who knows everything,†
and even foreknows everything, hesitates, how rash is the haste of one knowing only the past, and who neither listens nor inquires! A wise man said, 'One who hesitates shows his unwillingness',[14] a point to be considered in distributing burdens as well as benefits. The serpent bites in silence, but some have the announcement of excommunication in their mouths as they arrive on the scene; they forsake inquiry lest there be any objection, and proclaim a sentence already decided.

God has complete knowledge and foreknowledge of all things.
When our first parents became the first transgressors of a law they
†Gn 3:8 received under the terrible threat of death, he came walking,† not
running. He called them and asked the requisite questions; he did not disown them, but only their guilt. Excusing them somewhat, he punished them by a merciful punishment—they would toil for their food and bear children in pain. He wanted them to anticipate physical death, and in some measure the death of the soul, which is to expiate sin, lest they undergo a more serious punishment afterwards. Of them the prophet says, 'They take no part in human toil, and are
not plagued like other people. Therefore pride has gripped them;
†Ps 73:5–6 they are covered with their iniquity and impiety'† in evil deeds and
infidelity. Our merciful judge clothed them in the skins of dead
†Gn 3:21 animals,† in place of the pitiful loincloths of leaves they had sewn
together for themselves, as an indication of their own mortality.

Because you are lukewarm, says the Lord, *I will begin to vomit*
†Rv 3:16 *you out of my mouth.*† The figure of speech is appropriate, because

[14] Seneca, *De beneficiis* 2.5.4.

water that is tepid, rather than hot or cold, causes nausea and provokes vomiting.[15] 'Behold, I will myself pronounce my judgment'† †Jr 1:15–16
against you, says the Lord through the prophet. Behold, I myself will speak bitterness, and I will answer neither your questions nor your pleas. But I will impress on you, by my word and secret inspiration, and also by reading and hearing sacred scripture, the extent of your iniquity and the extent of your crimes and offences, which stem from transgressing my laws and commands. You have done what I forbade, and omitted to do what I enjoined on you. *I will begin to vomit you out*, to show you how hateful and abominable you are. I will begin, and, unless you repent, I will vomit you out completely. But if you return to your senses, I will stop.

You say, I am rich, and well-provided for, and need nothing.† You †Rv 3:17
are speaking from a heart filled with pride, as you talk to yourself. We may reply like a father to an adolescent son who has told him what he says to himself: 'You are speaking to a fool who is not wise'. What you are saying to yourself you rightly blush to tell one who is wise, lest he answer a fool according to his folly.† You speak, †Pr 26:4
magnifying yourself inwardly, while the psalmist says 'that a person may not presume to magnify himself'.† †Ps 10:18

A human is of the earth,[16] formed from lowly slime.[17] He ought to be lowly and not proud. Perhaps you speak, and are not ashamed to use your magniloquent tongue† among others; perhaps †Ps 12:4
you do not speak but your deeds speak for you. Perhaps you are given to humble speech, but are haughty.† Or you may be aware †Rm 12:16
of your weakness, and, corrected by the light of truth, you may speak humbly, giving an outward appearance of piety; but you show another side, a vain side, to those around you, and want them to ponder your thoughts and your words.

[15] Pseudo-Alcuin, *Commentariorum in Apocalypsin libri quinque* 3; PL 100:1113C. Haymo of Auxerre, *Expositionis in Apocalypsin Beati Iohannis libri septem* 2.3; PL 117:996BC. Rupert of Deutz, *In Apocalypsim Iohannis apostoli commentariorum libri XII* 2.3; PL 169:900D–901A.

[16] *Homo . . . ex humo est.* Isidore of Seville, *Etymologiarum libri XX* 11.1.4. Lactantius, *Divinae institutiones* 2.10.3; CSEL 19:147.

[17] *ex humili limo humilis.* Augustine, *De Genesi ad litteram* 6.1.1; CSEL 28:2. Bernard of Clairvaux, *Sermones de diversis* 31.2; PL 183:623D.

†Rv 3:17 *You say, I am rich, and need nothing.*† He seems to be speaking of earthly goods, but this is evidently untrue, since the richer people are the more they need. They need faithful friends, energetic helpers, shrewd counselors. A few, very few indeed, may find all they need from their own resources and lack nothing. They may appear to need neither guards for their goods, nor goods for the guards, neither barns for their grain nor grain for their barns. The rich man whose fields produced abundantly would not have asked, 'What shall I
†Lk 12:17 do?'† if he needed nothing, nor would he have remained content with his plan, even if he had not heard, 'Fool, this night do they
†Lk 12:20 require your soul'.† He may tear down his barns and build bigger ones, but nevertheless he will find that he still needs something, and is on the verge of getting it.

But he will never get what flees from him. As poets express it, the nose vainly pursues the scent of apples, and the lips sweet draughts.[18] Nothing less than God will fill a soul created in God's
†Gn 1:26 image.† And so, a rich person provided for by ancestral wealth, or by what he has acquired by his own industry and toil, is lying if he says he needs nothing, and he deceives himself if he believes it.

With regard to spiritual goods, it is all the more evident that no one in this life, among the hot or the cold, and especially among the lukewarm, is rich enough, or well enough provided for, to need none of them. Therefore to the angel of Laodicea who says, *I am rich, and need nothing,* the Lord says reproachfully, *and you do not know that*
†Rv 3:17 *you are poor, wretched and miserable, blind, and naked.*† Someone poor
†Mt 5:3 in spirit is not wretched but happy;† to such belongs the kingdom
†Mt 19:14 of heaven.† One afflicted by harsh necessity is poor and wretched. *And you do not know that you are wretched and miserable,* wretched in reality, miserable in appearance. Although you do not know and admit it, although you deny and contradict it, you cannot hide your wretchedness and need.

By what has just been said, *You say, I am rich, and need nothing,*
†Rv 3:17 and this statement, *and you do not know that you are wretched,*† we are given to understand that this misery is unprofitable and unacceptable to God. There is a misery of those who truly listen, who admit

[18] Horace, *Satiress* 1.1.68.

without reserve and humbly deplore their own wretchedness, who confidently implore and effectively strive to be worthy of divine mercy and compassion. The Lord would never have reproached this angel and his disciples with this misery, would never have censured them for it, but would rather have been pleased with it. That person is wretched who lives in a wretched and wicked manner; he is miserable who omits to remain obscure, whether he can or wants to do more. Impenitence makes a person whose sins are unforgiven wretched; wantonness makes one whose sins are uncovered† miserable. Every fault, every mortal sin, makes one wretched; every sin that is manifest and leads to judgment makes one miserable. †Ps 32:1

Poor, blind, and naked.† No one should think that the poverty of spirit so magnificently praised at the beginning of the Lord's sermon [on the mount] when he said, 'Blessed are the poor in spirit, for theirs is the kingdom of heaven',† is being demeaned. Nor is the one who said once in his lamentation, 'I am one who sees my own poverty under the rod of your wrath',† like this one who does not know that he is poor. And he who counseled, 'Remember, son, we lead a poor life',† wanted his son to become an imitator of one who saw this poverty rather then one who did not know it. Deceitful riches† have only a deceitful power to make a person rich. †Rv 3:17 †Mt 5:3 †Lm 3:1 †Tb 4:21 (4:23 Vulgate) †Mt 13:22

But how can a person not know that he is blind? Certainly in a physical sense no one can, but many can in a spiritual sense, as prophets were once called 'seers'.[19] Would that those among us who do not see may see, beloved, and may those who see never become blind! May we, in our lack of sight, at least see that we do not see, may we know that we are blind, as it is written: 'If I have been ignorant, my ignorance is before me'.† *Blind*, he says, *and naked.** You are blind, lest you see, naked that you may appear; you are blind lest you see, naked that you may be seen. Going down from Jerusalem to Jericho you fell among thieves who left you stripped and naked.† †Jb 19:4 *Rv 3:17 †Lk 10:30

The words under consideration here can refer to four vices opposed to the four virtues. The inertia opposed to fortitude makes

[19] Isidore of Seville, *Etymologiarum libri XX* 7.8.1.

a person wretched and miserable, wretched when in the grip of allurements, and miserable when overcome by troubles. The world sets up these twin battle lines against the faithful when it flatters them in order to deceive them, and resists them in order to break them.

Perhaps here we may mention the two battles that David won against the Philistines. On one occasion he attacked face-to-face at the Lord's command, and on another he went around in the rear and
†2 S 5:23 came on them from opposite the pear trees.† Clearly we must resist allurements, since we overcome troubles better when we realize that our momentary and light afflictions work for us an eternal weight
†2 Co 4:17 of glory.† One who puts down useless thoughts rises up opposite the pear trees, opposing rather than consenting to them, for they increase and exaggerate the trial of afflictions.

We can take the pear trees to mean steep mountains that rise like a flame, for pear and pyre are related.[20] Or, it can mean the kind of tree that rises in a similar way. In either case, an exaggerated description of all the troubles of this present life only increases them. He who is tempted by the apple tree is tempted by the pear tree too, since that kind spreads out instead of growing straight up. If we follow another reading, where 'weepers' appears instead of 'pear trees',[21] the meaning becomes clearer still. One who ruminates assiduously on the Lord's word is like a person who goes round to the rear from opposite those who weep, and against the impatient thoughts sown by wicked angels.

†Mt 5:4 (5:5 Vulgate) 'Blessed are those who mourn, for they will be comforted'.† Now is the time to move into action, as soon as the sound of one walking is heard in the tops of the pear trees, or above those weeping. This is the sound of him who said long ago through the prophet, 'O all you who pass by the way, look and see if there is any sorrow
†Lm 1:12 like my sorrow!'†

Reprehensible poverty comes not from a lack of goods but from intemperate desires. A man wise and experienced in these matters said, 'People have enough at hand, but sweat over what

[20] *piros* (pear trees) . . . *ignis enim pyr dicitur.*

[21] *flentium* in place of *pirorum.*

is not necessary'.[22] Without prudence a person is blind; without righteousness he stands naked. To see, to foresee, belongs to prudence, and the prophet asks the Lord that his priests be clothed with righteousness.† Similarly the Apostle says, 'Clothed †Ps 132:9
in the breastplate of righteousness'.† Righteousness renders to each †Ep 6:14
his due.

The words of the blessed Malachy, bishop of Ireland, apply to this fourfold division of virtues. He recommends, 'spurn the world but spurn no person; disdain yourself, but disdain to be disdained—these are the four goods'.

Temperance spurns the world, and refuses its desires; it considers vain and fleeting what this world holds out, and even what it promises. Righteousness spurns no one because it renders to each his due.[23] A person governed by prudence disdains himself, and turns from his own will; he judges no one more harshly than he judges himself. He fully knows why he angers and displeases himself; he knows what to condemn and censure in himself. He removes himself from the company of those who love themselves.† He reproaches †2 Tm 3:2
himself for many things, he chastises and afflicts himself, mindful of the saying: No matter how great a person's ruin, he is only a human.[24] To disdain being disdained is magnanimity, for the greatest rewards are promised to those bearing insults: 'Blessed will you be when people hate you and exclude you and cast out your name as evil'.† One cannot be both disdained and embraced by masses of †Lk 6:22
people, but it is a good thing to be despised by the despicable, to remain unmoved by their reproaches and contempt. Pleasing such as these means living basely—if anyone indeed could please them in their baseness.

I urge you, says the Lord, *to buy from me gold refined by fire, that you may become rich.*† Perhaps among humans this type of urging is †Rv 3:18
suspect; the more one person urges something on another, the less is he persuaded. But no one need cast suspicion on the kind merchant who has no need of our goods.† He is not looking for any price we †Ps 16:2

[22] Seneca, *Letters* 1.4.11.

[23] Bernard of Clairvaux, *In octava Epiphaniae* 4; SBOp 4:312.

[24] Hildebert, *Carmina miscellanea* 129; PL 171:1438C.

may pay, but he wants our salvation; he has already redeemed us at the incomparable price of his own blood.

Would that what he urges may persuade us, may lead us not only to desire but to obtain what he holds out to us! Faith seems
†Rv 3:18 to be meant by *gold refined by fire*,† faith tested in the furnace of
†Pr 17:3; Si 2:5 many afflictions, as gold is tested in a furnace.† We must enter the
†Ac 14:22 kingdom of God through many afflictions.†

Moreover, because faith is, in the Apostle's words, 'the substance
†Heb 11:1 of things hoped for and the conviction of things unseen',† its cost to us is contempt and renunciation for things present and seen. The more avidly a person hungers after these, and clutches them, the less he deserves them. And so, the righteous person lives by
†Rm 1:17; Ga 3:11 faith,† rendering to each his due, devoting himself wholeheartedly to heavenly things while estimating those of earth as nothing. Things that now are and then are no more, especially since this 'now' is so brief, and eternity when it comes will be without end, have meanwhile only a seeming reality and no subsisting solidity. Why are they not more correctly reckoned among things that are not rather than among things that are?

†Jm 2:20 And to be sure that their faith apart from works† not be dead, just as works do not live apart from faith, he adds: *that the shame*
†Rv 3:18 *of your nakedness may not be seen* you *put on white garments*,† that is, perform actions that are genuine and pleasing to God. When at the Lord's rising an angel, whose face was like lightening and whose
†Mt 28:3 garments were white as snow, appeared† to commend fervent faith and a life of grace, we can take the whiteness of the garments to mean heaven's joyful solemnity. Just as *gold refined by fire* refers to faith, so do *white garments* bespeak hope. A person who has already to some extent put these on lives in that eternal joy by meditation and desire. Nor does *the shame of* his *nakedness* appear, for he has grasped that blessed promise by the joyful anticipation of hope. The Lord speaks of this to his church: 'On that day you will not be put to shame over all your deeds by which you have transgressed
†Zp 3:11 against me'.†

And because love is greater than faith or hope, although
†1 Co 13:13 *1 Co 13:8 these three now abide,† love alone never fails.* We apply the following to love: *Anoint your eyes with ointment that you may*

see.† If an eye is present where there is love,[25] we can reasonably take †Rv 3:18
the two eyes to be the two precepts of love of God and of neighbor.† †Mk 12:30–31; Mt 22:37, 39; Lk 10:27

An *ointment*†a capable of opening the eyes even of a man born blind was made from a mixture of the Lord's saliva and dust†b because †aRv 3:18 †bJn 9:6 nothing so attracts the mind of any of the faithful to the twofold commandment than diligent meditation on the Lord's incarnation. Saliva comes from the head, and, as the Apostle says, 'God is the head of Christ'.† Therefore saliva is divine wisdom. The dust with which †1 Co 11:3 it was mixed is our flesh created from dust. Thus the ointment the angel Raphael used to restore Tobit's sight was made from the gall of a roasted fish† to signify death's bitterness, that is, the sufferings of †Tb 6:9, 11:11–13 Christ. Faithful and devout meditation on the Lord's passion anoints the eyes with this ointment.

Those I love I reprove and chastise.† The Lord consoles the angel of †Rv 3:19 Laodicea for his earlier reproofs, that he may believe that they came from love, not from hatred. He rebuked him seriously for serious reasons. Now his zeal toward them abates, and he is no longer angry at them with that anger that is the restoration of love. He does not reprove them, but he calls them into his presence to look continually at the countenance they were born with in the mirror of truth. He does not chastise them, punishing them with gentle blows that he may make amends for them and cleanse them from their iniquities.

Therefore be zealous† for the greater gifts; *be zealous* for what †Rv 3:19 is holy, pure, lovely, of good repute, what stems from virtue and praiseworthy discipline.† *Be zealous*, remain firm in your heart, and †Ph 4:8 faithfully promise me in my ministers that you will strive to live more perfectly for the future. *And repent* for the past, for sin, if you wish to be without anxiety regarding what you have atoned for. You must first block up the openings through which filth flows so freely, and then drain off the stagnant water shut up there. May he mercifully grant both these gifts to us, Jesus Christ our Lord, who extends to us this twofold invitation—who with the Father and the Holy Spirit is one God over all and blessed forever. Amen.

[25] Richard of Saint Victor, *Tractus de gradibus charitatis* 3; PL 196:1202D.14. 24.

Sermon Twenty

Behold I am standing at the door knocking. If anyone hears my voice and opens the door I will come in to him, and eat with him, and he with me. To the one who conquers I will grant to sit with me on my throne, just as I have conquered and sit with my Father on his throne. Let anyone who has an ear hear what the Spirit says to the churches.† †Rv 3:20–22

B*EHOLD I AM STANDING at the door knocking. If anyone hears my voice and opens the door I will come in to him, and eat with him, and he with me.*† It is the Lord, beloved, it is the Lord! †Rv 3:20 Why do you delay? Why are you sitting down? Why do you not get up and run? Why do you not fly to open to him? Why does not one run faster than another? Where is Peter's faith, where is his fervor—as soon as he heard that it was the Lord, he put on his tunic, for he was naked, and threw himself into the sea!† †Jn 21:7 Happy was Martyrius, who reckoned he was carrying a leper he found outside to the monastery, but he was bearing the Lord of glory. Rightly did

the abbot, to whom this was revealed, order the brothers to run and
open the door quickly![1]

Today, Lord, your prophet Isaiah describes your own martyrdom
which we celebrate; he presents you as one like a leper, struck down
†Is 53:4 by God and humbled.† Why are you standing outside?* Why are
*Gn 24:31 you knocking? Why are you asking and waiting for the door to be
opened to you? Are you not the one who instructs us to go into
†Mt 6:6 our room and shut the door and pray?† Truly we must pray without
†1 Th 5:17 ceasing,† as he said, as he taught, since we must pray always and not
†Lk 18:1 grow weary.†

†Jn 20:26 Do you not enter by closed doors as you will?† Come in, blessed
†Gn 24:31 Lord, why are you standing outside?† Are you not the one who
†Rv 3:7 opens and no one closes?† If it was your angel,* we ought, as we
*Ac 12:15 read of Peter, to run and open the door quickly. And if the maid
was so happy that she did not open the door for Peter but hurried
†Ac 12:14 instead to spread the news,† how should we treat the one who is
standing, knocking, and waiting for us to open to him? What if
we should experience this from the Song of Songs as we wait: 'I
†Sg 5:6 opened the bolt of my door, but he had turned aside'?† Woe to
those wretched and foolish virgins who hear as they knock sadly on
†Mt 25:12 the closed door, 'I do not know you'.†

†Rv 3:20 *Behold*,† he says. I am not speaking to you of what is to come.
I am telling you what I am presenting to you now. 'I am the one
†Is 52:6 speaking; behold, I am here.'† I am the one, not some herald or
minister of mine, not some prophet, not an angel. Why do you
†Pr 8:31 delay? 'My delight is to be with the children of men'.† 'With desire
†Lk 22:15 I have desired to eat this Passover with you'.† Let no one let this
opportunity pass, no one trust in the activity of others, no one lose
courage through negligence. *If anyone opens,* he says, *I will come in
to him*, whoever he may be. [Jesus] sent into the city for a certain
†1 P 1:17 one, without respect of persons,† with whom to keep the Passover.*
*Mt 26:18 Nor did he keep the Passover alone, but with his disciples, as the
Song of Songs has it: 'Open to me, my sister, because my head is
†Sg 5:2 covered with dew and my locks with the drops of night'.† *Behold I*

[1] Gregory the Great, *Homiliae in Evangelia* 2.39.10; PL 76:1300B–D; CS 123: 366–367; *Be friends with God: Spiritual reading from Gregory the Great* (Cambridge, Mass: Cowley Publications, 1990) 56–57.

am standing at the door knocking. What astonishing honor! And what astonishing stubbornness in anyone this mercy and meekness do not lead to repentance!

A door obstructs[2] and stands in the way. Even though the door stands in his way, still he stands and knocks. He is knocking with benefits and goads, with promises, warnings, and examples. Behold, today he is standing and knocking so as to split rocks and even open tombs.† Woe to us if we be found harder than rocks, more heedless and hopeless than those interred! Impenitence, impatience, disobedience, and ingratitude close the door. A door is closed to keep what is inside in; it is closed to keep what is outside out. Impenitence does not let out an admission of guilt, and impatience will not pay sin's penalty; disobedience does not let in salvation, nor does ingratitude let grace come in. Sorrow and fear open to let the former out; desire and joy open to let the latter in. †Mt 27:51–52

The sorrow of repentance does away with guilt, and one who truly hates sin escapes from it. In the same way a strong fear of what is to come makes present difficulties easy, just as in barely tolerable cold, or in no less heat, a person used to say that he had seen far worse than both, and was doubtful whether in those places of punishment he would not pass from melted snow to excessive heat. It is no wonder when, in the present, we perceive that frozen or burned parts of the body are healed and refreshed by cold water.

So too those impelled by love to move toward life enter upon the narrow way, which is obedience without delay, so that since they hold nothing dearer than Christ† they imitate his example of obedience. And, as nothing is more contrary to grace than the vice of ingratitude,[3] so there is no surer way of obtaining grace than a holy and happy spirit of devotion, for this is joy in the Holy Spirit.† †RB 5:1–2 †Rm 14:17

Faith opens to allow obedience to enter—faith that works through love,† as we know. Humility opens to grace, as it is written: 'God resists the proud, but gives grace to the humble'.† Patience too in trials, so they may pass—for it is hard to kick against the goad;† †Ga 5:6 †Jm 4:6; 1 P 5:5 †Ac 26:14

[2] *Ostium dicitur ab obstando.* Isidore of Seville, *Etymologiarum libri XX* 15.7.4. The text continues: *et obstare est contra stare. Cui igitur ostium obstat et contra stat, ipse tamen astat et pulsat.*

[3] Bernard of Clairvaux, *Sermones de tempore* 2.1.; PL 183:339C.

and repentance for sin. We read that nothing is so excusable that it cannot become criminal if we welcome it, and nothing is so criminal that it cannot be excused when we do not.[4] Nothing is impossible
†Mt 17:19 for those who believe;† nothing is out of range for the humble, nothing intolerable for the patient, nothing unpardonable for the penitent. And perhaps this pertains to these four virtues: 'Open to me, my sister' through faith, 'my friend' through humility, 'my dove'
†Sg 5:2 through meekness, 'my immaculate one' through repentance;† and in all these mercy, giving everything, and striving to please me in everything.

Let us listen, then, to the voice of one who says, *If anyone opens*
†Rv 3:20 *the door* to me *I will come in to him*.† Perhaps you gave him an opening by contrition of heart, and he thrust in his hand; or perhaps he made the opening for himself by thrusting in his hand so that your
†Sg 5:4 stomach may be moved at his touch† and your conscience be struck by his power and action. Perhaps too confession of sins opened a little door, but he, a giant of twofold nature, wanted a house door opened to himself. For one like him, only the enlargement of love offers a wide enough entrance for the habitation of Zion to rejoice
†Is 12:6 and praise, because great in it is the Holy One of Israel.† A person opens a door for him who sees all things naked and open before
†Heb 4:13 his eyes;† a refusal to think things through, loose living, obstinacy of will, despair of amending, fear of reparation, shame at confessing sins, all these close a conscience to him. But now, to those who
†1 Co 2:2 know nothing but Christ Jesus, and him crucified,† whose minds
†Sg 5:2 are filled with nothing else, he shows his head covered with dew,†
†Ep 5:23; Col 1:18 that is to say himself, who is head of his body, head of the church.†

Our present life is night, and its tribulation is like dew in comparison to the future life. Would that none of us may fear dew and hoarfrost of this kind, or snow will burst upon him who is going to pass from melted snow to excessive heat. His head was covered, completely covered, with this dew when nothing was missing from all that Jewish impiety could think up. His locks are the masses of blessed martyrs tightly bound to his head, and they too are covered

[4] Hugh of Saint Victor, *Allegoriae in Novum Testamentum, Exegetica dubia* 2.16; PL 175:791A. Richard of Saint Victor, *In Cantica Canticorum explicatio* 25; PL 196:481D. Gracian *Decree* d. 25; c.3.

with the drops of night.† He asks entrance for them and for himself, †Sg 5:2
that the memory of his suffering and of theirs may penetrate our hearts. Thus it is that no altar is consecrated without their sacred remains, nor is the saving victim offered, of which the Lord gave his disciples a symbol at the supper, and later the reality.

Breakfast, we note, is the first meal, and supper the last. The mysteries of the law were like a breakfast. To [those mysteries] the eternal priesthood according to the order of Melchizedek passed down under oath in the form of bread and wine, because no repentance will henceforth change it. A lamb used to be eaten at the supper. It was a type of the sacrifice that will never be superseded.

Would that our beloved would come in to us, would come into his garden and find there the fruit of his apple trees to eat.† Would †Sg 5:1
that our souls would keep for him all the apples, new and old, so persevering in our former zealous ways as always to progress by new increments of virtue. Would that everything worthy of being offered to him may be kept, may be seen by him, and repaid by him, since no fee comes from anyone else. Would that when he comes to eat with us he may find honeycomb with his own honey to eat, his wine with his milk to drink, and may say to us too, 'Eat, my friends, and drink, and be inebriated, my beloved'.† †Sg 5:1

He eats with us if he is pleased by our lives and our devotion; he has us eat with him when he refreshes us by a share in his own sweetness. This is the hidden manna he promised to give to the one who conquers.† This sweetness the prophet extols from his own †Rv 2:17
experience: 'How abundant is your sweetness that you have hidden for those who fear you'.† You have perfected those who hope in †Ps 31:19
you, who do not presume to eat their own suppers alone, where they are inebriated with wormwood, but who wait for the supper you deigned to promise. He with whom you now eat at his poor little supper will one day eat with you. He will be pleasing to you in his humble state even to his life's end, O Lord, and he will henceforth be pleased by your endless happiness.

Not only, he says, will this one eat with me when I come in to eat with him, not only will he eat with me, but he will also reign with me, and I will make him *sit with me on my throne.*† But †Rv 3:21
this will happen only when he completely conquers, *just as I have*

conquered and sit with my Father, when he conquers the evil one,
†1 Jn 2:17 when he conquers the world and its desires,† when he resists the
devil and forces him to flee, when he overcomes both armies that
the world marshals against the elect. For the world opposes him to
break him, and flatters him to deceive him. Thus the prophet prays
on the steps of the ascent, 'Lord, deliver my soul from evil lips and
†Ps 120:2 a lying tongue'.† The world and its evil prince do us more harm by
suggestion than by deed; the threat of both is more dangerous than
the blow, the promise than the delivery, as they always possess less
than we expect.

†Jb 7:1 Vulgate Brothers, our life upon earth is a warfare,† but another life will
follow in heaven. If this warfare proceeds victoriously, there will be
a blessed supper, tranquil repose, full rest, and eternal glory. Would
†Rv 3:7 that he who opens and no one closes† would open our ears now
†Rv 3:22 that we may hear *what the Spirit says to the churches.*† The Spirit calls
†Jb 42:5 the churches together; let us obey him by the hearing of the ear.†
May we hear what he says, what he commands, what he urges;
may we hear him when he corrects us, for the true and truthful
†Jn 15:26 Paraclete bears witness to our spirit.† Would that we may hear what
†Rm 8:26 the Spirit says now, so that, as he helps our weakness,† we may
†1 Tm 1:18 have faith and a good conscience,† and may fight the good fight.†
Then, with victory complete, the same Spirit may speak to us in
that repose promised us, so that each of us may henceforth rest from
†Rv 14:13 his labors.† Would that we may hasten to that rest* and be found
*Heb 4:11 †Mt 25:21, 23 worthy to enter and be conducted into the joy of our Lord,† who
is God blessed above all forever. Amen.

SCRIPTURAL INDEX

CISTERCIAN TEXTS

Bernard of Clairvaux

- Apologia to Abbot William
- Five Books on Consideration: Advice to a Pope
- Homilies in Praise of the Blessed Virgin Mary
- Letters of Bernard of Clairvaux / by B.S. James
- Life and Death of Saint Malachy the Irishman
- Love without Measure: Extracts from the Writings of St Bernard / by Paul Dimier
- On Grace and Free Choice
- On Loving God / Analysis by Emero Stiegman
- Parables and Sentences
- Sermons for the Summer Season
- Sermons on Conversion
- Sermons on the Song of Songs I–IV
- The Steps of Humility and Pride

William of Saint Thierry

- The Enigma of Faith
- Exposition on the Epistle to the Romans
- Exposition on the Song of Songs
- The Golden Epistle
- The Mirror of Faith
- The Nature and Dignity of Love
- On Contemplating God: Prayer & Meditations

Aelred of Rievaulx

- Dialogue on the Soul
- Liturgical Sermons, I
- The Mirror of Charity
- Spiritual Friendship
- Treatises I: On Jesus at the Age of Twelve, Rule for a Recluse, The Pastoral Prayer
- Walter Daniel: The Life of Aelred of Rievaulx

John of Ford

- Sermons on the Final Verses of the Songs of Songs I–VII

Gilbert of Hoyland

- Sermons on the Songs of Songs I–III
- Treatises, Sermons and Epistles

Other Early Cistercian Writers

- Adam of Perseigne, Letters of
- Alan of Lille: The Art of Preaching
- Amadeus of Lausanne: Homilies in Praise of Blessed Mary
- Baldwin of Ford: Spiritual Tractates I–II
- Geoffrey of Auxerre: On the Apocalypse
- Gertrud the Great: Spiritual Exercises
- Gertrud the Great: The Herald of God's Loving-Kindness (Books 1, 2)
- Gertrud the Great: The Herald of God's Loving-Kindness (Book 3)
- Guerric of Igny: Liturgical Sermons Vol. I & 2
- Helinand of Froidmont: Verses on Death
- Idung of Prüfening: Cistercians and Cluniacs: The Case for Cîteaux
- Isaac of Stella: Sermons on the Christian Year, I–[II]
- The Life of Beatrice of Nazareth
- The School of Love. An Anthology of Early Cistercian Texts
- Serlo of Wilton & Serlo of Savigny: Seven Unpublished Works
- Stephen of Lexington: Letters from Ireland
- Stephen of Sawley: Treatises

MONASTIC TEXTS

Eastern Monastic Tradition

- Besa: The Life of Shenoute
- Cyril of Scythopolis: Lives of the Monks of Palestine
- Dorotheos of Gaza: Discourses and Sayings
- Evagrius Ponticus: Praktikos and Chapters on Prayer
- Handmaids of the Lord: Lives of Holy Women in Late Antiquity & the Early Middle Ages / by Joan Petersen
- Harlots of the Desert / by Benedicta Ward
- John Moschos: The Spiritual Meadow
- Lives of the Desert Fathers
- Lives of Simeon Stylites / by Robert Doran
- The Luminous Eye / by Sebastian Brock
- Mena of Nikiou: Isaac of Alexandra & St Macrobius
- The Monastic Rule of Iosif Volotsky (Revised Edition) / by David Goldfrank
- Pachomian Koinonia I–III (Armand Veilleux)
- Paphnutius: Histories/Monks of Upper Egypt
- The Sayings of the Desert Fathers / by Benedicta Ward
- Spiritual Direction in the Early Christian East / by Irénée Hausherr
- The Spiritually Beneficial Tales of Paul, Bishop of Monembasia / by John Wortley
- Symeon the New Theologian: TheTheological and Practical Treatises & The Three Theological Discourses / by Paul McGuckin
- Theodoret of Cyrrhus: A History of the Monks of Syria
- The Syriac Fathers on Prayer and the Spiritual Life / by Sebastian Brock

CISTERCIAN PUBLICATIONS

TITLES LISTING

Western Monastic Tradition

- Anselm of Canterbury: Letters I–III / by Walter Fröhlich
- Bede: Commentary...Acts of the Apostles
- Bede: Commentary...Seven Catholic Epistles
- Bede: Homilies on the Gospels I–II
- Bede: Excerpts from the Works of St Augustine on the Letters of the Blessed Apostle Paul
- The Celtic Monk / by U. Ó Maidín
- Life of the Jura Fathers
- Maxims of Stephen of Muret
- Peter of Celle: Selected Works
- Letters of Rancé I–II
- Rule of the Master
- Rule of Saint Augustine

Christian Spirituality

- The Cloud of Witnesses: The Development of Christian Doctrine / by David N. Bell
- The Call of Wild Geese / by Matthew Kelty
- The Cistercian Way / by André Louf
- The Contemplative Path
- Drinking From the Hidden Fountain / by Thomas Spidlík
- Eros and Allegory: Medieval Exegesis of the Song of Songs / by Denys Turner
- Fathers Talking / by Aelred Squire
- Friendship and Community / by Brian McGuire
- Gregory the Great: Forty Gospel Homilies
- High King of Heaven / by Benedicta Word
- The Hermitage Within / by a Monk
- Life of St Mary Magdalene and of Her Sister St Martha / by David Mycoff
- Many Mansions / by David N. Bell
- Mercy in Weakness / by André Louf
- The Name of Jesus / by Irénée Hausherr
- No Moment Too Small / by Norvene Vest
- Penthos: The Doctrine of Compunction in the Christian East / by Irénée Hausherr
- Praying the Word / by Enzo Bianchi
- Rancé and the Trappist Legacy / by A. J. Krailsheimer
- Russian Mystics / by Sergius Bolshakoff
- Sermons in a Monastery / by Matthew Kelty
- Silent Herald of Unity: The Life of Maria Gabrielle Sagheddu / by Martha Driscoll
- The Spirituality of the Christian East / by Thomas Spidlík
- The Spirituality of the Medieval West / by André Vauchez
- Tuning In To Grace / by André Louf
- Wholly Animals: A Book of Beastly Tales / by David N. Bell

MONASTIC STUDIES

- Community and Abbot in the Rule of St Benedict I–II / by Adalbert de Vogüé
- The Finances of the Cistercian Order in the Fourteenth Century / by Peter King
- Fountains Abbey and Its Benefactors / by Joan Wardrop
- The Hermit Monks of Grandmont / by Carole A. Hutchison
- In the Unity of the Holy Spirit / by Sighard Kleiner
- A Life Pleasing to God: Saint Basil's Monastic Rules / By Augustine Holmes
- The Joy of Learning & the Love of God: Essays in Honor of Jean Leclercq
- Monastic Odyssey / by Marie Kervingant
- Monastic Practices / by Charles Cummings
- The Occupation of Celtic Sites in Ireland / by Geraldine Carville
- Reading St Benedict / by Adalbert de Vogüé
- Rule of St Benedict: A Doctrinal and Spiritual Commentary / by Adalbert de Vogüé
- The Rule of St Benedict / by Br. Pinocchio
- The Spiritual World of Isaac the Syrian / by Hilarion Alfeyev
- St Hugh of Lincoln / by David H. Farmer
- The Venerable Bede / by Benedicta Ward
- Western Monasticism / by Peter King
- What Nuns Read / by David N. Bell
- With Greater Liberty: A Short History of Christian Monasticism & Religious Orders / by Karl Frank

CISTERCIAN STUDIES

- Aelred of Rievaulx: A Study / by Aelred Squire
- Athirst for God: Spiritual Desire in Bernard of Clairvaux's Sermons on the Song of Songs / by Michael Casey
- Beatrice of Nazareth in Her Context / by Roger De Ganck
- Bernard of Clairvaux: Man, Monk, Mystic / by Michael Casey [tapes and readings]
- Bernardus Magister...Nonacentenary
- Catalogue of Manuscripts in the Obrecht Collection of the Institute of Cistercian Studies / by Anna Kirkwood
- Christ the Way: The Christology of Guerric of Igny / by John Morson
- The Cistercians in Denmark / by Brian McGuire
- The Cistercians in Scandinavia / by James France
- A Difficult Saint / by Brian McGuire

- A Gathering of Friends: Learning & Spirituality in John of Ford / by Costello and Holdsworth
- Image and Likeness: Augustinian Spirituality of William of St Thierry / by David Bell
- Index of Authors & Works in Cistercian Libraries in Great Britain I / by David Bell
- Index of Cistercian Authors and Works in Medieval Library Catalogues in Great Britian / by David Bell
- The Mystical Theology of St Bernard / by Étienne Gilson
- The New Monastery: Texts & Studies on the Earliest Cistercians
- Nicolas Cotheret's Annals of Cîteaux / by Louis J. Lekai
- Pater Bernhardus: Martin Luther and Saint Bernard / by Franz Posset
- Pathway of Peace / by Charles Dumont
- A Second Look at Saint Bernard / by Jean Leclercq
- The Spiritual Teachings of St Bernard of Clairvaux / by John R. Sommerfeldt
- Studies in Medieval Cistercian History
- Studiosorum Speculum / by Louis J. Lekai
- Three Founders of Cîteaux / by Jean-Baptiste Van Damme
- Towards Unification with God (Beatrice of Nazareth in Her Context, 2)
- William, Abbot of St Thierry
- Women and St Bernard of Clairvaux / by Jean Leclercq

MEDIEVAL RELIGIOUS WOMEN

edited by Lillian Thomas Shank and John A. Nichols:

- Distant Echoes
- Hidden Springs: Cistercian Monastic Women (2 volumes)
- Peace Weavers

CARTHUSIAN TRADITION

- The Call of Silent Love / by A Carthusian
- The Freedom of Obedience / by A Carthusian
- From Advent to Pentecost
- Guigo II: The Ladder of Monks & Twelve Meditations / by Colledge & Walsh
- Halfway to Heaven / by R.B. Lockhart
- Interior Prayer / by A Carthusian
- Meditations of Guigo II / by A. Gordon Mursall
- The Prayer of Love and Silence / by A Carthusian
- Poor, Therefore Rich / by A Carthusian
- They Speak by Silences / by A Carthusian
- The Way of Silent Love (A Carthusian Miscellany)
- Where Silence is Praise / by A Carthusian
- The Wound of Love (A Carthusian Miscellany)

CISTERCIAN ART, ARCHITECTURE & MUSIC

- Cistercian Abbeys of Britain
- Cistercians in Medieval Art / by James France
- Studies in Medieval Art and Architecture / edited by Meredith Parsons Lillich *(Volumes II–V are now available)*
- Stones Laid Before the Lord / by Anselme Dimier
- Treasures Old and New: Nine Centuries of Cistercian Music (compact disc and cassette)

THOMAS MERTON

- The Climate of Monastic Prayer / by T. Merton
- Legacy of Thomas Merton / by P. Hart
- Message of Thomas Merton / by P. Hart
- Monastic Journey of Thomas Merton / by P. Hart
- Thomas Merton/Monk / by P. Hart
- Thomas Merton on St Bernard
- Toward an Integrated Humanity / edited by M. Basil Pennington

CISTERCIAN LITURGICAL DOCUMENTS SERIES

- Cistercian Liturgical Documents Series / edited by Chrysogonus Waddell, ocso
- Hymn Collection of the…Paraclete
- *Institutiones nostrae:* The Paraclete Statutes
- Molesme Summer-Season Breviary (4 volumes)
- Old French Ordinary & Breviary of the Abbey of the Paraclete (2 volumes)
- Twelfth-century Cistercian Hymnal (2 volumes)
- The Twelfth-century Cistercian Psalter
- Two Early Cistercian *Libelli Missarum*

STUDIA PATRISTICA

- Studia Patristica XVIII, Volumes 1, 2 and 3

CISTERCIAN PUBLICATIONS

HOW TO CONTACT US

Editorial Offices & Customer Service

- **Cistercian Publications**
  WMU Station 1201 Oliver Street
  Kalamazoo, Michigan 49008 USA

  Telephone 616 387 8920
  Fax 616 387 8390
  e-mail cistpub@wmich.edu

Canada

- **Novalis**
  49 Front Street East, Second Floor
  Toronto, Ontario M5E 1B3

  Telephone 416 363 3303
  1 800 204 4140
  Fax 416 363 9409

U.K.

- **Cistercian Publications UK**
  Mount Saint Bernard Abbey
  Coalville, Leicester LE67 5UL

- **UK Customer Service & Book Orders**
  Cistercian Publications
  97 Loughborough Road
  Thringstone, Coalville
  Leicester LE67 8LQ

  Telephone 01530 45 27 24
  Fax 01530 45 02 10
  e-mail MsbcistP@aol.com

Website & Warehouse

- **www.spencerabbey.org/cistpub**

- **Book Returns (prior permission)**
  Cistercian Publications
  Saint Joseph's Abbey
  167 North Spencer Road
  Spencer MA 01562-1233 USA

  Telephone 508 885 8730
  Fax 508 885 4687
  e-mail cistpub@spencerabbey.org

Trade Accounts & Credit Applications

- **Cistercian Publications / Accounting**
  6219 West Kistler Road
  Ludington, MI 49431 USA

  Fax 231 843 8919

Cistercian Publications is a non-profit corporation. Its publishing program is restricted to monastic texts in translation and books on the monastic tradition.

A complete catalogue of texts in translation and studies on early, medieval, and modern monasticism is available, free of charge, from any of the addresses above.